AIRMAN ABROAD

Airman Abroad

National Service Letters
Egypt, Kenya, etc., 1953–1955

Hamish Brown
2590848

Whittles Publishing

Published by
Whittles Publishing Ltd,
Dunbeath,
Caithness, KW6 6EG,
Scotland, UK

www.whittlespublishing.com

© 2023 Hamish Brown

ISBN 978-184995-540-9

Printed and bound in the UK
by Halstan Printing Group, Amersham

Out of a dateless darkness pictures gleam,
But are they memory or only dream?

Masefield, *Wanderings*

CONTENTS

INTRODUCTION

Those who went through National Service are now likely to be Saga louts, so before long first-hand knowledge of those 16 years between 1947 and 1963 will disappear. There is little written about National Service – and most of what there is, is by those who became officers – so one justification for publishing these 'letters home' is that they will give a record for how it was – for one squaddie anyway. What writing there is, overwhelmingly concerns the army, who after all bore the brunt of the fighting in Korea, Malaya, the Canal Zone, Kenya and Cyprus, and who took the vast majority of conscripts.

No two stories could ever be the same and this particular squaddie, perhaps hardly typical, was abroad for his two years, and served in the more civilised ranks of the Royal Air Force. There are many thousands who look back to their National Service days with loathing, and many considered them a waste of time. I think, though, however harsh, or because they *were* harsh, those years served a social (and therefore economic) usefulness. Oddly enough, it was often lads from 'working class' backgrounds, who had been coddled at home (with regular jobs and insular social life) who felt most out of their depths whereas the 'posh' boarding-school boys had already experienced something similar to forces life in their schools, with their communal activities and often unfair treatments. All certainly had their ears opened to a widening vocabulary.

People in the armed forces today will find my experiences odd, partly because today all three services are far too technical to be lumbered with unskilled entrants. National Service was at least unbiased: everyone did it, whereas today's forces are a chosen career.

This book is thus something of a dip, an all sorts, as, within the framework of the straightforward RAF discipline, my young life played out its innocent absorbing of experiences. Of course, that innocence wasn't realised then. We didn't question. We accepted what we were told, did our work, made what we would of our freedoms, accepted our medals and, over the decades now can look back on those National Service years with some nostalgic warmth. Rereading my letters of the time gives a veracity which later remembrances could never match. I also suspect many more unpleasant experiences and frustrations were not reported home – and, remember, I was still in my teens when posted off to Egypt. I'm surprised at some of the things I *did* report.

We servicemen were such tiny cogs in the machine of Empire, whose workings were already being subjugated to impossible stresses. Having no power, we were uncorrupted, we were young and optimistic, could sing, 'I'm riding along on the crest of a wave, and the world is mine'. I feel I made a good use of the opportunities: my two years in the RAF provided a sort of self-education opportunity –and 'the longest paid holiday of my life'. In the simple letters home I record the busy activities of a worker ant, knowing nothing of the self-serving ends and chicanery of the Empire's graveyard governments. With hindsight, it was strange to be in the Canal Zone in those rearguard years (and Kenya the same) when we Browns had experienced the Japanese invasion of Malaya and the fall of Singapore, the first stroke in counting out the British Empire. In the Zone and Kenya we conscripts were all just normal, narcissistic youths out for a good time. And we did have a good time, most of the time, in this crash course of growing up and taking on responsibilities. Even a lowly telephonist mattered. The experience did us no harm – *au contraire*, for me it was a valuable rite of passage experience. The story may not be important but it is unique, and I hope interesting. I certainly found my two National Service (NS) years memorable.

All the letters I wrote to my parents as a boy during World War Two, from schools in Malaya and South Africa, showed the *aerial* battles, scenes with the RAF shooting down swastika-marked opponents or sending their ships to the bottom of the sea. Airmen were to win 32 VCs during the war – most, sadly, posthumously. I grew up reading about the derring-do of Guy Gibson and the Dam Busters, of Leonard Cheshire and Douglas Bader (heroes being portrayed in all those splendid black and white feature films of the fifties and sixties, with Kenneth More, Richard Todd, Jack Hawkins, John Mills, Alec Guinness *et al.*) And wasn't the RAF the first-ever such force in the world? The Royal Air Force (well, flying) was what fascinated me as a boy and in the last years at school was to have a practical application, as I joined the RAF Section of the Schools CCF (Combined Cadet Force). More on that shortly.

Reading between the lines there are plenty of glimpses of the hard graft and binds of life in the forces. That I went through the mill without ever being on a charge says something of my willingness to pull my weight, I was capable at my work on the switchboard, always turned up sober, mucked in and got along fine. I'm grateful for the necessary self-discipline those years instilled, and for the chance to enjoy such widely different experiences in very different countries, with some very good muckers who taught me the tolerance of companionship. And how we talked!

Some friends have been surprised at my not following up the chance of a commission, having been designated POM (potential officer material) but, if successful, that would simply have meant being stuck with the suffocating protocols of a lonely admin post, being a dogsbody – and having to put up with the boozy, hierarchical yet juvenile ethos of an Officers' Mess. As an airman, in contrast, I would have far more freedom in my time off and far less hassle when on duty. Not even the difference in pay would tempt – though I did resent that we NS victims were paid less than regulars for the same work.

The controversial NS conscription had originally been meant to last just a few years, but it took the horrors of the Korean War (which only ended in July 1953) and the 1956 Suez debacle – and the changing nature of war itself – to see NS end, in 1962. In that time over two million teenagers were given uniforms and pocket-money wages and sent off to defend, and to fight, and perhaps die. And we went, didn't we?

Thinking of the Korean War, up in the Bathgate Hills in Central Scotland stands a replica of a Korean temple, which is a memorial to that horror. The names of those who died are displayed in the temple, while round it are planted 1,090 birch trees, one for each British fatality, most of whom (88 per cent) were National Service conscripts aged 18 or 19, at the time still too young to vote – but not to die.

There is plenty in what follows that now makes me squirm besides the young man's earnestness, but it would be false to alter any of the opinions we expressed. This is how it was then. In some ways reading these letters was like meeting another person, someone encountered before surely, familiar yet posing as an unknown airman, simply writing home as anyone might. Yet that's not quite true, I'm sure; I wrote more often than most. Often, if unconsciously, I was writing for the sake of writing. Now and then I've included verses written at the time, their words perhaps giving sharper indication of feelings.

Many letters have been lost and I have perforce used memory to fill gaps. Where my memories are verifiable, I'm glad to note off-repeated yarns have not strayed far from veracity. The fact that they are in letters anyway removes much of the manipulations of memory. I have cut out references to many people, at home and abroad, who had no continuing part, keeping to a limited family and particular friends. I have removed the constant thanks for letters and parcels received, and the various purely family endearments and comments which ended letters. The sometimes wobbly spelling has been corrected and some duplications removed. Letters can be presumed addressed to my parents in Dollar unless otherwise shown. An address is only given for the first letter at a new location and thereafter is omitted. I include my sketch maps of the Canal Zone, Jerusalem and Kenya as they were then. Some of my letters had drawings in them, and a few of those have been reproduced. In order to minimise the narrative flow, words or acronyms that anyone with military experience and/or of a certain age might reasonably be expected to know appear as footnotes, but explanations that add to the information are in [square brackets], and longer notes and commentary are marked at their start with an asterisk, *. A few topics, more detailed yet, appear as appendices.

Most of the various forms of note give the background to matters in the letters, or reminiscences not written about at the time, but many more notes have been added, sometimes extensively, on the historical/political realities of the Zone, Cyprus, Jerusalem and Kenya. History has always fascinated me, and while I was out there I lapped up the histories of the bloodthirsty Cyprus and Jerusalem centuries, little knowing how, so very shortly, those two places – and Kenya – would once again be unhappy history in the making. These commentaries give the letters an even greater feeling of our squaddies' innocence.

Much was purposely kept from public knowledge – and from us, as well – being, sometimes, both incredible and discreditable. Fake news is nothing new. Politics is a far dirtier game than war – and the politicians make sure others carry the guns. If I was an innocent young man then, I am an angry old one now.

As there are frequent references to money, note that £1 in 1953 is at the time of writing worth 5p or, putting it in another way, what £1 would buy in 1953 would in 2021 cost £19.53.

My National Service was very much 'a game of two halves'; extraordinarily different in Egypt's Canal Zone and in Kenya, the former with such constrictions and the latter with all East Africa calling. Neither was without a troublesome, sometimes bloody, background, but that made little practical difference to a Signals Section telephonist, whether at work or at play. Egypt's constraints gave more time to study and read, an inner world much of the time, whereas in Kenya, there was so much to *do*, so many activities with so many friends – friends who would be friends for life. In the Zone it was far less sociable, and no long-time friend came out of that spell in the desert. This is a tale of 'the desert and the sown'.

Here then is what one gauche nineteen-year-old wrote, warts and all (though my publisher has replaced two terms likely to raise hackles in some with 21st-century sensitivities). Do not judge me, then, with hindsight, any more than I do myself. Wince I may, now, at some parts, but I can also laugh. They were days of great fun, hard work and hard play, making the most of opportunities and, because there was no need to state it, pride in being in the Royal Air Force.

> *Shades of the prison-house begin to close*
> *Upon the growing Boy,*
> *But he beholds the light, and whence it flows,*
> *He sees it in his joy;*
> *The Youth, who daily farther from the east*
> *Must travel, still is Nature's Priest,*
> *And by the vision splendid*
> *Is on his way attended.*

(from Wordsworth, 'Ode on the Intimations of Immortality')

Hamish Brown,
Burntisland, 2023

1

Square bashing: in the UK:
23 October 1953–4 February 1954

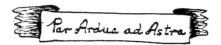

My enlistment date was 23 October 1953. I was briefly at RAF Cardington, near Bedford, for kitting out, then went on to RAF Hednesford in Staffordshire, a camp high in the woody hills of Cannock Chase, for square bashing. (Hednesford was a good Viking name, *Hedin's Ford*.) My hope was to receive an overseas posting, something most wanted to avoid. (Stationed near home and a good local pub was the dream for most.) Although I had asked for the Far East, where I had been born and had already travelled, I was posted to Egypt, but it could equally well have been RAF Leuchars, next to home in Scotland. There was no known logic behind postings.

Linking the letters are comments and explanations which, of necessity, are lengthy to start with, as people and concerns at home and in the RAF are introduced. Various things, so taken for granted then, have no meaning at all 60 years on. The NAAFI was the Navy, Army & Air Force Institute (founded in 1921) which provided many home comforts and facilities for forces personnel. So separated are civilian and forces' lives these days that I had to check if the NAAFI still exists. It does, and is still called the Naffy.

RAF Hednesford was a big sprawl of dark wooden huts. The photograph I took through the entrance on a grey day with smoke and mist makes the scene akin to some wartime POW camp, (World War Two was a recent reality for my age group) but RAF Hednesford was by no means a gloomy place, whatever the structure. In a group photo our hut of 22 all are smiling broadly at the camera, the corporal i/c[1] included. We pose in front of a Spitfire. A picture of our Flight 5 (120 airmen) is equally cheery. We belonged. That I remember so little is probably due to the mixture of a good intake, reasonable corporals, my own fitting in and the RAF being more reasonable than what we heard of square bashing in the army. I can still fold towels and blankets quickly and neatly, just as taught.

---

1 In charge. For expansions and definitions of technical terms and slang, see Appendix 1.

Left: The Tiger Moth in which I had my spin at the RAF Hawarden Camp

Right: Hawarden display 1952. A Lancaster Bomber

We were an extraordinary cross-section of the country's teenagers, from all social backgrounds, from every corner of the land, and we can thank the National Service for much. We rubbed along well. There was a lot of laughter and a lot of boisterous ragging (on one occasion a poor victim was locked in his locker and dumped out on the parade ground). My pocket diary one day noted 'friendly riots in dorm'. Boys will be boys. And being 'genned up' from a CCF background was quite an asset: I knew things like the IA[2] of a Bren gun, while marching well was second nature. I'd already been bawled at by teachers and prefects, had already learned forces' practices and procedures – and how to fit in with unchosen people and situations.

We had visited RAF Leuchars from school, and I had gone to summer camps at RAF Hullavington in 1951 and RAF Hawarden in 1952. At these we seemed to spend a great deal of time swimming, shooting and flying. I was mad keen on swimming, was already a good shot (both brothers, while in the CCF, went to Bisley), and I grabbed any chance of going aloft, whether in a Lancaster bomber, Chipmunk or Tiger Moth. I recall being at the controls of a Tiger Moth when we passed over what looked like a bomb crater and my instructor, behind, pointing: 'Tiger Moth. Prang. Last week.' Nevertheless, I've always had an affection for the Tiger Moth, which entered service in 1931, and was still a trainer for World War Two, the last RAF biplane; 8,500 were built.

Some called up would resent the interruption to careers begun, if not deferred, yet others found a stability in the ranks and learned trades which could be taken up thereafter. Remember, this was the colourless world of food rationing and utility clothes and furnishings, but was also, like life everywhere, any time, good in parts, bad in others. Undoubtedly many youths today would benefit from a disciplined form of service and we see the beneficial results in such bodies as the Scouts or those challenged by the Duke of Edinburgh's Awards scheme or even community opportunities based on outdoor activities, music, crafts, gardening. The key is *interests*; busy, engaged, committed youths are not going

---

2 Immediate action: what one did when it stopped firing.

to be into drugs and violence and all the other destructive options available today. (Yet it is these very inspiring possibilities that are cut and cut by governments and authorities – who then probably spend more money coping with the results of their unimaginative acts.) I'm just astonished today to see, against the odds, the extraordinary range of talented young people, whether climbing mountains, making music, setting up businesses, breaking records in sports and athletics. And they have come from every background imaginable – or unimaginable.

Just how *everyone* was sucked into doing their two years National Service can be seen in the experiences mentioned in (auto)biographies of people as diverse as David Lodge, Michael Caine, Fred Trueman, Michael Parkinson, Tam Dalyell, Jackie Charlton, Ronnie Corbett, Michael Heseltine, Leslie Thomas, Peter Hall … Some liked the experience, others did not. (Brian Blessed experienced a great deal of bullying both during square bashing and after, endured soulless work, and bitterly resented time and talents misused.)

I went into the RAF for my two years straight from school. There wasn't much option as I was not academically qualified for university, nor did I particularly want it then – or afterwards. Being free of school was a glad release. The RAF held no terrors for me, for I had knocked about a bit – and taken knocks – so was confident of coping with whatever came. There are flashbacks and added notes to give something of my own background; how these two years fitted into my life as a whole – which can only be viewed now of course.

As cadets at school we were often visited by regular officers for lectures, and NCOs would bring along bits of machinery, armaments, air cameras and the like. Even then the RAF was becoming highly technical. We received more than a ration of lectures on the Internal Combustion Engine – the 'infernal combustion engine'. One poor visiting sergeant was obviously out of his depth and waffled on, to our glee, when questioned about the 'pestenulator' – a word we had invented for such occasions.

My knowledge of the Ochils came in useful one desperately hot Friday afternoon in summer when we were issued with a radio and sent off on an exercise over the hills. The radio was a box-like affair, very heavy and had to be carried like a backpack. The exercise did not appeal: climbing up and over White Wisp and checking in from the given six-figure references on our route card. By the time we had reached the top of the town's Burnside most of our uniform was tied round us as we sweated from that modest effort. The road to the castle would be sweltering. 'To Hell with this!' I thought and put forward a proposal which was agreed to by acclaim.

As a schoolboy I'd roamed the Ochils for years and explored the glen, then a doubly attractive lure as it was supposedly out of bounds, and I had explored every corner. The toil up was lightened by the prospect of what I suggested, and before long we were splashing about in one of the secretive pools of the Dollar Burn. That *was* an afternoon to remember! And the routine checks? No problem. At the appropriate times I climbed up to the edge of the wooded glen where we'd dumped the hefty radio and reported on our mythical manoeuvres. I doubt if the officer i/c had ever climbed White Wisp; and my descriptions of topography and views could not have been faulted even if he had been a hillgoer. There was a final ironic twist. We reported back with well-wetted hair (an oversight, that) only to hear our officer gloat to another teacher, 'I certainly made them sweat!'

With this background, square bashing was neither surprising nor intimidating:

'You're in the RAF now, Brown!'

The last photo before call-up

Three letters from RAF Cardington survive:

RAF Cardington

23.10.53

The safe arrival of 848 Brown is hereby reported.

My pal Bill Blakey and I had a compartment together until the last minute when another bloke stumbled in – obviously having had a good booze-up just before. He fell asleep and just about set himself alight with the cigarette he was smoking. At Kilmarnock when he woke (10.30pm) he jumped up and grabbed his case believing it to be at Kettering (which we only reached at 6.30am!). There we changed trains, and finally reached Bedford at 8am.

It was an uneventful journey – I woke up every time the train stopped: Kilmarnock, Dumfries, Annan, Carlisle, Keighley, Leeds, Sheffield, Derby, Leicester and Kettering. I woke fully at five and went along to the 1st-class toilet at the other end of the coach and washed etc.

What a flat place this is! The highest hills are the railway embankments. It became very misty and very cold and we were all thoroughly miserable except our friend from the Gorbals who was still quite happy. We're a very mixed bunch: boys just out of school, boys just out of university and all the variety expected of folk from John o'Groats to Land's End. There are some pretty awful types, but mostly good lads and we've enjoyed ourselves, so far. All we've done is being issued with bedding, and cutlery, and filling in forms. I caused quite a stir with our family genealogy, me born in Ceylon, for a start. They've probably put you, Maw, down as a full blooded Siamese! And when they heard D [brother David] was born in Japan they gave up and put us all safely down as British. Don't know the address yet but, as we are only here for seven days, please don't bother writing.

25.10.53

It's raining again and I've just had to sprint from the Dining Hall. Very good lunch, and more than sufficient, absolutely nothing to grouse at, though some do. We seem to have nothing but free time. We spent most of the day of arrival on our backs, and the far-travelled Scots party needed it. At odd times on Friday and then on Saturday morning we got pushed through various procedures: X-rays, medicals, security talks, information, church meetings etc. [I'd already had a medical for the RAF in Edinburgh at the end of August.] There were also the unsparing medical films.

As for Church, all of us (about 2,000) were marched to the parade ground and split up into C of E, RC, Jewish, and OD (Other Denominations) and were given a talk by our respective Padre. Ours, OD, is a Flight Lt Methodist. I've practically lived in the Kingsway Club, which is next door to the church, it being smoke-free and providing table tennis, darts, mini organ, radiogram, piano and numerous armchairs. I played 15 games of table tennis last night before staggering off to bed. Church this morning (all voluntary nowadays) and a very good Service. OD here proves to be Scottish –there are English Presbyterians, Methodists, Baptists, Congregationalists, Brethren – and even one Christian Scientist. Padre has a good Scots name and a fearful English voice.

LATER, IN CLUB. Singsong on one side of me, Monopoly on the other and ping pong's crash-bang through the wall. Chap opposite is a bit homesick and near tears. Trying to cheer him up. He's never been away from home for more than a night or two – at this age! Mail is pounced on. Going to stop; want to join the singing.

29.10.53

Enclosed a Baggage Insurance chit for my civvies which were posted on the 28th. If they haven't arrived after 15 days you can claim. We had a farewell beano in the NAAFI last night (cost me 5d for a glass of lemonade yet some people spent *pounds* on beer). When my RAF Savings Book reaches you please keep it till you get my next address. I'm saving one shilling a day (30/- per month) which is automatically put into the book before I get my pay. In the middle of cleaning so must stop.

* On a spare afternoon at Cardington I recall someone suggested a walk up the hill and I, the Scot, after a look round, quite innocently asked, 'What hill?' From the flatlands of RAF Cardington a batch of us were sent on to RAF Hednesford for our square bashing. Up on Cannock Chase, it was a distinct improvement scenically.

2590848 A.C.2 BROWN, H.M.,
FLIGHT NO.5, HUT 181,
WING. NO.1, B SQUAD,
NO.11 S. OF R.T.,
RAF HEDNESFORD,
STAFFS.

31.10.53

The above is my new address. Cannock Chase is rather like Scotland only not so high. There is nothing but trees, trees and more trees. If it's not raining, it's very misty and always icy cold (five blankets on the bed and we are still chilly). We arrived by train and lorry yesterday and have had a busy time. We are all choked with the feeling of colds resulting from injections and vaccinations – so are feeling miserable. The billet is a good one and the fellows a decent crowd. My pal Billy Blakey, who I travelled south with, is in the billet, as beds were allocated alphabetically. He is in the next bed swaddled in blankets and also trying to write.

Seems quite an efficient camp. Regulars say the weather is always bad. There are chances for games and riding is one of the official options – and it looks an excellent spot for that. I also put my name down for rugger and swimming. There are clubs, NAAFI, theatre and

The entrance to RAF Hednesford which was not nearly as bad as the view might suggest

gym, so free time goes fast. There is a 36-hour leave coming along sometime but that is hopeless for Scots getting home. Could you please send me two padlocks (1½" wide) and one of those basin stoppers that will fit any hole. Basins never have stoppers. Discipline is good and strict and you'll get a frightful bollocking for little things. I'll have to stop and get on with bulling[3] boots etc. We're all comically sniffly and groggy – hence the afternoon off. I'll write as soon as I feel better, and warmer. Write soon, and give all the news (Crail etc).

Yours, 2590848 – which is what we become here. Just numbers.

2.11.53

Just had the billet inspected by our Officer. I was billet orderly for the day. I saluted him and gave the rigmarole: 'Sir, 848 A C 2 Brown, Billet Orderly, Sir. Hut No. 181, 5 Flight B Squadron, I wing. Billet ready for inspection, Sir.' (As though all that wasn't pretty obvious.) I fell in behind with note book and pencil. He was quite pleased, and well he might be – we'd spent hours cleaning the hut. Name was Jeffries, so nicknamed 'Judge'. Very keen. I have the afternoon off to go swimming. Back on Friday I had a good walk on the hills. Yesterday was Remembrance Day Parade – drizzle and a sorry march past, a squeaky Last Post and failing loudspeakers. Dollar CCF would have showed them up. Still it kept 7,000 of us busy freezing for an hour.

Good lot in the billet and feeling fine and fit. Three Dollar boys here: last year's head boy, Charlie Millar, 'Gnome'; White from Dunfermline (you know his father), and Norman Crosthwaite. We were all RAF at school of course. We usually meet up in the NAAFI for nights. Sunday papers are obtained by all of us paying in a penny and, with the collection, purchasing all the papers on sale. A pal gets the *Sunday Post* sent on. I go through the *Sunday Times* as I'll get tested later on current affairs. Sleep like a log, eat like a horse – and all the fun of the fair. Life as cliché.

---

*Not reported home, I recall one lad, a Jehovah's Witness, rather pushed his magazine, *Watchtower*, at us, so one day he was given a watchtower. While he was fast asleep two tables were made to straddle his bed and on this were stacked every piece of furniture in the billet. A placard was placed at his head, 'Here's a watchtower for you, mate!' He took it well.

Another memory. In the centre of the billet was a stove (for heating the place) with the coal held in a large galvanised bucket. It was always empty first thing in the morning. Reveille in the freezing cold was unpleasant to say the least, but our Corporal Bristow had

---

3 Polishing – to a high degree of shine.

his own way of forcing us out of bed. He brought a kettle and poured water into the bucket from a great height. Within no time at all everyone's bladders responded!

5.11.53

The sun shines at last. The district looks even better than I thought: very upsy-downsy and covered in woods – rather like Killiecrankie. The only blight is that wherever you look you see coalmines and chimneystacks. Looking out now down a lovely valley I can see seven. Stafford (Wedgwood country) is only nine miles away and at night the whole of the Midlands is a sea of light. Still very cold, and always is, and will be, as we are so high up. I'm longing to get a ride on one of the station nags. Had a game of rugby yesterday and will have Saturday off playing for the Station's second team.

Our Passing Out Parade is on the Tuesday before Christmas. We get about 7 days leave then, as well as the Christmas and/or New Year grant. Please send Tom and Anne's address so that I can invite myself there for my 48-hour pass in two weeks' time. There was a Passing Out Parade today and it was impressive.

Our dress is 'working blue' and denims, and we certainly do work – till we're blue! Drilling with the frost white on the ground is not fun. We are lucky with our corporals; they are real characters. The officers are a mild lot in comparison. There are terrific arguments between the six Scots and the dozen English (not forgetting one Taffy). It always ends with the mob of us going for drinks at the NAAFI. There's nobody really obnoxious. Lots of clubs, sports, and cinema and theatre, take up all spare time – when we're not cleaning brasses and bulling boots and scrubbing floors and oiling rifles and polishing woodwork and shining windows and ironing uniforms and sewing denims and chopping wood and eating meals etc, etc, etc. The billet atmosphere is redolent with the smell of warmed boot polish, steamy garments being ironed and all the assorted cleaners (endless Brasso) – and sweaty, smelly us. Under Judge Jeffries is Sgt Thomas whom we rarely encounter. Our real mentor is Cpl Bristow i/c our hut 181, not a bad guy at all. The other corporals are Gill, Crawford, Thomson and Holt – a mixed bag. I think we're lucky.

10.11.53

Now the hour of 06.45 and I am writing while queueing for breakfast which seems even more disorganised than usual. One mercy is that they rarely have porridge, for they can't make it properly. We have cornflakes usually made soggy with warm, sweet, milk. Eugh! Always famished of course but can't really grouse – as POMs we do get let off some things.

Send on requested items please; they are eagerly awaited; don't forget a case or grip (small) of some kind. Thanks for the sweets, rags, and padlocks. It's icy cold as usual. We have 2 extra blankets but are bawled at if we dare light the billet fire – to save work. (Most wouldn't know how to light a fire anyway.)

I had my first ticking off today. Bill and I went up at lunch time to the post box, then were standing looking at a map of the station when a voice roared out of the Guard House, 'Come here, you two.' We went and got a bollocking for 'not being at attention' while looking at the map – the map so displayed we had to bend down to read it. You just grin and bear this sort of inanity. Of course we are always open for the catch-all of 'behaviour prejudicial to good order and discipline' – so we don't even smile at the wrong time!

Coming home, I doubt if I can manage it on the day we pass out. If we leave at 11, it would be bus to Stafford, train to Crewe, change to Edinburgh, train to Dumf,[4] bus to Dollar. But when is the last bus to Dollar?

I got highly praised for a Bren gun stripping (knew it anyway). The periods I least enjoy are gym (strangely enough) because so much of the time is taken up changing. Drill is fun, the DI[5] being reasonable. The Education lectures are interesting, and Defence and so on are not bad. We never seem to stop filling forms.

I passed my RAF Swimming Proficiency yesterday. We went to Walsall Baths. Late back, so we had a special tea laid on: 'a good thing' for the food is not good (and not enough of it). The NAAFI gets well visited. Everyone gets parcels, so we just manage. NAAFI supplied beer but not spirits, not that I care.

Had a walk on Saturday in the hills – up and down narrow lanes and up on proper moors. Still haven't found who is in charge of riding. Now we have our permanent passes we can go anywhere after tea on weekdays and out till midnight on Saturday – and all Sunday. Not very much daylight for wandering, but cheering to go into one of the towns for an evening. Haven't been to the pictures yet; no good films. Have had some games of rugger. You always get time off for sport!

Today two home letters, books and other things arrived – from Cardington. Does Ian want me to keep his letters? I think I may have to send much of my washing home as it is so badly done here. Others have received some back and can't get into most of it. Poor chap on next bed is almost choking himself trying to get his collar on. [Detachable collars and studs were the bane of our lives.]

Pen nib broken, so excuse pencil scribble. Starting to clean billet for CO's inspection in the morning so will have to stop till later. I had to use my Housewife[6] to invisibly mend a snag on a shirt sleeve. Can't have that, can we?

---

4 Dunfermline.
5 Drill instructor.
6 Sewing kit.

LATER. Our Flight Officer (P.O. Jeffries) came in this evening and we had a good time pulling his leg. He gave as good as he got. If he'd come five minutes earlier he would have found most of the hut round the for once blazing stove eating hot buttered toast (illegal of course)! Half an hour before and he couldn't have got in as all the furniture was stacked up at the door end in order to bull-up the floor.

our drill instructor!

Writing this in the Writing Room in the NAAFI after our supper. The room can knock spots off many homes for cleanliness and tidiness: lovely deep chairs and thick carpet, writing desks and other furnishings in light-coloured wood with green curtains to go with rust-coloured upholstery. I like the way you tell me to practise drawing in my spare time. What spare time? I did a caricature of a lecturer once – only he saw it – and wasn't amused. Enclosing one of our DI. Good bloke too. 'Cooms from Oodersfield way.'

I was asking what the chances of going abroad were and the Careers Officer said not bad, if you apply. After Christmas I start anything up to two months' training in a trade before being posted finally to some station. Once posted, however, there is not overmuch work, unless I become an officer – and we are all POMs here. Out of 450 in our intake (intakes once a week) perhaps two will become officers. I don't want to be one, as you know. For all of the technical branches they want degrees and diplomas for this and that, and if that isn't needed the shortest service wanted is three years and so on and so on.

How is Paw's knee? Glad to hear your hand is better, Maw. Weather here is mixed but I'm fine, no cold or anything. I bashed an elbow pretty badly at rugger but it is nearly normal again. You seem to be rebuilding the Crail cottage. Give Hamid a pat.

---

* Several family holidays had been spent on the Fife coast before Father bought a small fisherman's cottage down near the harbour at Crail. I had made most use of it between school and call-up, and loved 28 Shoregate dearly. A big basement where fishermen stored boat and nets used to have salt crystallise on the beams after damp weather. We installed a toilet there, reached by going out the front door, round the corner and through another door into this basement. More than once I was enthroned when the whistling kettle let rip. As like as not the old dear across the street would nip over and switch it off before I could manage. (A companionway down was to be one of the first alterations!) I used to make some pocket money by doing watercolour sketches of the scenic harbour and leaving them on the doorstep with a note: Ten shillings. Please put money through letterbox'. Hamid was our dog, a smooth-haired fox terrier. The Hamid came from brothers *Ham*ish and Dav*id*. He was all terrier terror, though protective of the endless Siamese cat families that marked the Dollar years.

Big brother Ian had graduated in 1953 from St Andrews University, so, deferment over, was promptly called up. Thus, in my last summer at home, he was at Eaton Hall, the army's stately home near Chester, for officer training. His written requests and thank you letters and describing courses, etc, all had a familiar ring. Basic training was just that: square bashing with brass knobs on, his setting of a mansion no doubt more becoming. Now and then he was asking if I was yet in the RAF, and by the time I was square bashing he was at Bordon, the REME training centre, and thereafter was stationed in Germany. Young brother David would miss the joys and sorrows of National Service.

It can be seen that our regime was by no means harsh (Loch Ossian youth hostel was far more primitive!) and one just tolerated the bull: spit and polishing boots or buffing them with a hot spoon, ironing soap into creases of trousers and tunic, keeping clothes clean and neatly folded and trying not to get Brasso on everything when shining buttons and cap badge. (Remember the button stick?) Of course there were the odd lads who could never do anything right, *haunless*[7] rather than *gormless*, and the NCO's cane would unerringly point to the sin and it would be a fizzer[8] again. We didn't paint coal, cut grass with scissors, or suffer other excesses as half-expected. We did have one lad who simply could not organise his rights and lefts: 'By the left quick march' and out would shoot both right leg and right arm. For most people swinging the same arm and leg together is nigh impossible but there is usually one practitioner in any intake to drive the drill NCO crazy. They are usually 'excused' in the end, and at their passing-out parade must sit rather sorrowfully, watching.

11.11.53

I've decided against cousins Tom and Anne for this weekend as they are not easy to reach. Out of our Flight (about 120) there are only two of us who don't want to go away, [on a weekend pass] so we are going walking and exploring over the weekend – it's good walking country, this Cannock Chase.

My elbow is fine now. Practically all we do here I've done before, so no shocks. The weather has improved greatly. Beautiful sunrises often coming back from breakfast. Beautiful sunsets going to tea. Art Club, Monday; Film, Tuesday; Church Club tonight, Thursday, a bit of table tennis, then the camp empties and we either hike or lie abed reading, our hut forgotten even by our corporal. I thought of going to London but I'd rather get out into the country for a day or two. Have to change for P T soon. I've plenty of vim, compared to some. Saturday afternoon last Bill and I had endless games of table tennis as we had the

---

7 Handless in good Scots, or 'all thumbs'.
8 A charge, usually leading to punishment.

place to ourselves. (Every game was close and really strenuous.) *I am the only one left out of our 22 in the billet who has not been on the black list or cookhouse.* No doubt I'll be there soon as the fact stands out glaringly on the board. My personal drawer got commended by the inspecting officer – believe it or not!

13.11.53

Just on dinner time. As on last pay day we Bs get off early so have this half hour free. Last dinner was, for the first time, adequate – of course I was serving and when everyone is served the servers take as much as they like. We had soup, corned beef, brussels, roast and mashed potatoes, gravy and turnip, followed by a trifle à la Air Force. Sounds OK but is overcooked and tasteless.

Two Education lectures, drill, pay this morning; all fun. Enclosing the broken pen nib. Muckersie have them, so please send a new one. Thanks for the *Sunday Times* – arrived this minute. Most people are filling in 36-hour passes now. We Scots look on in envy. Two beds along is a chap from Anstruther. This morning our corporal called us a 'shower of (pause) tadpoles', which got a laugh. Wonder how often he's used it? He's good at his job though, without needing to play the tyrant. Comes and socialises sometimes at night. So we want to do well for him.

Lunch Parade call, so cheers from your ' 'orrible likkle man'.

Mother, Father, Colin Angus and a selection of Siamese cats at Dollar

* I often referred to my parents as Maw and Paw, from 'the Broons', characters appearing in the *Sunday Post*, that idiosyncratic D C Thomson publication which also sported Oor Wullie, all (then) drawn by Dudley T Watkins. They also published the *Beano* and *Dandy*. Big brother Ian's nickname at school had been Beano. Tom and Anne were cousins, both doctor specialists in sexual diseases, something that both fascinated and appalled. When I'd come back to Scotland as a boy from South Africa during the war I had a horrific collection of boils. (There were times I could not sit down.) Dr Tom managed to obtain

Square-bashing. Cpl Bristow's intake, HB (4), Bill Blakey (5)

some of the new wonder drug, penicillin, and on one visit to Devon Lodge gave me a course of treatment: endless injections up and down my thighs, one every four hours, day and night … They lived at Burnley at this time. Perhaps my lack of concern at the constant injections in RAF days had something to do with this initiation. We had a day out of camp to go the RAF hospital at Cosford (Staffs) for a yellow fever injection. That should have hinted at what would come. You don't get a yellow fever jab for a UK posting.

The reference to sunsets on one occasion could have seen me on jankers.[9] We were returning 'home' from an hour of 'Left! Left! Left, right, left!' on the square, I one of the three at the head of the column, when we came over a rise to be presented with an overwhelming blaze of red sunset, one I've never seen bettered in a lifetime of world-wandering. I stopped dead in my tracks, so the column piled up in disarray behind me. Two things probably saved me: one, this was the saner RAF, and two, what had stopped me had all of us, Cpl Bristow included, looking at it in amazement. The whole western sky was on fire, the reddest of reds, shot through with orange, with glowing clouds stirred into the molten mix, an overpowering wonder, almost alive and ready to overwhelm us. Nobody had ever seen anything so awesome. I stammered some reply to 'You, Brown, what the eff do you think you're doing?' Everyone just stood awhile, and then we were quietly told to get into line again and march on, heads high and hearts singing. I wonder how many still remember that unforgettable moment touched with glory?

9 Military punishment, often meaningless.

LATER. Preparing for hut and Flight Photos. We're in the billet, four billets in our flight, four flights in our wing, two wings in the squadron … About 500 arrive and depart every Thursday. Lucky; the rain arrived after the photo session.

24.11.53

Writing this in one of the offices in the Station Headquarters. Now 3pm (or should I say 15.00 hours?) and I've just been away for a big can of tea for the officer next door. We have our cups out of it when he has drunk his fill. I am here as we are on our Fatigue Week and do all kinds of odd jobs. I'm in an office as I'm hardly fit for anything else: to start, I've been piling up a horrible throat, this morning I got cramp on a leg and it is now very stiff. Going to breakfast I fell in the dark and so have a nice hole in a hand and wrist then, at the fire station in the morning I was chopping wood and just about chopped off a finger. Yesterday I pulled a chest muscle when I got a 2cwt[10] bag of sugar to catch (if I had not held on it would have fallen on someone). So now you see why I am on light duties, and very nice it is compared to yesterday's outdoor painting in an icy wind. I'd a wet game of rugger the other day (some of us have unusual notions of fun).

Did I tell you that I was at a Gilbert and Sullivan *Gondoliers* on Wednesday? [Rugeley Amateur Operatic Society] A sudden arrangement, and Bill and I jumped at it. Very amateurish, but worthwhile. Supper out, and we crept into bed – legally – long after lights out. Going to Birmingham on Saturday, a club tomorrow evening, film on Thursday, so plenty to do, Bill and I usually together.

EVENING. In bed. Excuse the scrawl but my index figure is bandaged. Doesn't let me off the spit and polish, though. Thanks for the nib. Can now write in ink again! How is your [garden fork-] speared hand, Maw? Let me know Ian's address please. Made pals with a cairn terrier that wanders about. Pets are allowed, I noticed [presumably for permanent staff]. I'm still not in trouble so ain't I pleased! This afternoon I ended up showing a brass hat round the camp. Being late for tea I got in with the staff lot and so had over 50 damsons with my custard. Quite a good camp library; I'll be there tonight. I've bought a pile of RAF Christmas cards – special ones for our use, with the station's crest.

The weekend was a bit lonely but very restful to do things just when feeling like it. Queer to be carrying on *comme ça* when the rest of the camp still slog past the billet under orders; my being here, but not of it. Breakfast on Sunday was at 08.00. Far too early! So I made a pile of honey pieces instead and left them handy by my bedside. The mice got them! Everyone getting ready for bed now; we all settle down quite early. Some are up 'betimes', and are not popular! I get up just before 06.00 and do all that is needed in the same time as those up at 05.00. More used to it, I suppose. There's a bit of a riot going on so I'd better go and join in or I'll be tipped out of bed too.

---

10 hundred weigts, i.e. 102 kg.

* Horseplay was always a feature of any billet and was simply part of that bonding (in self-defence!) which saw each flight by the end of square bashing determined to prove the best. There were always the odd lads who simply could not do a decent layout, or arrange their bed-space for inspection properly. Others would help out. All through my National Service years I was struck by the general decency of people. But always people.

> *I envy solitude*
> *and silence among the coloured hills.*
> *I envy wind and stars*
> *and all the gossamers of life*
> *that man can see but cannot touch*
> *or rule, or legislate.*
> *Waves are not asked to queue,*
> *Nor mountains wait.*

26.11.53

You should see the billet just now – 20% of them are flat out and most of the others are very groggy – just another little jag of a needle, and away they faint. I'm just very stiff in the left arm and am going out to our Church Meeting in a moment or two. Bill is going to bed. I've never heard the billet so quiet. I've just been dishing out cups of tea to the most unhappy. There's a good film on tonight but if Bill isn't a bit healthier I don't think I'll bother. Boy! The groans and aches and pain, but all of our billet still managed to parade this morning. (Some from other billets were called for by the ambulance.) My finger is out of bandage and into sticking plaster. Only aches and pains from the arm – and throat cold. I volunteered for overseas today, but all rests with Postings Office, Gloucester, and they'll do what most suits them. I wish lunch would hurry up – I'm always hungry even though I stuff to full capacity each meal. The other Dollar boys passed out today and it is under four weeks now till we do. How quick this week has gone – not that we've learnt much – though we brushed up on sweeping floors!

28.11.53

Had a wonderful weekend. On Saturday there was a rumpus because someone said something he shouldn't have to a NAAFI girl. The NCO i/c cancelled 36-hour passes and kept us waiting till someone owned up. Don't know what really happened but our crowd were just chuffed to be off for the ten to two train to Birmingham. The centre of Birmingham is attractive and there are some impressive buildings. We went round the Art Gallery (Bill and I) and an Exhibition, then tea and the big Christian Rally which was a bit American-ized but good all the same. The Birmingham starlings are amazing. On one old, floodlit church the slatted windows were lined with them and every bit of jutting out masonry was covered. The bare trees were so covered with birds they looked as if covered in summer leaves. And the noise! I've never heard anything avian like it. We were in our crowd again coming back and crept in past 11 o'clock. Too lazy to leave camp for church today and went twice to our own OD kirk. I went to C of E Evensong the other week, but the man's very pedestrian. This evening we played table tennis after church, then went on to the NAAFI for a snack supper. 'So to bed'!

I'm out of the following, so could you please send: 1 small Lux, 1 tin Brasso, 1 Kiwi black polish, 1 bar Palmolive soap, 1 chunk *washing* soap, and Vick. So much on there's little time to read. The CO was pleased with our inspection on Friday. Bill is engaged, so he gets mail nearly every day.

6.12.53

Away in Birmingham yesterday with a fearful rush. We had to do without lunch, but well worth it to hear *Madama Butterfly* at the Theatre Royal. We enjoyed it very much and, in the evening, *Il Trovatore* as I'd been lucky in obtaining tickets. Wonderful singing and encores and curtain calls all the way through. People were standing at the back. When I've finished this I'm going to book *Faust* on Saturday evening and *The Barber of Seville* as a matinée. Padre has just arranged a bus to take 30 of us to the *Messiah*. Big do with Birmingham Orchestra and some well-known singers like Isobel Baillie. 'Be getting real cultured, so I will' with operas, Gilbert & Sullivan, Shakespeare, Messiah etc. Carl Rosa Company was good and I crept into bed at one this morning. Our church had a Methodist Communion today which we stayed for. More or less the same as ours.

We had a five-mile cross-country run up on Cannock Chase, which most found an effort. For me it was more pleasure than penance, off over the misty, fresh landscape, and of course I'd done six such runs this year at school and romp the hills anyway. I kept quiet about that and gained an undeserved reputation as a fit b… I'm actually astonished how unfit many are; sedentary backgrounds.

We were in the gas chamber one afternoon last week, and this week we have two days on the range. Time's running out quickly and I'll soon have to start worrying about getting home. Blood-doning too, today. We are volunteered! I'm rarely at the Naffy as I can't afford snacks with all this culture just now! Tell D I'll give him his birthday present at Christmas when I am home. Very sad to hear about Chali, poor old puss [our old Siamese tom]. Will

Crail be liveable-in by the New Year? I'll have to stop now and do my weekly blanco-ing. I got sent to the cookhouse last Thursday – but not for any crime; just my turn. Spent 90 minutes washing up in the tin room – what fun! My leave will be till 11th January definite or a week more if it is made embarkation leave. Last year leaves were messed up by snow. We might have a rail strike of course. Drill test and assault course done. P.T. one next week. We had a hilarious GCT[11] film on 'Shapes, shine and shadows' which I saw years ago in the CCF (as would Ian). A more recent one was dated 1943! Thanks for letters and Crail news.

---

* No more letters survive from Hednesford. I was 'out' earlier than expected (presumably with the overseas posting news through), various leave entitlements, and Christmas also to be fitted in. Missing the passing-out parade wasn't a glad release; rather, I was peeved, for I had worked hard to earn it, was looking forward to the biggest chance probably in all my two years to march in a big parade and swank at being in the Royal Air Force. I was even more pissed off when left kicking my heels at RAF Innsworth before finally being flown off to pastures new. Ironically, or because of this, my finishing time in the RAF would be earlier than expected. And *that* did me out of climbing Kilimanjaro.

RAF Hednesford no longer exists. In 1956 it was used to accommodate Hungarian refugees who had fled when the Russian tanks ended their chances of freedom. Now the site is part of the attractive Cannock Chase Country Park.

A few letters survive from RAF Innsworth, where I largely kicked my heels waiting to go overseas. There was one to a friend written during the grim journey from Scotland to Gloucester. How servicemen hated Crewe station. The top page of the letter is missing but it was written to Colin Chapman, one of several school friends who went on to become reverends – C of E (but I never held that against him). He was one of a party of us from school who sat up in the Ochils to read aloud through St John's Gospel in one session. We had both recently acted in Ian Hay's *The Housemaster*, myself miscast as the cold head, the Revd Edmund Ovington. (*She Stoops to Conquer* and *Arsenic and Old Lace* had been earlier plays I'd helped with at school.)

Crewe Station 18.1.54

Crewe Station at four in the morning – can you think of anything more miserable? I've waited here before – but it has always been in the summer and a few degrees above freezing. I tried to sleep after Preston but was too cold. Just had a cup of tea – vile British

---

11 General Classification Test.

Railways stuff. We left Stirling at 9.23pm. There is a lad beside me. He has just married and is feeling rather unhappy. He's doing what I'm doing – only he did not volunteer for overseas, not with a pretty wife back in Scotland. He showed me two wedding photos, and has been talking about her all the time.

Above the door to the refreshments room and standing out on the keystone of the arch is a carved face which might well be the face of an old Grecian god. There is a wreath on the head and the eyes are fixed ahead and the mouth gives the impression of unpleasant laughter. Perhaps he is the god of melancholy laughing at all the miserable squaddies wandering about. (Excuse this flight of fancy but I've got to do something to take my mind off my chittering flesh, and I could never face another cup of tea like the last one.)

I will be quite glad to reach Birmingham and have breakfast. At least I know Birmingham, and I think I'll manage two or three hours in Gloucester before going to the RAF Station – lunch too, perhaps, for a last symbolic touch of civilization! My hands are becoming too cold to write, my nose is running, my ears are tingling.

LATER. Gloucester. The Tudor Café. 10.45. At last I can sit over a coffee and relax for a wee while. I feel about all in and can hardly keep my eyes open. I'm almost too sleepy to feel like eating. Packed journey from Crewe to New Street, Birmingham. I felt almost at home in Birmingham Station, having been in it most weekends while square bashing at Hednesford. I sat and dreamt of the four operas I'd seen, I heard the singing at the Rallies again, and pictured the café we went to most visits – and Bill and I will never forget the weirdo who told us of it.

We were in for the second week running and we wandered about looking for some new café that was not a self-help. We came on a place that called itself a Wine Parlour or something like that but it also had a menu for teas. While dithering on the steps this character appeared, dressed in white jacket and dark trousers, the jacket ripped in one place, and we could see a great hairy chest. His collar was missing and his tousled hair hung right over his eyes in matted strands. He had not shaved for days and face, hands and clothes were filthy. He came up to us and in an undertone said, 'If you two lads are wanting a good meal cheap, I'll tell you the place … Don't come in here … Down there and turn left …' We took his advice, more to get away from him than anything else; still the place he suggested was good and we went each week after that. I wonder if he was paid to send along likely looking saps like us.

From Birmingham to Gloucester I was one of seven forces men in the compartment, and had my first taste of what I shall have to put up with for a long time, the almost competitive and constant foul language. One started and soon they were all swearing away every few words. I was too weary to sleep, so I sprawled and watched the sun rise. For three minutes it was wonderful: the great red wall of cloud, then the red turned to white and broke up to go sailing overhead, the pearly sky on the horizon became blue and the sun shone through to glisten the frosty world. There is no snow here. It gradually stopped in the north Midlands.

I staggered out of the station and wandered into the town centre. Half past nine! Over 13 hours travelling. I went into a café for a cup of tea but it was a dirty place, full of litter and bus drivers and ticket collectors. I went over to the bus stance to leave my luggage but it did not open for another quarter of an hour. I waited, and in the end managed to ease myself of most of my burden. Horrible kitbags. I went to the Cathedral and met one of its ministers, or whatever you call them. His name was Mac … (I forget what) and he comes from Loch Aweside. He invited me to come in any time and I said I would if I could. Gloucester seems a pleasant town at first sight – and how English. I feel quite a foreigner here, being hardly able to understand some of the accents and the look of the place is so different. I go to Innsworth on a 10 past 12 bus. I could not find the name on a map I have, but it is only 4d on the bus so it cannot be far. There is an old Elizabethan Inn over the way. My buttons I spent so long polishing yesterday are all tarnished already.

Well, my young scholar gypsy, I must stop and drink while my coffee is hot. Mr Holmes said once during leave that I looked better in uniform than in shorts – but a kilt is best. I am going to have one for my twenty-first birthday, and it will be a Macmillan tartan.

---

* Mr Holmes was W K Holmes, a retired reader for Blackies, poet, author, local historian, and a long-suffering friend of mine. He was the only adult I ever met during wanderings in the Ochils in those post-war years, and his modest book, *Tramping Scottish Hills,* was an early treasure of mine. From Egypt, and later Kenya, I would contribute early attempts at articles to magazines, and after any appearing, I'd receive a postcard of encouragement in his spidery handwriting. Hamish Macmillan Brown duly received a hunting Macmillan kilt for his 21st birthday: which could also be regarded as a *leaving* the RAF present. Alas, some years ago I outgrew it!

2590848 a.c.2 BROWN, H.M.,
DRAFT No. 904,
HUT 102,
5. P.D.C.,
RAF INNSWORTH
GLOUCESTER.

18.1.54

Another long-winded address.

I have no idea how long for, so you could send cake and towels. Rather a tough journey down from Scotland – absolutely no sleep, and now I have the bad luck to be on night duty at reception, which means no bed tonight either.

Gloucester is charming. I had a look at the Cathedral and some of the old Elizabethan-type houses. Going to try and take 40 winks on some blankets in the corner. No snow here, but cold, except in this room, which is like an oven.

I'll write in a day or two.

21.1.54

Well, things are settling down somewhat. It has been rather hard, though, for the 30 of us doing the jobs of 300. Yesterday morning I was storeman, yesterday afternoon I was a runner, yesterday evening I was a clerk. We are starting again this morning, and I have managed to wangle my way onto the clerk's job again.

My precious knife fell out of my bag in a lorry the other day but was found and I got it back. We are becoming much busier. About 300 more people came yesterday, which should ease the work a bit. I have been put on as permanent staff until I go. Interesting work.

On Sunday afternoon if we can get off, some of us will go and visit Cheltenham. There is not much time in the evening. Did I tell you that I will be flying out? That will be interesting, but I think sea would have been even more so. Reading in the paper last night of two more RAF plane crashes – one on our route! I wish they would let us know where exactly we are going. The food here is excellent; even the moaners can't find anything to grumble at! Yesterday's breakfast was fried egg, bacon and tomato followed by fresh grapefruit and cereal, bread, *butter* [still rationed in 1954], and marmalade. Lunch: soup; bacon, liver (lovely thick gravy too), beans, tomatoes, chips, onions, cabbage; and a choice of a custard tart or two baked apples and custard, also biscuits and cheese. What an improvement compared to Hednesford. The weather has been dry with a nice nip in the air at nights. Champing to be off. Egypt will be a bit warmer!

Your parcel arrived to-day. Mail is the thing people look forward to most here, and I was delighted to find a slip for myself while sorting the mail (which has been my job to-day). Enjoying myself here. Every evening I go to the church room as there is always a good crowd of lads and lassies – and tea and biscuits and singing. I've made good friends with a wee lad, Ken Mullis. First bumped into him in a bookshop (Haynes) in Cheltenham. Can't write more – I want to join in the activities. Most importantly, I may be off on the 2nd February, so better not post to here later than this coming Friday. Did I tell you both Ken and I found silver threepenny bits in our helping of the cake? Last night was chilly. This morning my towel at the head of my bed was like a board, and buckets in the corridor were frozen solid. But at least the ground is firm. There's been much of interest here really, which I should have written about. Now I'm being yelled at to make the char, so this will be my last scrawl from here – and from England.

* At Innsworth, the Allocation Unit, we were issued with long johns and greatcoats for the Canal Zone, which was laughed at as a typical forces cock-up over gear: 'Woollies for Egypt!' But we soon found it otherwise when on guard at 02.00 under the biting night cold of the desert. Ken and I kept in touch for several years. He joined me, Colin Chapman and brother David on SU cycle tours I led in Scotland a few years after demob, and went on to become a Methodist minister. He then made contact 50 years later!

The two weeks of RAF Innsworth soon passed, with nothing much to remember – except the food. Why was it so good there? Both in Egypt and Nairobi it was pitiable; the main, constant moan of the NS years. We did see *Call Me Madam* and *Francis Covers the Big Town* at the cinema, and tested various denominations of worship in the camp and in Gloucester. Ken flew off to Germany, then I was moved to Hendon, squeezing in visits to the National Gallery and the Tate and seeing the fine film of *Julius Caesar*, a performance somewhat grander than Hednesford's! We flew in a York from Stansted, had a stopover at Luqa in Malta. (The name is from St Luke who, with his buddy, St Paul, was shipwrecked there in AD 60.) We had a leg stretch and were off again, and reached Fayid in the Canal Zone at dawn. From there we were taken to El Hamra and finally I ended up at RAF Deversoir.

A JOURNEY TO MAKE

I have a journey to make
Beyond the shores of time.
I have a journey to make
Which only can be mine.
Will I make it in fine array
With banners in my van,
For we must make of journeys
Whatever proof we can?
Will I make it singing, glad,
My youth made strong,
Or will it be a murmured thing,
An old and broken song?
It frightens me to hoist a sail
Or foot a mountain way,
Yet the journey comes to every man
As night becomes the day.

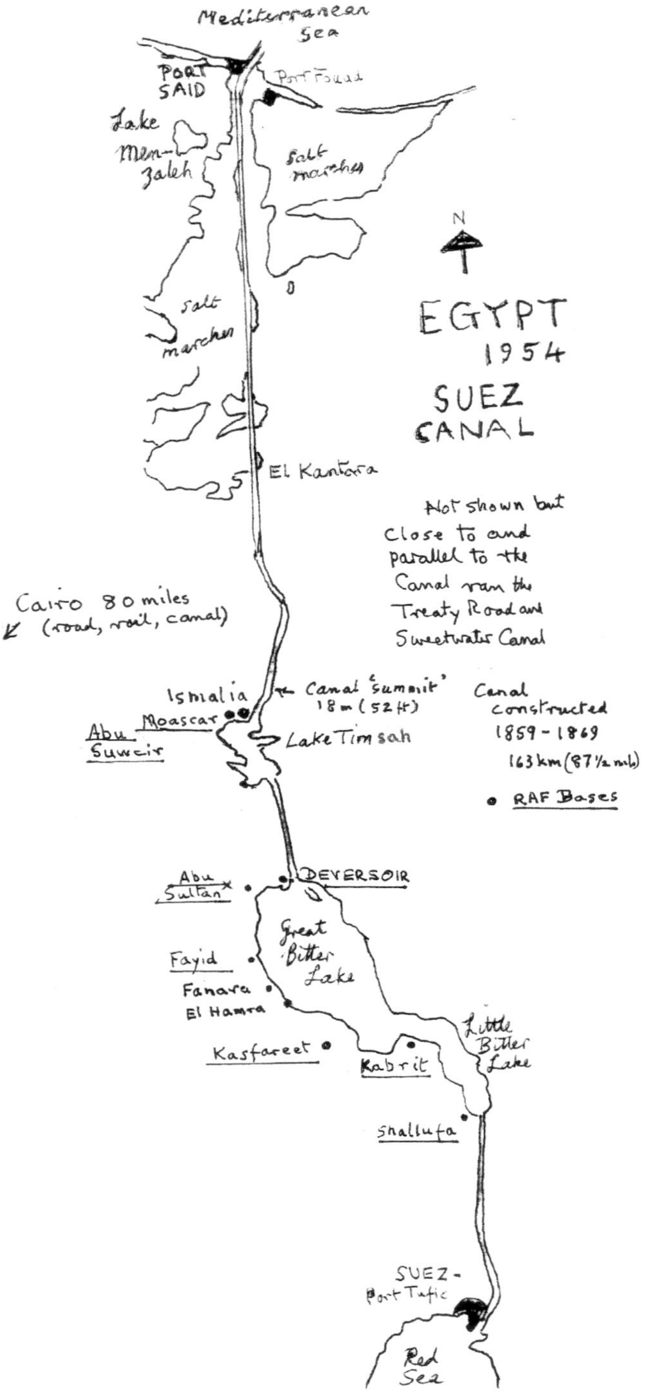

Mediterranean Sea

PORT SAID

Port Fouad

Lake Men-Zaleh

salt marshes

salt marshes

N

EGYPT
1954
SUEZ
CANAL

El Kantara

Cairo 80 miles
(road, rail, canal)

Not shown but
close to and
parallel to the
Canal ran the
Treaty Road and
Sweetwater Canal

Ismalia

Moascar

Abu Suweir

Canal "summit"
18 m (52 ft)

Lake Timsah

Canal
constructed
1859 - 1869
163 km (87½ mls)

RAF Bases

Abu Sultan

DEVERSOIR

Great Bitter Lake

Fayid

Fanara

El Hamra

Kasfareet

Kabrit

Little Bitter Lake

Shallufa

SUEZ - Port Tufic

Red Sea

2

The Zone, 1: Reacting to realities:
5 February–5 May 1954

LANCASTER

1953 had been quite a memorable year, with Stalin dead, Elizabeth crowned and Everest climbed. I, more modestly, led Scripture Union friends on a cycle tour, went to Inter-School camps at Dounans and Scoughall, managed 8th out of 60 in the school Cross Country, helped at the Scottish Beekeepers Association stand at the Highland Show in Alloa and earned my first-ever wage packet clearing up the showground, cycled to see my Aberdeen girlfriend, and enjoyed one last day on the Ochils as a schoolboy. My RAF Christmas leave was spent in Dollar and Crail – and another 'last day' on the Ochils before heading abroad.

The Mau Mau troubles were causing concern in Kenya, and Jomo Kenyatta and others were jailed, troops were flown in and a state of emergency declared – not that I probably noticed at the time; I, half-expecting to go to Singapore, had been more concerned about jungle warfare in Malaya. Egypt had seemed a disappointment, but with hindsight was surely a much more 'cushy billet' than Malayan jungles.

King Farouk had been booted out of Egypt, which was of direct concern. The unrest saw us being pitched into something of a war zone. I never did any trade training, as I'd expected in the UK, and arrived in the Canal Zone on 5 February 1954, to be turned into a telephonist. Most National Service trades in the RAF were either highly technical with long training courses or were humdrum: clerking, nursing, storemen and the like. I'd ticked typist and photographer on the list of options. At this period 27 per cent of the RAF were conscripts: 187,000 regulars, 69,900 conscripts. By the end of NS 388,907 of us had been called up into the RAF (and 90,700 to the navy, 1,320,972 to the army). In the Zone there were ten RAF stations, 34 army bases and two dockyards.

At RAF Deversoir we slept in a Signals Section circle of Nissen huts, half-sunk in the sand, and between each hut was an army tent for those whose job it was to repair our equipment when it failed – an even cushier job for army personnel who in the Zone were often badly looked after, and their morale low. The tents were standard ridge tents but with brick walls and solid bases, the soldiers sleeping on camp beds. We had iron beds (eventually), but the bane of all bedding was the presence of bedbugs against which we waged a continuous war with DDT powder. A lifetime on I can still recall the smell of squashed bedbugs. Ants were everywhere too, and flies in the summer – but worst of all were the cockroaches. Showers were primitive at one stage, with a bucket arrangement with a chain like an old-fashioned toilet; pull the chain to tip the bucket and eke out the precious water. Standing naked below this contraption one day I pulled the chain and, instead of water received a shower of cockroaches. Every hut had a big water *chati* at the entrance, a tall, porous clay Ali Baba jar wrapped in hessian, the cloth always wet with evaporating water, so the contents stayed deliciously cool. The drips falling onto the sand ensured every chati had a small patch of greenery under it, like a miniature garden.

It would take a couple of hours to walk round the camp. The 7-mile perimeter was marked by a tangle of barbed wire between barbed-wire fences, yet one morning the soldiers next door to us woke to find the locals had stolen the tent from above them as they slept, and had vanished over the wire. The soldiers were put on a charge for losing army property.

I've never really liked beer, and whisky set me retching (why, shortly) so it was easy enough while doing my two years simply to say I was teetotal. Initially there was pressure applied ('Oh, come on, mate!') but I was thrawn.[12] No. I can see how youngsters became so easily beguiled into excess. Peer pressure is insidious, but I'd long before come to have little but contempt for it. National Service was refreshingly free of what I considered the hypocrisies of school. Boozing was a major pastime but abstention was never held against me. I was no holier-than-thou Christian and could be as roisterous as any, and was known as a bit of a prankster. (Read the last paragraph of my time in Egypt for one memorable leg-pull of mine.)

I was not allergic to whisky (never heard of that one) but on one of my teenage Irish cycle tours I'd pedalled right across the flat middle of the country from Tralee to Dublin and arrived with what cyclists called 'the knock' – tummy muscles in a knot – and my Aunt Sis gave me some whisky to ease the agony. Nothing could have been worse on an empty tummy, and it was decades before the smell of the stuff didn't have me wanting to boke [be sick].

We had squadrons of Vampires and Meteors on the station, and the Vampires often carried extra tanks of fuel to give them additional range. The tanks, when emptied, were dropped, and the locals would bring them in out of the desert and sell them. I became part of a consortium which had built a catamaran, the hull made from the beaten-out drop tanks. We sailed on the Great Bitter Lake next to the camp. The Suez Canal also passed the

---

12 Stubborn.

RAF Deversoir. The PBX arrowed (behind the HQ block), MT compound in the background

camp and it was always an extraordinary sight to see a liner gliding along as if land-borne, towering over the palm trees that lined the waterside. On the opposite side of camp we looked over to the euphemistically named Sweet Water Canal, a substantial canal of fresh water brought from the Nile in 1863 to provide drinking water (and irrigation) along the length of the Suez Canal, south of Ismailia. Canals on both sides of camp did relieve the flat desert monotony with a certain amount of welcome seasonal greenery.

I used my time to the fullest under the trying circumstances, and read endlessly and also began to write seriously. During those long night duties when very few calls were made, the exchange could be quite a social spot. The duty officer on his rounds would stop for a cup of chai and the sort of literary chat not likely to be met by a junior officer in his Mess. The table would be covered in books and papers. At 0300 hours rank was not very important, and school had given me an intensive dislike of rank-pulling. So I read and read and scribbled and scribbled. Some day I would show them! One of my worst efforts I'm sure was hundreds of lines modelled on the *Kalevala* about a hero I named Vanaga Rive. Fortunately, that is all I can recall. All my money went on books. Everyman Classics were only two bob[13] after all, and by not smoking or drinking I had some money. I can recall later, when teaching, a senior member of staff rather grumpily asked how I, a very junior teacher, could afford to go off climbing in the Alps all summer. There was a £50 travel allowance in those days which was just adequate, but when I challenged him to work out what he spent on cigarettes in a year it was a considerably greater sum. There were far too many good things for me to be doing (even in Egypt) ever to be tempted to follow the crowd. And there were always others who thought the same. Those were happy times of freedom within discipline.

I was periodically caught by guard duty, which meant being on the gate (interesting) or perimeter wire (boring) or stuck up on a tower for a couple of hours. There was one night post which everyone else hated; a hole in the ground stuck out a mile in the desert beyond the wire where one sat with eyes level with the ground so anything moving would be outlined against the stars and reported. I was usually able to swop round in order to have

---

13 Shillings: two bob could come in the form of a two-shilling coin (aka florin) the same size and shape as a 10p piece, but then of course worth *considerably* more than now.

On guard; well, posing at the billet entrance

this spot, which entailed being driven out and then collected two hours later. Most people feared the dark and isolation. I loved it. Some nights I would just sit and watch the glittering glory of the desert sky. Sometimes there were flickering electric storms shimmering silently, sometimes a cold biting enough to crack rocks, but most nights I would lift the phone and find which mucker[14] was on the switchboard and have him plug in to Radio Moscow, thereby ensuring me a two-hour fix of classical music. I never once had to report movement out in the desert.

We were rather cooped up in camp, though Deversoir had the blessing of the Bitter Lakes for swimming and sailing. The camp NAAFI could be supplemented with visits to Fayid or Ismailia, but Ismailia was too often out of bounds, depending on the state of 'British Out' activities by the Egyptian nationalists. I'm surprised there were not more problems, what with no civilian, female, or outside interests, the punishing climate and – for most – perhaps too much free time. For many there was nothing to do except get pissed. Behaviour among the ranks, however, always seemed to be decent. Compared to army infantry establishments we were more purposeful – there were aircraft to fly and service – so morale was fine. The Vampires' whining or roar had the same accepted comfort of a nearby railway line at home. It was the biggest thug in the hut who walked a seriously homesick lad to the door, an arm round his shoulder, and wished him well. Coming back in he said, 'Fucking lucky bastard; going home.' On the whole we put on a 'good show'.

Between the end of World War Two and the mid-fifties British forces had been deployed in policing, garrisoning, giving humanitarian aid, or fighting serious-enough wars in – wait for it! – Northern Ireland, Germany, Austria, Trieste, Greece, Cyprus, Malta, Gibraltar, Libya, Egypt, Sudan, Somaliland, Ethiopia, Eritrea, Palestine, Jordan, Iraq, Aden, Kuwait, Bahrain, India, Ceylon, Malaya, Singapore, Indonesia, North Borneo, Hong Kong, Japan, Christmas Island, British Guyana, British Honduras, Belize, Guatemala, Barbados, Jamaica, Bermuda, Gold Coast, Cameroons, Togo, Zanzibar and Kenya. This 'peacetime' demand created Britain's biggest-ever worldwide military duty, sucking in two to three million men. In those pre-technical days, conscription could hardly be avoided. In the 'graveyard' of the Canal Zone in 1951, 14 squadrons had a strength of 152 aircraft and something like 60,000 army personnel. Britain's retreat only became clear in retrospect. The government made sure of hiding the reality of the Zone years.

---

14 Mate.

Much of this was new to me when I began browsing through these letters – and I learned much from Douglas J. Findlay's *White Knees, Brown Knees* (Discover Press 2003), who himself was stationed at Deversoir. The *Road to Suez* by Michael T. Thornhill (Sutton) 2006 is a full account of the Zone story leading up to 1956. The curious might like to know what went before that, so the following is a brief historical summary. Appendix III tells the saga of building the Suez Canal itself.

1869 saw the Suez Canal open after ten years of hard construction. As the canal cut 6,000 sea miles off the route from Britain to India and other map parts then tinted red, it was of vital political and commercial interest to Britain. French interests suffered a setback when in **1875** the wily prime minister, Disraeli, pulled off a deal to buy a controlling interest in the Anglo-French Suez Canal Company from the bankrupt Egyptian khedive,[15] Isma'il Pasha, for £4 million. (The Egyptians themselves were left out of any profit-sharing from this asset in their own country!) In **1882** British forces landed in Egypt ostensibly to help the Egyptian government quell a rebellion (which had seen 50 Europeans killed) – and stayed.

In **1928** the Muslim Brotherhood was founded with the objective of ousting Britain from Egypt. **1936** saw the signing of the Anglo-Egyptian Treaty (by the then Foreign Secretary, one Anthony Eden) which freed the country from being a British protectorate but gave Britain control of the canal's defence for 20 years. A force of up to 10,000 troops would be maintained in the Suez Canal Zone. The RAF maintained the right to overfly Egyptian territory.

During World War Two, **1939–1945**, British Military HQ was moved to Cairo and troop movements were unrestricted, as was the setting up of bases – anything, in fact, to see the defeat of the Axis forces in North Africa.

1946 saw tensions rising again and Britain agreed to withdraw to the Canal Zone once more. An Egyptian call to quit completely in 1949 was rejected. Extremists thereafter would turn to terrorism and attack British troops and installations. **1947** saw Palestine partitioned, the unhappy solution to years of fighting there between Jews, Arabs and Britain. In **1948** the state of Israel was founded. Displaced British forces from Palestine were posted to Malta, larger numbers to Cyprus and most to the Canal Zone (further breaking the terms of the treaty numbers permitted). Egypt was naturally nervous at this possible Cold War target in its midst, but even then safeguarding the oil supply from the Middle East, vital for Britain, was seen by the British as the over-riding priority. Open conflict soon followed. The Egyptian prime minister was assassinated, and a year later, **1949**, the leader of the Muslim Brotherhood was killed in retaliation. In the Egyptian General Election of **1950** the Anti-British Wafd[16] party was swept to power. Riots in **1951** saw many British women and children in the capital being evacuated. Guerrilla forces, with the Cairo government's tacit approval, took control of Ismailia and increased attacks in the 'occupied' Zone. (One Egyptian newspaper was offering a reward of £100 to anyone who killed a British officer.) Heavy fighting would see 30 deaths by January **1952** when, in turn, British forces besieged

---

15 Ruler.
16 *Hizb al-Wafd*, Delegation Party.

and overran the police HQ in Ismailia with the loss of 46 Egyptian lives – and four British; 886 prisoners were taken.

There followed serious rioting in Cairo ('Black Saturday') when 37 Westerners were killed, and shops, banks, hotels, nightclubs (and the iconic Shepheard's Hotel) were looted and burnt. Troops in the Zone were alerted and others flown in from Cyprus, besides a squadron of RAF Vampire fighters. In July General Neguib as figurehead (Colonel Nasser the real plotter) seized power in a military coup, and a few days later the ineffectual King Farouk abdicated, replaced by an infant son. **1953** saw endless talks in Cairo leading nowhere, and British families were once more advised to leave Egypt. The infant King Fuad was deposed in turn. Egypt was declared a republic.

Early **1954** saw Neguib sacked, reinstated, and finally ousted by Nasser, who would be Egypt's strong man until his death in 1970. It was eventually agreed that British forces would vacate the Canal Zone by the end of 1956. The evacuation of the Zone got under way. In October 1954 an attempt on Nasser's life led to a clamp-down on the Moslem (now Muslim) Brotherhood.

So that was the where and what so many Suez erks[17] were facing: the reality of being in the Zone, and not really knowing just what was involved. The British government duplicity kept the emergency quiet for its own political ends, falsifying statistics and even refusing to award a service medal (till shamed into doing so – 50 years later). Churchill called the period 1951–1954 the Battle of the Canal Zone. In all 200,000 of us would be there over the years – hardly the minor trouble spot the politicians claimed. Twice as many were killed in the Zone as died in the Falklands War.

And afterwards?

In **1956** Nasser survived another assassination attempt, and nationalised the Suez Canal's Anglo-French Suez Canal Company, this partly as retaliation for Britain and America refusing to help finance the Aswan dam – which also drove Nasser to happily accept Russian aid. The last troops left, then 4½ months later came the debacle of the 1956 invasion of Suez by Britain and France (abetted by Israel), only to withdraw again following international, and especially US, condemnation (the US had been kept ignorant of the invasion plan). Eden then resigned and Harold Macmillan became prime minister. Britain was no longer the leading foreign power in the Middle East. In 1958 the canal was nationalised by Egypt, which paid over £E38 million[18] compensation to the Suez Canal Company's shareholders. Today, the canal (bigger, better) still operates effectively, with far greater demands, under efficient Egyptian control. More about the canal in Appendix III.

In 1952 Kenya, as well as Malaya, were escalating 'problems' for Britain. France was fighting in Indo-China, King George VI died, in 1953 Stalin died and the Korean War ended (July) – not that any of that was discussed in letters home. (Sweet rationing coming to an end had a more practical implication.) British forces were still engaged in Malaya, and would be till In-

---

17 Squaddies then; now, veterans.
18 £E was Egyptian pounds, at the time approximately equivalent to pounds sterling.

dependence in 1957. And just as the Canal Zone saga was ending, Cyprus was changing from an ex-pat haven and holiday venue into another bloody zone wanting Britain out. I was lucky to have seen Cyprus before it blew up, to have been in the Zone while RAF Deversoir was being run down, and to have enjoyed East Africa with the hellish Mau Mau largely a spent force.

RAF Deversoir

Canal Zone

5.2.54

Journey over – thank goodness. We landed at Fayid very early and then trucked down to El Hamra and then to this place later in the day so RAF Deversoir is to be my prison for good now – all sand, tents and barbed wire. Days are as hot as the hottest Scottish summer, but cool, now, 8pm. I'm just going to turn in as I'm rather weary.

We all have a 24-hour guard stint about one night in nine. There are floodlights all round the edge of camp with machine gun boxes at important points. You go in pairs at all times – and armed when out of camp. Dangerous Ismailia is not far up the road. The Sweet Water Canal is next to us and *the* Canal (and Lake) is over the road – a promise of good swimming and sailing. A railway also runs up and down the length of the canal. We have full working days on Mondays and Fridays; on the other days we only work mornings and the rest is free [so we were informed, rather optimistically as it proved]. We have jet aircraft here too, so there is plenty of noise. The food is rotten and the NAAFI very expensive. Money here is 100 piastres = £1 Egyptian (very similar to English one). There is also NAAFI money – coins made of plastic! All I've done today is find my bunk. I'm lucky in that I have a hut and not a tent. I will send my address as soon as I know it. Most people seem fed up with not having enough to do – and hate the confinement. I think I will be at an advantage with many varied interests and plenty of swimming. Time will tell how I get on.

2590848 a.c.2. BROWN, H.M.,

SIGNALS SECT.,

(HUT J.6.)

R.A.F. DEVERSOIR,

M.E.A.F. 25.

7.2.54

That is now my address. Long lie-in this morning, then I went to our Church for the OD service. In a few minutes I'm going again to the C of E Evensong as it is the only evening service. There were about 20 in the congregation. Since arriving I have done nothing but collect signatures on my Form of Arrival. That will take till Tuesday. I've read most of my spare time, but the billet gets so stuffy – and noisy. At Innsworth we just wandered up to the club hut; there is none here. I'm longing to get in for a swim. I get paid on Tuesday. We have a little extra for the difference in prices. I am writing this small, as a letter goes up from 2½d to 6d if it is overweight. It is funny, but fruit is hard to get, in fact where we are is bad for everything. Ismailia or Fayid seem to be the shopping centres – but one can't go anywhere singly, which is a bind, and Ismailia, the only big town, is Out of Bounds.

Even with all our spare time there is a local[19] who comes in and dusts, sweeps, makes beds etc. Most lads just lie on their beds and read cheap books and comics, only stirring for an odd card game, drink or picture visit. What an existence! I'll have to see I keep my mind busy. Now, the things I'd like you to send please: a lot I'm afraid. Most lads have sent home for stuff. [The list was mostly clothing, but also water colour paints, brushes, pens, inks and paper. Books were also requested: from poems of Donne, Browning and Rupert Brooke, to a pocket dictionary and my French-language Bible.] A pot of home honey would be very welcome too as we get nothing to put on our stale bread but slushy marg.

LATER. I have just come in from Evensong: about 40 present and a very good service. I suppose it is natural for the C of E to be bigger, but all the same under 100 churchgoers in a place this size is pretty poor. In my billet the lads aren't interested. I nearly got lost again coming back from Church in the dark. All one sees are millions of lights and circles of similar huts and tents. I wandered for about half an hour trying to get home to J.6. I had a good laugh over it with the others. The dark is very beautiful – and frightful too. I was standing on the church veranda watching the lights twinkling away down the lake and, across the other side, the low hills were dark against a starry sky. The moon lit up everything and it all looked so peaceful – until a rifle shot rang out. I went into the church then. Another lad came in. He put his rifle behind the door and laid his bayonet and ammo pouch on the next chair. That more or less sums up the faces of this place. A lad who has lived all his life in London, say, must find this an awesome spot. I rather like it, though naturally missing the green hills of home.

The lad who sleeps next to me has just started his evening serenade with his guitar. He can play tunes that really pull the heartstrings then can crash onto the raucous pop stuff I don't

---

19 Publisher's note: the author, as was common practice then, used the terms 'local' and 'native' or the slang 'wog' and 'Gypo' interchangeably; however, with regard to modern sensitivities only the first, 'local', is used in the letters.

much care for. His other occupation is poring over an encyclopaedia. There's a Taffy and a Jock always at each other's throats. The rest are fairly normal. I can hardly write for watching our guitarist's bare toes beating time to the 'Teddy Bears' Picnic'. We have a dud wireless, too – but no lockers. The hut is half-underground so as not to be blown away or buried in storms. We go down a passage to get in. All the buildings are supposedly mosquito-proofed; some of the married bungalows seen from the outside are nothing but mesh netting. The sand gets into everything – even into bed with one. I brought a bit of bread back from tea so as to put honey on it. It was quite gritty to eat, and the stormy season has yet to come. Things are fairly quiet in the Zone just now. Here's a wee plan of RAF Deversoir. [Hasn't survived.]

The chief of air staff was here this morning, and everyone lay and watched an air display put on for him. Even the RAF regiments' guns were fired in a mock raid. Lovely sunny weather was guaranteed!

12.2.54

Do you know you can get Forces Air Letters from the Post Office which only need a 2½d stamp? The sea mail parcels need a declaration form. (Mine will amuse!) Money is tight; one big cost is the sailing club's monthly sub. I am joining. It is the most active club and very good. Some boats are crewed-out already, and sailing. Half a dozen of us were down at the point yesterday and sat munching peanuts and watching the tankers steam up the canal: *San Felix* of London, *George Livanos* of Panama, *Emma* of Genoa and others. We came back along the shore, and, surprise, surprise, I collected half a dozen shells. We sat and drank *assis* in the club and watched the elegant native boats splashing about in the breeze. An old man was sitting in the stern of one, stolidly puffing at a long pipe. They try and sell us all sorts of things and we fend them off in our best newly-learnt Arabic. (They grin great white smiles at our attempts.) One chap I'm friendly with left a note on my bed this morning, spelling my name 'Haymish'. Mish is the native slang for 'lad' or 'waiter', and I still get caught in the NAAFI when someone else calls out 'Hey, mish!'

I was at the dentist this morning and had a bad tooth filled. He nearly had to pull it out, but said it would spoil my nice grin. I waited two hours before being seen, so it's a wonder I had any grin left. Ah well, I can again enjoy a long cool drink of *assis*. Don't ask what it is; predominantly orange but with other things added. An excellent thirst-quencher. The creepy crawly things are coming out now as spring advances. I got a big bite in the middle of my back from a huge black ant, and one lad keeps scarting[20] as he's covered in big lumps down one leg – from insects unknown.

I began work today. Never felt so lost as when I was dumped in front of the telephone switchboard with all its wires and plugs and discs and so on. Work will be interesting. I was

---

20 Scratching.

warned that the NCO i/c was a beast but I find him alright. (He's let me off early parade tomorrow.) His instructions were all clear and helpful, so eventually I'll be genned up.[21]

What would you say to me having a trip to Jerusalem – RAF time, flying, and still being paid? This would be for a Moral Leadership Course, which the OD churches run. Jerusalem! Wow! It will have to wait two months at least till I get my sparks[22] up on becoming a.c.1. A visit to Cyprus, too, would cost nothing for leave. Transport is free and if I stayed with Aunt Nellie I would have no accommodation to pay – but that's quite a bit ahead, certainly not till after she returns home from the UK. Is she with Sis and [daughter] Margaret? When does she return to Cyprus? How are all the animals: dogs, cats, piglets, goldfish? Someone wants to go a walk round camp, so I'll stop. I hope we don't get shot by the guards. It's quite dark, just on 8 o'clock. Fabulous stars, unbelievably brilliant, as if painted in.

---

* I have omitted much of this purely family chatter as being 'Nogi' (not of general interest), a term sometimes declared by parents at home mealtimes to contain three loquacious boys. However, you should find enough explained to make sense of the references in letters. I didn't exist in limbo.

15.2.54

I've been writing letters all night – and itching; round ankles, waist and elbows. I'm all bites, and they itch and itch and ITCH! I am settling down to work and had a second shot on the switchboard this afternoon. I felt all thumbs and an awful fool but the Cpl Supervisor seems pleased. Book learning steaming ahead too, and a merry crowd to work with. I had the bad luck to be on Week-End Guard after a morning on work – so 16.00 Saturday till 18.00 Sunday ruled out Church. On guard, camp was very quiet, not a mouse stirring all night. We hunted an intruder (thief?) in the morning, but he escaped onto the busy Sweet Water Canal road through a huge hole in the wire. Quite cold at night and our greatcoats were useful. Wonderful antique trains chugged past at times. Glasgow-made, Jock claims, he from Glasgow of course. Last century I reckon (the trains, not Jock).

NEXT DAY. Mail! Piles of it: three from home, one from mucker Ken in Germany, two magazines and all the enclosures. I was delighted, and after dinner went rushing down to the point and read them there, and slobbered orange juice all over them. I was on the board this morning again and will be every day. Did quite well. The mail is collected by us for all Signals folk, so we in the exchange have ours right away.

---

21 Know my stuff.
22 The trade's badge, sewn onto the upper arm of the uniform.

There was a fine yacht at the point and we watched it going off gracefully. Shortly after two great clumsy native boats banged past. One stopped, and what a din. A family joined it with a few bundles and mats, pots and pans – and a primus – their total worldly goods perhaps. How lost the young girl looked, and how worn the grandmother. It was rather sad and led on to a long discussion about comparative civilizations. Our conclusion? We're all fairly happy really with our varied unhappy lots. My pal Ken from Germany says he has a wonderful place, RAF Fassberg, miles from anywhere, but near the Russian Zone border.

20.2.54

I'm scribbling this in the main Guard Room while waiting to go on Guard. I managed second shift which means I can make Church in the morning. I met the Padre properly on Thursday, and he will try his best to get me to Jerusalem. I have just been informed we have 21 (not, as I thought, 14) days' leave in the first year of National Service. Last night I saw the film *Pickwick Papers*. Jimmy Hayter in the leading role is a Dollar F.P. [former pupil]. Hopefully, I'll see *The Prisoner of Zenda* and *The Conquest of Everest* this week. Funny how a run of good films comes all at once. On Thursday I was in the married quarters. It felt quite odd to sit in a civilised, ordinary house with a sergeant, his wife and a squadron leader, and all calling each other by first names. There's just no civilised social facilities for us on camp.

Some people got a shock when heavy rain fell and the sand became a foul mud, cloying pounds of muck on shoes. Not fun. I am on Pumping Station guard duty overnight. One person stays on a tower shining a searchlight over the Sweet Water Canal and the Station, and another patrols underneath. On from 20.00 to 22.00 and then 02.00 to 04.00 and in the morn, 08.00 to 10.00, then 14.00 to 16.00. (That's how time is given here, to be completely clear.) Enjoying the work; longer time on board now – and by myself. The rain played havoc yesterday; put 20 lines out. Longing for 'civvy' clothes as 'blue' is too warm for running about after working hours.

I was stuck up on my tower for 08:00–10:00 guard and, with its reflecting corrugated iron roof I frizzled. Very interesting watch with comings and goings up and down the Sweet Water Canal: kids selling peanuts, a runaway donkey, veiled women with pots on head, old men and young kids (2-legged and 4), all busy until it became hot. At night you could see the eyes of foxes or dogs glowing across the fields. Very green fields, but in the distance sand again and at the canal a row of trees over which the masts and funnels of boats appear to ghost along with no visible water connection.

We have no lockers yet, and dust gets into everything in the hut. We're putting in a complaint about no proper beds and lockers, as we should have them; a task for tomorrow when we have a half-day. I shrug rather than rage. I get a leave pass for this weekend, which gives me Friday evening to Monday free, an entitlement as I was on guard over at Station Stand-down last weekend.

25.2.54

Your air-letter (and David's) written on 19th arrived today, taking just three days, according to the postmark. I'd been champing for mail all week, and then today I have mail from nine different people – delighted!

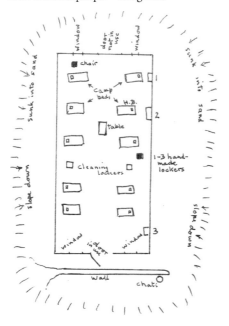

This is a plan of our billet. As you can see it is sparsely furnished – 10 beds, 2 lockers, 9 bed-mats, 1 brush, 2 chairs. The rest we have acquired ourselves. I spent yesterday afternoon improvising a shelf. A big tin would be handy to keep perishable things sand-proof. I made useful hooks out of my kitbag hasps, but am still living out of my kitbag so to speak. Ten in the billet and a nice crowd on the whole. On my right is a boy called Oz (Oswald), then, working round, there is Den (Dennis) who plays the guitar, Fred who is mad on Scouts, Snap who is mad on making things, our Cpl who is mad on lying in bed, Taff who is mad on his wife, Tom who is maddeningly quiet, and Jock who is just plain mad. Jock and Oz have both had twenty-firsts this week. I missed out John who sleeps opposite and came at the same time as I did. He spends half his life writing to his girl. He's youngest, a nice lad.

I am up at six and have to be in the PBX[23] by 07.00. I work at the board 07.00–08.00, and now, sometimes, other shifts. I'm one of the lads now and we have quite a time. Very pally with two others in the exchange who have similar tastes. They, John and I go swimming together. The land is quite green (for about half a mile) as it is watered by the Sweet Water Canal which is just a big dirty ditch. The many palms have great straight trunks and tufted tops. People tether out goats every morning to feed. Hens start crowing at 02.00!!

Tell David not to bother with my reproductions of paintings. I bought dozens when I dashed round the National and Tate Galleries. I have a board on which I pin two or three,

---

23 Private Branch Exchange.

and change them now and then. Thank goodness for all the Art Appreciation classes at School. I'm always being asked questions about them. I've early Italians up just now: Botticelli, Fra Angelico and Giotto. I can hear a football match going on outside; a good cool afternoon for some exercise. There was boxing last night, with some good bouts. Almost tea time. John is preparing for Guard. Two others are writing and the rest have gone for a walk 'round the wire' – like POWs.

There is always something of interest; now we hear Neguib has resigned and, of course, all sorts of rumours are about. That was first thing this morning. Everything then went haywire in the PBX. A line went dead while an air exercise was on, and it was one panic after another. The OC's number blinked and friend Jessop gaily plugged in and yelled, 'Sorry, line engaged!'

A fisherman drying his nets while a ship moves along the canal behind

before actually being asked anything. Things had calmed down by when I took in mail. Going out to supper tonight.

The Rupert Brooke I wanted was *The Complete Works* which I had with me at Innsworth and left there with a French-Maritime WRAAF at the club. She was to send it on to Dollar, so when it comes please forward the book on here. You do have a lot to put up with, with *two* of us doing NS. Ian, of course, can have luxuries, being a wealthy officer and a gentleman and not a lowly erk.

4.3.54

On Saturday morning a group of us went down to the canal to sunbathe and watch the boats go by, amongst others a Russian tanker, a Clan Line boat from Glasgow with two railway engines on deck, and one boat piled high with timber. The other day I saw the *Orcades* go past on her maiden voyage. I didn't think her lines all that graceful. I, of course, could boast of having twice sailed through the canal.[24] Sunday was a nice restful day. Church twice, as usual, a VIP (vice-Chaplain in Chief or something like that) taking morning service. On Monday afternoon I went on guard again. We had the hottest day since last summer and I felt (and looked) like a beetroot by the end of four hours in the blazing sun. We brought some peanuts from a wee blind native boy. You know how in the Bible we read of sheep following the shepherd? Here we see it. Rather an amazing sight, all the goats and sheep trotting along behind the women. The canal is more a disgusting drain than anything

---

24 Appendix V explains when.

The shell we try not to step on.

else. We're told a few soldiers have ended up in it, but it does allow a swathe of greenery. The water comes from the Nile across 80 miles of desert to Ismailia and Lake Timsha then runs down past us all the way to Suez. In the lake we just float, float, float (very easy as the water is super-salty). We have a favourite spot where we can dive off rocks into chest-high water. You keep your feet off the bottom though as there is a wickedly spiky shell which will puncture a foot. Back for early tea and then most of the evening I was in the Padre's Office. My watch had been playing up, and a lad there fixed it in a couple of minutes. He had four on his wrists. He is the C of E organist as well. I go to both C of E and OD functions – always some good company in the office, and tea, and often someone has a cake from home. Camp meals could be so much better with very little effort. Writing this while off-board. Been on an hour and dealt quite easily with one 'rush' period.

Yesterday we had our longest swim. We never want to come out. The water is not very nice if you swallow any – and is like bee stings in the eyes. At some season the water rises and fills the marsh just in from the strand. It is drying out now and leaves great white stretches of salt, and the sand, too, crunches saltily underfoot. Goats and sheep wander about under the care of black-draped women who have long shiny veils hanging from their noses. It is all very picturesque, and with the clear blue water and the waving palm trees on the point the scene is just waiting to be painted.

We swim out to meet the liners and to be buffeted by their wash. The cleanest boats are never British. Norway have a large percentage of the tonnage, mostly in tankers, and they are always smart and clean. Here is the list of those that passed up on Sunday afternoon: *Ville de Diego-Suarez,* le Havre, cargo boat; *Batory*, Gdynia, smallish passenger boat; *Manchuria*, Copenhagen, liner; *Rhodesian Castle*, London, liner; *Americi*, Greece, liner; *Waziristan*, Sunderland, tanker; *Clan MacKinlay*, Glasgow, cargo boat; *Amalfi*, Naples, tanker; *Bjørgsund,* Oslo, tanker; *Ampenan*, Rotterdam, cargo boat; *Genie*, Monrovia, tanker; *Maid of Pinto,* Malta, wee cargo boat. There were others but that lets you have an idea of the interest of the canal. A Russian tanker refused to reply to our yells and waves. We always chatter and wave to ships (and sometimes wish we were on board). We usually miss those going East as they pass in the morning and we are often at work then. [Over 13,000 ships a year were passing through the canal at this time.]

I spent two evenings building a locker-cum-wardrobe-cum-desk-cum-bookcase. It is most impressive with door knobs, cubby holes and a line of books – the structure mostly made of scrounged orange boxes. All I need is some drawing pins and hinges. I hope a pal can find them in Fayid. The towns are not so dangerous now. Someday I'll have to make a visit. I'm becoming quite tanned, a very pleasing brown. I'm told that some army lads got severe sunburn (when off-duty) and they received a fizzer as it was made out to be 'damage to Government property'.

* Appendix III tells about the building of the Suez Canal, but another story is worth mentioning, concerning one John 'Rob Roy' MacGregor, an eccentric, evangelical Victorian canoeist who would claim to be *the first to pass from Port Said to Suez by water*. He paddled his canoe, *Rob Roy III*, from Port Said on the Mediterranean to Lake Timsah – as far as the Suez Canal had been completed at the time – then swapped over to make use of the Sweet Water Canal south to Suez and the Red Sea – hence his claim. He then took his home-made craft to Cairo to descend the Nile and eventually took it to the Holy Land to explore Bible-mentioned rivers and the Sea of Galilee. This was to prove the last of many canoe ventures, all over Europe and the Baltic, and led to a book *The 'Rob Roy' on the Jordan (1869)*. At Suez he was interviewed by a fascinated journalist from the *New York Herald Tribune*, one H.M. Stanley. Hearing Stanley was off to Africa, MacGregor gave him a letter to deliver to his 'good friend David Livingstone' (whose African book MacGregor had illustrated).

Kyernia

6.3.54

(from Aunt Nellie)

My dear Hamish,

Our letters have crossed as you thought they might. Sis and Margaret arrive on April 15. I have never had three of the family staying before and it will be fun (Margaret only had two weeks and had departed before we arrived). I told Cystalla (the maid) today that you were coming. She had a crush on your dad. Maybe he tipped her well.

In winter all the amateur artists in England seem to come here. Believe me, most are very amateur. (I was advised against bringing 'painting truck' with me) Kyrenia is very pretty admittedly. You'll find the sea here a bit more chilly for bathing. I wait till May for bathing. Waring's beach is only five minutes' drive from here.

The first of thousands of freesias are out along with irises and nasturtiums. I sell them, I sell anything to raise money for the Red Cross. I've just refooted golf stockings for a wealthy bachelor on condition the Red Cross benefits. There's a party to meet the new Governor. The Matthews are driving me down. They remember you in extreme Colombo Youth. They said you were a wee devil. I can believe it. They have built opposite me, happy neighbours to have.

Buses and shared taxis come over from Nicosia. My telephone number is 252 Kyrenia, and everyone knows me if asking: first house past the football ground and if I am not in and house not standing open the key is under the mat. People are honest here. Have you got a kilt? Bring it for dances if you have. If I want to feel young I go to the Dome. For the decrep the Red X hires wheelchairs, bed tables and less polite objects.

I know your bloke [Air Commodore] Boyce here, a nice chap, took over the command of the Air Force from Bowling. But you'll hardly be moving in such exalted ranks. You will find the two years a great experience. I always feel glad I trekked about the Far East [she had lived in Perak, and travelled to Bangkok for my parents' wedding in 1926], and even South Africa [as a nurse, wife of a military doctor, she met those – including us! – who, fleeing the Japanese, were arriving in SA from Malaysia and Singapore.] You'll be sick of the sun some days but then think of the misty days in Scotland. Scotland is always there. A Church circular tells me to cut out smoking, alcoholic drinks, cinemas etc. Thank goodness I was brought up by a Presbyterian. I've already had a sherry.

Take care and enjoy life.

Nellie

Deversoir 12.3.54

Thank goodness my civvies have come – so uniform only needed when working. Thanks for that. Just finished tea and what a difference the home-made jam made; stale bread with Dollar strawberry on top of a slice. A dog-handler who visits got a piece.[25] When I asked him if he'd like a piece he asked, 'A piece of what?' When I called a mate 'glaikit'[26] on the switchboard the other day he took it as a compliment. Jock and I enjoy saying things like 'Whiles, we're gey drouthy' or 'I'm right scunnered with night binds', or 'Some of yuse is peely wally'.[27] Not the same in English, is it?

Last night our evening in the Padre's office was less cheerful, for a P O Coutts, just 21, who had been confirmed last Sunday, crashed his Vampire. There was very little of him to bury today, and they have not yet found his head. Very sad – he was such a nice young lad. [On April 2 a Valetta crash saw the three crew killed.]

Started to re-read Axel Munthe's *Story of San Michele*, easily in my books top 12. In the hut we all have top 12s for books, records, pictures, paintings etc, depending on our interests. Someone's list rarely fails to reflect the person, and yet there are surprises like one boy who spends most of his days engrossed in comics who puts down 'The Hound of Heaven' as his favourite poem. My favourite piece of verse just now is Fitzgerald's free translation of Omar Khayyam's *Rubaiyat*. Reading it out to pals in the billet. I woke everyone up one morning by shouting out the start of the poem at the top of my voice. (It *was* rousing time.) A variety of accents and adjectives told me where I could go.

Must take this chance to wish Paw and Ian all the best for the 14th and the 16th. Many happy returns. Are there any leather goods or articles that I could bring back as belated presents?

---

25 Sandwich.
26 Stupid, idiotic, foolish.
27 Very dry; fed up with night shifts; pale and wan.

One may not have Cyprus leave till resident here six months. I want to go earlier, so put in a request for special permission and it went right up, signature on signature to the CO Deversoir who added his, so I have special permission to apply for 'compassionate leave'. (That will tickle Aunt Nellie.)

My trade test not far ahead now. There are many worse 'trades' than being a telephonist. 'Signals' are a good lot. I suppose some intelligence is needed!

P.S. Here's the *Rubáiyát* start, if you don't know it.

> Awake! For Morning in the Bowl of Night
> Has flung the Stone that puts the Stars to Flight:
> And Lo! The Hunter of the East has caught
> The Sultan's Turret in a Noose of Light
>
> [Edward Fitzgerald's 1879 translation of the *Rubáiyát of Omar Khayyám*]

16.3.54

We managed to acquire three dozen drawing pins after ages of searching in Fayid. They cost a fortune, but I can now pin up lots more reproductions [of paintings] as a bright background to my bookcase-cum-locker. I helped sort out mail yesterday as they were very busy with a large pile of sea mail. There were a sad number in broken condition. I had a letter from Bill Blakey. He is on a 31-week course – radar mechanic. He was a teacher and has just given up trying to fathom why a student of the classics has been given such a highly complicated mechanical job. Ken in Germany works in Air Traffic Control.

Yesterday another parcel (also bashed and leaking sweets). The shirt fits perfectly and has passed the billet critics! The painting stuff was safe. The honey was a surprise, and led to me giving the billet a lecture on bee-keeping for *over an hour*! I wondered at having a dog but the thought of leaving it behind puts me off. There are a lot of dogs I'm making friends with, owned or stray, posh or pi.

Sailing this afternoon, and I dived off when half a mile out to swim back – a real treat. The troopship *Empire Orwell* (which I might have come out in) passed today on the way back to Blighty from the Far East. Rows and rows of brown army and airmen on it waving and shouting rude things. We got a rare tossing in its wake. Diving about the rocks inshore I was nearly run down by a gash[28] boat (not a felucca[29]) which came round a corner suddenly. I had dived in and was swimming underwater when it swept round, to my pals' horror, right over where I was due to surface. I came up facing it about six inches away! I know sufficient of the lingo to tell them what I thought! They were profusely sorry,

---

28 Un-noteworthy, rubbishy.
29 A traditional Nile sailing boat; very picturesque from a distance.

so I told them to '*maalish*' (forget it). That's near where we dive to find the magical wee seahorses and baby octopus. There were some nice natives who let us dive off their barge, which was moored about 500 yards away. We swam deep down to explore what are like sand hills on the bottom of the Lake. Underwater is the only place where we can be away from the stronghold of the sun. Interestingly, our Bitter Lake fishes are Red Sea ones, never Mediterranean species; they only reach as far south as Lake Timsah (Ismailia). The feluccas are the broad, load-carrying boats with the lateen sails one always sees in pictures of the Nile. They look so beautiful. We'll never see the Nile, though.

I'll hardly recognise the Crail house when I'm out. Are you leaving the floors as they are? Are you going to distemper, paint, or do what with the walls?

Ah, my checks now. Well, all our guards are still alive – and complaining at the *cold*. I'm in shirt sleeves. Yesterday was a hot enough day that just walking made us sweat. Everything has been tightened up: no going out after dark, and arms to be carried again while out of camp, and vehicle guards are doubled and dozens of other clampdowns – all following five people being shot last week. That has happened before, only this time officers are being aimed at specifically.

I'm reading a great deal. I was delighted to have found an excellent lot of big reproductions of Augustus John in a *Picture Post*. I've pinned them to my locker. Had quite a long chat tonight with a boy about art. Strange how you find them. I met another art enthusiast in another billet by noting two Watteau prints over his bed. My row of books also attracts some attention. Very few ever want to borrow one to read, though. Comics are the most many manage. Most lockers are covered in pin-ups – on the inside of the doors! A couple of good films gives a bit of conversation that is new – *The Cruel Sea* and *The Yellow Balloon*.

The 'Army Faults' cut the cables of our outside lines last night by mistake. What a commotion: we had 59 booked calls once they were back. Time to test those lines again. I passed my GCT test with flying colours so now can be trusted to work the PBX by myself.

---

* In 2005 I visited the Secret Bunker in Fife, one of those startling Cold War underground warrens in which the chosen would expect to survive a nuclear strike on Britain. Here 200 RAF personnel lived like moles year after year till the Cold War melted away. The Cold War ended just in time, for plans were afoot to replace this vast, costly (and useless) survival scheme with another one with more up-to-date technology. How out of date it all was I swiftly realised, for on entering I saw a WAAF (model) sitting at a telephone switchboard identical to the PBX I had known in the Zone half a century earlier. I could have sat down and taken over from her.

29.3.54

88° today. I wonder if the honey was granulated when it left the frozen north. It isn't now. We began Summer routine today so are up at 05.00, work 06.15 to 12.30 and then collapse down to the blessed water till it is cool enough to come home without pouring sweat. I swam from Africa across to Asia yesterday. (That sounds good, doesn't it?!) Still, I must have covered a good mile. Did you hear on the wireless about the trooper[30] *Empire Windrush*? We cheered her through not so long ago, and I even knew a lad who was on her, he having been here till a day or two before. I wonder what will happen now she is on fire for a second day? [She sank in the Mediterranean; for her story, see Appendix IV.]

It was not at all my fault being nearly run down by the gash boat. They are informed on a brightly painted notice, in English and Arabic, to give that point a wide berth. And it is quite safe swimming out to the big ships. There are buoys beyond which we don't pass. Three wee Egyptian corvettes tore through the other day. The dredgers blew their horns, the locals waved – and the Brits booed. The Bitter Lake is salty enough that grains stick to our hairy arms and legs. Presumably the fish etc are adapted to the conditions. Odd too, being so like a sea, but not having tides.

It's hard to think it is now Spring. These last few days have been really stormy, with rain and high winds. Last week the temperature was up to 90°[31] every day, so we went into tropical kit. Swimming yesterday was a thrill in a heavy sea, but great fun as the water was warm. The lake was the best place to be, as dust was blowing everywhere. Today the ground was slimy with overnight rain. I went for a skite[32] and sat down in the mud. Dollar must be pleasantly green by now. I wonder how Hamid will remember me. A worker in the PBX had a pi dog called Bongo. He went home and the dog was left to someone in the Equipment Section. Yesterday it wandered in with tail wagging, walked round sniffing hopefully at us all, and then slowly went out again, tail drooping.

On escort duty on Sunday (with my rifle, accompanying me wherever, whyever.) Can be a gharry,[33] car, Jeep – which has an upright bar in front to snap any wire strung across the road with the intent of doing bodily harm. Runs are always to other barbwired camps and never to towns, not that we'd be allowed to leave our vehicles. Sometimes in other camps we might have a break and wander round or find a cup of chai. Drivers always seem to have some Stella under their seats – the local-made beer.

---

30 Troopship.
31 ~32°C.
32 Skid.
33 Lorry, usually, but sometimes other vehicles.

2.4.54

Dear Ian

I rather envy you in Germany. Conditions there seem good nearly everywhere. German would be a worthwhile language to pick up, unlike the gash Egyptian here. This place, as you might guess, is a bit lethargic, but with temperatures on 90° even walking is a sweaty effort. The last few days have been cold and stormy (for here) with high winds and rain. We've gone into k.t.[34] – you should see all the white knees! My job is interesting and sometimes exciting. My test for a.c.1. comes up soon. The highest I could possibly reach is S.A.C. The supervisor (our big cheese) is only a Cpl and he's been in donkeys' years. It's just one of those 'trades'. We're all treated the same anyway and have a good time. Just finished pressing my shorts for Colour-hoisting tomorrow. Yesterday was the Commemorative Service for the formation of the RAF. That was a big do. Tomorrow is just for we Tech. Wing folk.

There's an awful din on the radio so I'm going to flee to the Reading Room to continue a pile of letters. I've being seeing quite a number of films since coming here: *Pickwick Papers, Prisoner of Zenda, The Cruel Sea, The Yellow Balloon, The Glenn Miller Story.* Some kind person back home has sent me a parcel with over £2 worth of books. I wish I could thank them. I read books endlessly and also write a lot. I had the experience of putting three dead drunk billet mates to bed the other night. Probably no worse than what you officers get up to. My now *qualified telephonist's* greeting, Sur.

6.4.54

I am now a.c.1;[35] passed with 81%. And, after all the fuss and bother I have a flight booked for Nicosia. Everything is wrapped round and round in red tape and piled high with forms. (Memo pads we have in the exchange are marked with the reference: 'wt.34898/P2714 16 000 Pads. 11/49 WA185 668/13 FORM 348 (Small) (Pads of 100 interleaved) – interleaved, no doubt, so everything is in triplicate.

The Chambers' Journals were good, if possible I'd like them sent regularly. The drawing paper has yet to arrive. The fellow artist in the PBX says it is unobtainable out here. Could you send me out a batch of Penguins from the study bookcase please? They are all lengthy works which should be read, so no time like the present when I do read and read, so *Don Quixote, Canterbury Tales,* the Rousseau book and *Vanity Fair.* I'm reckoned the billet swot, but I do entertain!

---

34 Kit, tropical.
35 Aircraftman 1st Class.

Tidy in civvies and holding the tape at the station sports. the church lies neahind

No requirements for once. D will be at Camp now I expect – lucky lad. You must cycle to Loch Ard and see the daffodils. [Aunt Nell would comment on loving Loch Ard too, having read my letter.]

We've just had the Station Sports. I was officiating. We had a very sweaty afternoon – it had to choose today to become really hot again. Running was just crazy – with people coming in gasping and collapsing with foam oozing from their mouths. [I was holding the tape for the races.] Most of the helpers were officers. Rather odd, then, having me being called 'Sir' so often.

I went down to Fayid yesterday and had lunch with about 20 others in the MMG[36] Homely Club. I can well see it becoming a weekly trip. I was back in time to go to Evensong and to chat with the Padre, who is just back from a fortnight's leave in Kyrenia. He says it is a wonderful place. I wrote to Aunt Nellie again not so long ago – she's a chronic letter writer; I can see why you are always owing her a letter. She seems to be determined to make me Archbishop of Canterbury at least!

Going down to Fayid you pass a beautiful mosque: a plain square edifice with a slender, ornate tower rising up from a corner. With the palms and sea beyond it is very striking. I'm sure the mud huts here are made in the same way as those of the Israelites under Pharaoh. The agriculture is all done by hand with hoes and bullock ploughs: all very Biblical and unchanged, yet going along the roads are other Egyptians in new big American cars – and in the town there are luxury shops. We get mobbed by street vendors and beggars wanting baksheesh. Occasionally we see tempting things, but most items are very shoddy and obviously for tourists. I met a lad who was with me at Innsworth: we've arranged to meet again. He, four others and I visited an army transit camp in the afternoon.

Lot of talk on the unhappy BOAC Comet going into the Mediterranean, near Naples: the third Comet disaster for the world's first jet airliner. They were only cleared to fly again a couple of months ago after the Elba ditching. So what now? Cuttings please. [In October the cause was declared to be metal fatigue in the cabin roof containing the direction-finding aerial. In America in July there was the maiden flight of the Boeing 707. The new world of jet airliners was being born.]

---

36 Mission to Mediterranean Garrisons.

2 Lt I.S. Brown REME
110 Tpt Coy RASC
BAOR 23
18.4.54
[brother, Ian]

Dear Ham,

What is a 'PBX'? The Forces love abbreviations, don't they? Would anyone else recognise my address as being in Germany? We are in Celle, about the size of Dunfermline, with Hannover 20 miles away. I have a small LAD (Light Aid Detachment): 22 men, 8 vehicles, 9 German civilians and quite a good workshop, to look after the 150 vehicles of the Transport Company. We are kept busy. Last week with the half the company on a two-day exercise they managed to crash three lorries.

We are on the edge of large forests, full of bird life and the odd fox or deer. I've already got lost. An old major in the mess has a tame squirrel, Irish setter and breeds tropical fish. The mess is comfortable and I have a simple room and could well be here as long as staying in Germany. On a visit to Hamburg we travelled on one of the autobahns and managed to average c. 75 m.p.h.

Before leaving, Dad and I spent a few days at Crail in the wee house down by the harbour. I rather liked it. The condition must have been deplorable when you first saw it.

Look after yourself and don't let any bloody local try to shoot you up.

Ian

21.4.54

Grand to have a letter from Crail. Could you two not manage together to Crail for a week? D and Gran would surely be alright together at Dollar? I enjoy getting all the papers. Really, though, could you write to Aunt Effie over her contribution; I haven't the nerve. She sent True Romances – three of them! Very sweet to remember me, but oh dear, the billet was in hysterics. You mention Dad busy with boxes – is the year up now? Let's know how much is collected all told for the Church fund. Was the thief who took the things from the Church ever caught? [Mother's hand had added, 'No!' in the margin. Father was church treasurer – so we boys got all the foreign coins in the collections, especially after the holidays when pupils returned to school from all over the world.]

There's a cub in our billet doing the Bob-a-job scout thing. I've just been looking at his card. He's done 14 jobs – seven cleaning boots and badges. He's busy on a pair now. Port Said is out of bounds due to that last killing, and so is Ismailia – but Fayid is OK. Easter weekend was most enjoyable, even if I spent the Saturday on guard. That night bind[37] gave a bright moonlit night and the searchlights over the bomb dump were unnecessary. I received another sun bath during the day. As half the guards are enough to see all round, the Cpl i/c and I sun-bathed or watched the ants. They come in all sizes and colours. We have black ones every bit as big as this –  – and then minute ones that you can only just see ⊙ Like that!

There are some that are transparent. A large crowd of wee ones were enjoying a sugared almond when a big black one ran up. In a minute it was staggering away with three small ones hanging on to each leg.

There was a string of camels wandering along the wire, and the green wheat is turning golden. No wonder there are wars: two of our lads intend to set it alight with a flare when it is ready for harvest. They won't now!

I was at four services last Sunday. I got a lift down to the St Andrews Church of Scotland in Fayid, then I went up to the MMG, where there was a service at 11.30. We had a lunch party for over a hundred, and what a meal. I felt full for the first time since my dinner in the Old Inn at Gloucester. I had a bowl of roses in front of me, and what a change things like a tablecloth, salt cellars, cups and saucers made! The afternoon service was even better than the morning's. The place was not big enough and the congregation overflowed out the doors. Must have been some hundreds. I was back in time to go to Evensong here. Our OD Padre has still not turned up. What a time to go off on a holiday! I have this week-end off. I need it. I work hard and try not to give in to ennui. Tuesday I get my pay for the Cyprus visit and in the evening had a meeting with the joint C of E and OD Bible Fellowship. Glad they've combined; our one OD by itself was just too small.

A group from the Church Fellowship at Deversoir. Back: Harry, Dave, Hamish, Ano. Front: Dave Lee, Norman, Padre Parry, 2 ANOs

By the sound of Aunt Nellie's last letter Aunt Sis will still be there. Cousin Margaret is in Greece. Hope she doesn't get caught in one of those earthquakes. Be nice to have the two anything but 'old dears' together. Please send the jacket here. It is chill at night and in the cinema (outdoors) we need our greatcoats. They keep screening outside as it stays too stuffy indoors after the heat of the day. There is a new u/t[38] telephonist; arrived yesterday

37 Night shift.
38 Under training.

and he's in hospital today. This is a fever year. Typhoid comes every three years. We are all to be given another jab regardless of how short a time we have been here. I'll have mine after Cyprus.

24.4.54

This may be a bit of a scrawl as it is being written while sitting waiting for *The Million Pound Note* to start. It's been a boiling day but already at 19.30 we have on several layers of jerseys and 'blue' as we sit under the usual starry heavens. I love the night sky – it is always so clear and black behind the millions of stars. Reminds me of Psalm 8.

I don't much care for the OD Padre. Last time he gave a silly attack on Science. He has not preached anything constructive yet. I stayed to C of E Communion now I've the permission of the Bishop of the Lower Nile!! The Padre would only let me partake if this Gilbert & Sullivan potentate allowed it. I'm not C of E after all. Tut! Tut!

This morning a Flying Officer and I got a lift by a Major and a Col. into Fayid. (The special guard allows a day off afterwards.) I was going down to the Church of Scotland club – Dumbarton House – to order two books. Fayid has a lido for 'Other Ranks' – us. Fayid is a ramshackle sort of place with buildings half-up or half-down and fountains that don't fount – one is an elephant with its trunk in the air but no water. Some odd smells. You could find your way around the Zone by nose alone. The Lido was noisy with black-headed gulls like Crail. Kites too ['Shite hawks' among the ranks] and one white whirl of egrets. Coming back, I had several lifts. Swam after lunch and gave up sunbathing due to flies. My pal Chris Barrett is back from Jerusalem. He gave me a wooden-covered Red-Letter Testament (one with Christ's words printed in red). He is a very nice young lad (says the old one!). Well, the adverts are nearly finished...

4.5.54

Deversoir is getting hotter day after day. I was a bit feverish last night so took a couple of aspirins and sweated it out. After lunch half the camp flocked down to the canalside at the Point, to cheer the Royal Yacht *Gothic* which was homeward-bound following the Queen and Prince Philip's post-coronation world tour. [The Royals were not on board, having flown from Aden to visit Kenya and thereafter flying to join *Gothic* again at Tobruk. The ship was the last of a quartet: *Coronthic, Athenic, Ceramic, Gothic.* The *Gothic* was launched in 1947, but in 1952 was being refitted to become the royal yacht for King George VI, but he died that year – so the Queen was the first to tour in her.] As it passed, the Marine Band on board struck up, a cheery little touch. A more impressive boat followed, the P&O *Corfu*.

I'll manage to scrape together £10 for Cyprus. Most people take about £30 but I've no lodging expenses, or things like smoking, drinking, night clubs etc which seems to be the island's chief attraction to many. We have quite a growth of greenery below the water *chati* just now. We are all advised to drink a lot. Salt pills are available. Cyprus will be a welcoming green of course. Just finished packing and have prepared uniform for slipping on. Tomorrow I deal with payments, fetch my pass, find when I've to report and see how I'm to get there. May have to go off with a rush and spend tomorrow night in Fayid – hence the packing and bull tonight.

Many happy returns, Maw. It seems no time since your last birthday – and I'll still be here on the next. Home is not valued till it is left so many miles away. A group of us are going to form a Dramatic Society next winter. Still hope for a Riding Club here. (Horses, not camels!) [At this stage there was obviously no inkling of Deversoir being run down or closed. No riding ever happened. I was to write the play, but it faded away along with everything else that had seemed so permanent about Deversoir.]

I'll write again soon.

Over Port Suez

6.5.54

Port Suez is dropping out of sight below the tailplane. The landscape is very hazy due to the heat, and the sea is the colour of our Church roof – a dingy blue. I've got a window seat over the port wing, and as the seats face the tail there is a good view – of immense, indifferent desert. Much better plane than the last, and more or less soundproof: a Valetta done in grey and cream with white cushions etc. Just had a squash and biscuits. Oh, it is good to be off. I spent over 1½ hours this morning waiting for transport. Good Transit station (efficient too) but we broke down on the way to RAF Fayid. All yesterday chasing documents that ought to have been ready a long time ago. *N'importe!* I'm in the air. I'm somewhere round 11–12 stones in weight, I find. A taxi to Kyrenia costs 4/- so I think I may use that. I'll have to change money, arrange return, and go through customs on landing, and we'll very likely be given lunch. I hope so. The flight is due to take 1 hour 50 minutes. Egypt is just a faint horizon, and an hour to go.

3

Cheering in Cyprus: 6–20 May 1954

Time, which we grasp
(though it will fly),
is quicksilver in the end:
not to be saved, not to lend,
but thrown, like rain, into the sky.

Cyprus was a very welcome break, but island life was far too busy for writing letters so for weeks afterwards I was adding comments and descriptions on Cyprus within my Deversoir letters home. This format became rather a distraction, so for Cyprus, and Jerusalem later, there are now separate chapters, with the letters collated. There is a chapter 'With Aunt Nell and I' in my collected writings, *Walking the Song* (2017) which mentions the Cyprus visit briefly and tells more about this indomitable personality. Cyprus notes are found at the end of this chapter.

I'd first met Aunt Nell in South Africa when my mother, my year-old brother and I arrived in Durban after escaping the Japanese in Malaya in 1942. Nellie Tull was a nurse and her husband a military doctor (who died before we met again). An uncle (her brother) and family also lived in South Africa. The Scottish diaspora often proved useful. Aunt Nell's sister, my Aunt Sis (Dublin-based), was in Cyprus during my visit, a happy coincidence. They both headed to Scotland immediately after my Cyprus visit so 'they will give you all the gossip' I wrote to my parents. I did write one letter home from Cyprus.

Kyrenia, Cyprus

7.5.54

O frabjous day! Callooh! Callay! I woke up over the mountains as the plane began to dance about in the thermals – and fell in love with the island on sight: mountains and forests and secretive villages and roads twisting on the heights or in and out of a coast of rocks and sands laced with white as seen from the plane. I'm just recovering from a tiffin of pork chops done in wine following a visit with Aunt Sis and neighbours to Nicosia for the market. Heavens! The smell of fruit, of growing things, the scents of Aunt Nell's garden of colours. (She sells cut flowers to a dealer, who sends them *by air* to Cairo, to raise money for the Red Cross.) Looking up to the sprawl of St Hilarion Castle on its crags while surrounded by rampaging nasturtiums, iris, freesias, anemones and antirrhinum five feet tall makes Egypt seem a dream from which I've surfaced, not realising how asleep I'd become. Aunt Nellie's hands are a bit shaky but, driving, she tears along the roads. Everyone does! Last night we dined in the Hesperides and tomorrow I've to be at the Dome Hotel with them for a Red Cross dance. So don't expect much in the way of letters!

Cheers, from your beamish boy.

---

* Aunt Nellie had written to Mother for my address back in February, writing mostly about her garden (the bees busy at the almond blossom) and complaining at much of the social life and the collection of old decrepits at the Dome. (She was probably older than most of these winter guests.)

I'm hoping for a letter from Hamish. I do wish he'd been sent here [Amen to that!] but being RAF he can come for short leaves. The RAF have holiday camps here too. He'll find Egypt quite an experience. I am very fond of Hamish, probably because I knew him at a nice age of eight or nine first of all in South Africa. Crystalla is a dear, but my housekeeping will probably shock Sis. What does it matter? A bit of dirt won't harm anyone. Life is too short not to have lots of good things to do. Tell Hamish he's expected...Misery [cat] has just deposited a bird on the rug.

Our time was split between exploring the island and constant socialising. After Deversoir days I was ready for both activities. Aunt Sis had lived most of her days in Galway and I'd stayed there on my first visit 'home' from my Ceylon birthspace, before ever living in Scotland. She had become more Irish than the Irish. Two years before my call-up I'd enjoyed a cycle tour in Ireland and a week attending the Dublin Horse Show (the great year when Col. Harry Llewellyn and Foxhunter were winning everything). Coming out from the Gate Theatre I suggested Aunt Sis moved off the middle of the road, to be told, 'This road's too narrow to have a middle.' Her daughter Margaret, intellectual, bilingual in Gaelic and

English, helped create Ireland's Records Office. Margaret had her ninetieth birthday in 2001 and the extended family gathered from all the corners of the earth. With the company at her party singing a rousing drinking song in French, I commented that it would sound better in German so she sang the remaining stanzas in German, translating as she went. (I was to inherit/dispose of her library.)

Aunt Nellie too would go on to live to a ripe old age. She was quite a handful and though tiny could overawe most of the family. She was actually great fun, for those who could stand up to her bullying. I called her 'the last of the memsahibs' or 'the last of the Raj', which she rather liked, I suspect. She wasn't so happy with the portrait I did of her with her ebony and silver-mounted cigarette holder in her mouth. She smoked till into her eighties, when the doctor told her it was not doing her lungs any good. She walked out the surgery and never smoked again (see Note *1, p. xx). Latterly she needed a wheelchair at Turnhouse Airport and I'd whizz her along the crowded alleys, with her whacking people on the bottom with her walking stick and calling 'Out the way! Out the way!' or 'Hamish, faster! Faster!' I often wheeled her through out-of-bounds areas to the aircraft in a way which would not be allowed today. She knitted woolly socks every Christmas for all the males in the family (chequered brown and white, or black and white) and it was two decades after her death before my last pair had to be thrown out. While knitting she frequently clattered her dentures and Father (her brother) would glare over his paper at the noise. She always denied this habit, so I recorded her doing so as proof. She was not amused. With her click-clicking needles I thought she would have made a good extra in the film of *A Tale of Two Cities*. Aunt Nell spent as much time as was legally permitted with us in Dollar (several weeks every year) and also with Aunt Sis in Ireland. Dollar was a small village and the shopkeepers were soon shuddering when Aunt Nell appeared; in Cyprus much of the shopping was done by bargaining and she saw no reason why Scotland should be different. She terrified our shop girls.

I was hardly aware of the political unrest being stirred up in Cyprus with the call for Enosis (Union with Greece) which had started seriously from about 1952 and would explode in December 1954. A state of emergency was declared in 1955 and the inevitable independence came in 1959. That hardly calmed matters, so a UN peace force was set up in 1964 to keep the fanatical Greek and Turkish Cypriots apart. Trouble continued; the Turks invaded in 1974 and have held the northern half of the island ever since. An outline of this unhappy history can be found as a Cyprus Note *4.

In my Deversoir letters I keep mentioning a book by noted historian Rupert Gunnis, *Historic Cyprus*. This pre-war guide at the time of my 1954 visit (and long after) gave the only thorough coverage to all the various sites and their histories. (It was reprinted in 1973.) Today all the major guidebook companies have Cyprus Tourist titles though most concentrate on the Greek area with less adequate cover for the Turkish north. I did find one helpful exception, Diana Darke: *Guide to North Cyprus*, 1995. I never really followed the island's political history after my visit, especially with the island partitioned. Decades on I was put off from returning by believing modern tourism development (as I'd seen along the Turkish mainland coast) would have destroyed what so appealed. I'm told this has certainly happened in Greek Cyprus, but not in the north, and that the north, cut off from international trade and tourism, remains incredibly beautiful, unspoilt and friendly. Lawrence Durrell, of *Bitter Lemons*, asked (at the time I was there), 'Could one ever do any work with such scenery to wonder at?' The Greek poet Giorgos Seferis also lived, and wrote, in Cyprus in 1953 and took his inspiration from the scenery and ancient history or mythology. The scenery, the long history, they have not changed. The history, so often seen in stone, was to fascinate me. Also rewarding is Colin Thubron: *Journey into Cyprus* (1975) which describes a 600-mile walk along the north, right out to the Karpas peninsula. That was how it was and, for the north, still is. Maybe it is not too late to seek this older world that bears the centuries so well.

I have naturally consulted various modern guidebooks to check on memory and they have all left me sad for another country which at the time of my visit was apparently peaceable, the majority content to have it so. Yet Cyprus was so soon to tear itself apart with the horrors of sectarianism, leaving, as always, a wake of cultural vandalism. Some of the guidebooks were quite political and scarcely mentioned Kyrenia and the Turkish part of the island. The division would see a renaming of parts, but I'll stick with the old names used when I was there in the happier times. Though the tensions were surfacing I was only a brief observer, a greedy culture seeker. Time and time again over the years I was to read that an ancient church I'd seen had suffered in the fighting and been left derelict or been pillaged, or precious murals were mouldering away. So I'll try and reconstruct my experiences to give something of the feel of exploring Cyprus in 1954, making something of a narrative out of the various notes home from Deversoir following the hectic holiday.

There is a perfect blend of landscape and building through much of the Mediterranean, and Cyprus was my first taste of it: the long history that has left sights and sites embedded in an unconsciously gracious landscape, a sun-blessed architecture of church and town and castle. Greek and Roman gods were likely to be met among the olive groves, and Flecker's 'Old Ships' sweep round a sunset point. To an impressionable lad let loose, Cyprus was a feast for the senses. It was often difficult to see if rugged house walls and tiled roofs were ancient, decaying or still being built. History did rather knock things about (still does!) and the worst-ever earthquake on the island had been in September 1953.

✳   ✳   ✳

Cyprus descriptions abstracted from letters written later in Deversoir, the first of them sent to Ian:

I flew to Cyprus on May 6th, well before the summer heat. It felt perfection after the Zone. The lack of guards round the airfield at Larnaka on touchdown felt strange as was simply taking a taxi in to Nicosia with its crowded streets and shops looking like those back home. A typical – manic – driver took me north over the hills to Kyrenia, yelling out the window at a poor girl on a bike and blaring his horn as the only concession to blind corners, of which there were plenty on the switchback road. I didn't really want to travel with my eyes shut.

The descent to white, bright Kyrenia was gripping, with grand scenery heightened by the bold castle of St Hilarion. And the sea! The sea! Olive groves affirmed the Mediterranean. Later I would wander by the harbour and under the great caramel-coloured walls of Kyrenia Castle. Cypriot men apparently needed three chairs for their endless coffee drinking: one to sit on, one to put their feet on and one for the small cups of thick coffee, their newspaper and anything else.

A leisurely bath, a real bed with clean-fresh sheets, peacefully reading till drowsy, window open to the scent of flowers and the far, repeating fluting of an owl (Scops?), curtains waltzing to a cool breeze that rustled the pepper trees. In Egypt one forgets such normalities.

My days started early, often with a walk or a ride (there was a beach below the house) after Crystalla, the tiny old maid, had brought a cup of tea then, after breakfast, visits and site-seeing tours, often with the Matthews from across the road or with Andreas, Mr Baxter's gardener/driver, there were picnics, swims at the Club (water that felt cold!) then back for the expat social whirl: watching boring bridge at the Murray's, tea with Mr Waring or Mrs Grove or the Killinglys', drinks at Lady Murphy's, dinner at the Dome Hotel, drinks on the Dufrees' yacht and one night a Red Cross dance with music by the Cyprus police band, the venue heavily decorated with roses and carnations. With the Matthews' daughter in London, I commandeered a young lass who had played the piano for the company and she taught me the samba. A Highland dancing team performed. Aunt Nellie happily danced an eightsome reel. She also won an iron, first prize in a tombola. In the raffle a self-conscious bald man went up to claim his prize of a bottle of hair shampoo. I would meet the nice girl again at a Folk Dancing night and there was more socialising when HMS *Owen* came in to the harbour. We also had American Square Dancing at the Club one night. There was plenty of ex-pat commenting on the Queen and Prince Philip arriving back from their world tour; all very patriotic.

We made several visits to the Dome, Kyrenia's notable hotel. I can recall a small boy, enthralled by the music, standing quite wrapped up in his world, smile on face, conducting with a posy of flowers in his hand. The refugee, King Farouk, fleshy folds almost hiding his swimming trunks, was not a pretty sight. A Mrs Scott called her modest home, the

Hamish: civilian in Cyprus

pun intended, Iona Cottage. [Most of the Brits were there because Income Tax was sixpence in the pound. Not all were wealthy. Aunt Nell for instance existed on an army doctor's widow's pension.] Cottage or mansion, many had accumulated what I regarded as treasures: ecclesiastical objects, furniture, ceramics, terracotta figures, paintings and the like. Kyrenia is something of an artist's paradise, every garden a heady mix for the senses: colours, scents and bird songs.

Among Kyrenia's accumulation of ancients I met a few oddballs: a female who travelled with us to Nicosia and spent the time tearing up bank notes, Lady MacWatt who asked Aunt Nell at a dinner if she had found Christ, so Aunt Nellie, putting on a Scots accent, exclaimed that she 'didna ken he wis lost', the man who prowled the streets talking to someone in his head, in a loud voice, emphasising points with a walking stick – alarming at a first encounter … Someone asked Aunt Nell if she was English and was told 'Scottish'. 'Ah well, that's just the same isn't it?' Got an emphatic 'No!'

We spent one market day in Nicosia. I drooled over oranges at five for a shilling. Lorries tipped out cascades of lemons as well, and stalls were heaped with potatoes, carrots, marrows, cucumbers, courgettes, artichokes, peas and French beans. There were heaps of figs and black olives, stalls of fish (known and unknown, tiny and huge), eels and octopus, mounds of giant water melons, honey, olive oil, Turkish Delight and halva were on sale. Pens held chickens, turkeys and guinea fowl, there were heaped panniers of hot, round loaves of bread. A far cry from bully beef and powdered potato. (Why *so* different?) Clothes, sadly, were just European in style but the arguments over prices were of the east. There was wonderful lace, silver and copper work and cruder pottery. Aunt Sis and I visited a stamp shop together, then, while the others had a siesta in the Windsor, I wandered the narrow streets and visited St Sophia which was a mosque, not a church. [All my letters from Aunt Sis tended to be about stamps. She sent me 'one of her best', which bore a portrait of Erskine Childers – the author of *The Riddle of the Sands*.]

St Sophia was a church originally (mainly 13th/14th century) but with the Arab conquest in the 16th century it was stripped of Christian symbols, was given uncomfortable-looking twin minarets, and became a mosque. There can't be many mosques with Gothic doors, traceried windows and Byzantine capitals. [A few years after my visit Nicosia would become as divided as Jerusalem and the mosque's name changed to Selimye.]

We also crossed the mountains on a flying visit to Limassol on the south coast, where we went for a boat trip after seeing part of a pageant in which a girl as 'Aphrodite' drove a flower-garlanded chariot pulled by four white horses. Thinking of the Aphrodite myth (the

Above: Aunt Nellie, at Limassol, Cyprus

Right: Stravrovouni Monastery

Botticelli image of the naked beauty drifted ashore on a scallop shell), this happened at a bay which we passed on that boat journey. No Aphrodite in the gentle foam that day, no *Horae*[39] to welcome, just four very plump, very naked middle-aged ladies disporting in the sea – in Aunt Nellie's opinion much more Rubens than Botticelli. Note *²

✳ ✳ ✳

About 2000 feet above Larnaca, perched on a crag, is the oldest monastery in Cyprus, Stavrovouni (AD 327), which we reached by a tortuous dirt road. I counted 23 hairpin bends in about 5 miles so I'm glad neither of the old aunts was driving. We saw both exotic bee-eaters and rollers. When we first came in sight of the monastery what we saw was a row of ten gables stuck together, a high window in each, just like a row of Scandinavian-style warehouses, but built of stone. But the belfry (in scaffolding) gave it away. A monk with black robes and a black flowerpot hat and a white Father Christmas beard brought out a precious altar cross which, he said, held a bit of the 'True Cross'. Aunt Nellie's comment was that there were enough bits of the True Cross in Cyprus alone to have needed the felling of a forest. The mother of the Emperor Constantine supposedly brought a part of the True Cross here from Jerusalem on her travelling to Constantinople. The monastery, which had been destroyed over and over again, so we were told, is 'modern', i.e. 17th–18th century. The view was terrific of course: toned plains, over which lines of hills rolled like sea breakers, while, to the SE we could see the sea.

---

39 Ancient Greek personification of the seasons of the year.

One run with the Matthews took us on wee roads along the Pentadactylos, the mountains translating quite appropriately as Five Fingers, very much how they look from Kyrenia: knuckles and digits of bare limestone rock breaking out of the brittle, dusty vegetation with ambushing flowers, rock roses and arbutus, and with a scent all of its own. I sniffed Cyprus contentedly; Cyprus has scents, the Zone just has smells.

Lambousa Monastery

We drove up and along and in and out through the sunny forest solitude to find an abandoned monastery, Antiphonitis (the name sounds like something nasty one could catch out here!) which has a charming 12th-century Byzantine Church. Looking down, it appears a chunky building topped by a helmet-shaped dome and with a Gothic arched arcade on one flank. It sits among ruins on a terraced glade. We saw a black and white Cyprus chat.[40] The church is a lucky survivor standing as it is, open and unprotected. It has the frescos of the colourful style that makes every church a priceless gem of early Christian art. Christ is portrayed against a deep blue background in the dome and there is the popular scene of the Last Judgement – with a many-legged devil in attendance.

❋   ❋   ❋

I walked or cycled out from Kyrenia into the hills whenever possible to see monasteries and the several splendid castles. One day I cycled 9 miles to Lambousa, with its three pepper pot churches. The landscape was bright with asphodel, oleander, cistus, with red flax, orchids and lilies, gladioli, rosemary and marigolds, and seeing hoopoe, bee-eater, crested lark, wheatear and 'l.b.bs' [little brown birds] I'll never identify. At Morphou, further west, over a big plain covered in olive and orange and lemon trees, I was to discover the popular Church of St Mamas. The church block is surrounded with arcades (4 arches each side) and topped with a tall pepper pot tower.

The church has gone through various alterations (up to 1725) but Gothic details remain: doorways, marble pillars and the saint's shrine. However, it is the bright 'iconostasis'

---

40 The *Cyprus chat* is now called the Cyprus wheatear, *Oenanthe cypriaca*.

(painted wooden barrier separating nave and altar) that is special, both Gothic and Venetian. The altar has marble columns with Byzantine capitals. But you'd need Gunnis, not me, to describe all this. What I fell for was the saint's white marble tomb, or, the icon rather, which shows him riding a lion with a lamb in his arms.

The legend is about an ascetic hermit who lived in a nearby cave, who objected to the imposition of a poll tax; after all, he made no call on anyone for anything and owned nothing. Soldiers were sent to arrest him and take him to the Byzantine ruler in Nicosia to be punished. On the way they came on a lion chasing a lamb. St Mamas at once held up his hand, which stopped the lion. He then gathered the lamb in his arms and climbed onto the back of the lion and proceeded thus into the presence of the ruler – and was

promptly exempted from the tax for life! There are more than a dozen churches dedicated to St Mamas in Cyprus and at one we saw the lion had a face so like a cow's that I copied it; and St Mamas seemed to have dropped the lamb for it wasn't shown. I'm sure something could be made of this story and I'm now toying with the idea of writing a play about St Mamas. An anti-tax saint should appeal to we ill-paid servants of the Queen out here.

❋   ❋   ❋

One of the longer runs (150 miles), on the penultimate day, was with Mr Baxter's Andreas. We happened to be talking about books and I mentioned *Popski's Private Army*, 1950 [a Reprint Society issue of his book came out in 1953], the story of the charismatic Vladimir Peniakoff who led his forces behind enemy lines in the desert in World War Two. Baxter knew Popski – and had introduced him to people in London who looked after him during his last illness. We travelled to Soli, Vouni, Lefka, up through Nikitari to the wee church with all the fresco paintings [Asinou] then over the forested hill to Spilia, down the fantastic Troodos road and 'home' via Nicosia. The Troodos go up to 6,399 feet.[41] It was almost too much for Aunt Sis so my planned last-minute shopping spree in Nicosia was cut short. After a day in bed she was her bright self when I headed for Deversoir, a very different 'home'. I did get a jar of orange blossom honey, however. (Didn't last long.)

Soli was a typical Roman site with its basilica with a mosaic and marble floor and a huge theatre scalloped out of the hillside. I estimated there's at least 20 tiers of seats (for 3,500 spectators, we were told). Soli was originally a Greek city, then Roman, but in the 7th century Arab raids meant it was abandoned, like Kyrenia, with people settling more safely in the hills.

41 1,951 metres.

The Arabs, like the Vikings at home – or the Spanish in the Aztec and Inca worlds – between them must have destroyed the best part of the world's fabulous artefacts and monuments. [What has changed? Think of the Taliban destroying the great Buddhas at Bamiyan in Afghanistan in 2001, or the several churches in Ukraine shelled by the Russians in 2022.]

After Soli we had a picnic which gave me the chance of a swim (the old dears don't) then it was up 800 feet to the site of Vouni, the only ancient Persian palace in the Med. It was destroyed in a fire in 380 BC. There is not much to see other than the foundations. Swedish archaeologists excavated here, and Soli, in the 1920s. We were shown round by the guardian (dressed like a bus conductor). The stonework is massive with thick walls, flights of steps and large water tanks. All the best things of course are in the museum in Nicosia – like the armless Aphrodite from Soli (not quite the Venus de Milo!) which is on many postcards. I'd like to have seen more in Nicosia but we never seemed to have time there. Aunt Sis told impatient Aunt Nell she was a bit of a Philistine when we were trying to find a specific feature at Vouni. Water was actually laid on throughout (over 100 rooms), there were WCs and even a sauna. Royalty did well for themselves even then. What a mess history is and, heavens!, Cyprus has had more than its share. Vouni was one of the sites we visited which appeared on the Cyprus stamps.

Asinou was quite my most favourite old site in Cyprus. It doesn't even look like a church as it stands like a solitary alpine barn on an open hilltop in the forest, just a rough-walled, simple rectangle building with an overhanging tiled roof. It dates to between 1099 and 1105 – when the Normans were roughing-up England.

The inside is simply covered with the most glorious mural paintings, many from Bible scenes of course: The Annunciation, Christ entering Jerusalem, the Last Supper and so on. There's one painting of Christ offering wine to six of his disciples, his gaze on Judas who has turned away. Sermons in pictures. Or history: the 40 martyrs of Sebaste [now Sivas] in Turkey who were left on a frozen lake to perish – and tempted to renounce their faith by the sight of steaming hot baths set on the shore. There's a painting of the church's donor who holds a model of the church which looks just as it does now. Lots of saints everywhere: St Helena as a queen enthroned, St George on a white horse, St Anastasia who was a poison-curer, and carries a medicine bottle. The church is dedicated to the Virgin Mary, so she is shown in all her imagined life – and after! If I've gone on a bit about Asinou (in Greek the mouthful Panaya Phorviotissa) it is just so magical, brilliantly, sweepingly beautiful. [Asinou is now a World Heritage Site, 'the most beautiful of the churches of the Troodos'.] I bought a booklet on it or I'd forget most of the names. I've only mentioned *some*.

Descending from the Troodos we saw the biggest historic church but didn't go in: the Byzantine St Barnabas and Hilarion. It is a bit stolid but topped with five domes and a tall bell tower but bits are early 10th century. This village, Peristerona, also has a mosque.

Leaving Kyrenia there were olives in flower and more carob trees which Aunt Sis said was our source of vanilla – from their pendulous pods. They are also called locust trees and it's suggested that they are the real locusts that the Bible has John the Baptist eating in the wilderness: 'locusts and wild honey' – but what was wrong with eating the insects. and you don't get trees in the desert? Aunt Nellie last autumn got £15 from selling carrots on her land. Out of curiosity I've just looked up honey in my concordance and find it is mentioned 36 times in the Bible. We did see rows of hives nearing Morphou, where the oranges and lemons are grown. I met a man, 'Honey' Thompson, who takes hives all over the place to catch the varying blossom flows – just as we took hives to the heather in Scotland.

I could happily live in Cyprus's climate. If there's blazing bougainvillea there's a decent ration of sun. Bougainvillea originated in tropical South America and was collected by an 18th-century navigator, Monsieur Bougainville, the first Frenchman to circumnavigate the world. It must have reached all round the world now. Like Australian eucalyptus (here too) which we had at Hill Crest. [in South Africa].

The village of Bellapais is a scattering of white cubes among the deep greens of almond and fruit trees with sparser grazing grounds above breaking into the wounds of rocky outcrops. Very Cezanne-ish. Bellapais proved as special as everyone said. The Aunts had been there, Nellie 'too often' (she *is* a Philistine). Difficult to convey what was special. I was going to say 'silence' but there's a background chorus from birds so it is more accurately 'peace', partly from the actual abbey buildings, half-ruined, half-alive, with gardens and a row of young cypress trees, partly from its lofty crag setting with such spaciousness of sky and sea (on some days you can pick out the Turkish coast, 60 miles away), and partly from the saga of its history. I was captivated. A blue rock thrush was a new bird for me, and a big black millipede was rowing along on its wavy legs. And the shrill of cicadas to me is the sound of sunny climates, just as chameleons and geckos mark the swing of day and night [see Note *3]. I twice walked the hour up to the site from Kyrenia, [Bellapais was called 'loveliest of Gothic abbeys' in Thubron's book. Lawrence Durrell was living in the village at the time, and his book *Bitter Lemons* pictures period and place perfectly.]

Left: Bellapais
Right: Aunts Sis and Nell in the cloister

And the history? It is essentially a Crusader creation. Disraeli wrote of it as a 'land famous in all ages. ... the romantic kingdom of the Crusaders. (Romance obviously requires plenty shedding of blood!) When Jerusalem fell to Saladin in 1187 the Lusignan King of Jerusalem had the Augustinian canons, who had guarded the Church of the Nativity, established here. A bit of the 'True Cross' was bequeathed to it, but all the treasures were carried off by the rapacious Genoese in 1373. The French Catholic Cyprus rulers had been very oppressive and, like most of the world pre-Reformation, had become godless and decadent, and Bellapais was in decline. When seized by the Turks in the 16th century they drove out the monks but allowed the village the use of the church. The locals also, alas, made use of the abbey's stone for building village houses. Britain did its share of vandalism by concreting the floor of the Great Hall in 1878 (intended for a military hospital). But much remains almost complete. One can climb onto rooftops, the refectory still has its striking fan-vaulted ceiling, the cloisters remain a haven, the church (much from the 13th century) is still a church, with the formal 16th-century iconostasis surviving and with a soaring wall of a belfry pierced by four arches – the highest eyecatcher of all. I wish I'd taken more photos.

※　　※　　※

Kyrenia is dominated by its castle, the perfect picture of what a castle should be. It bullies its surroundings, and was never captured throughout the island's bloody history.

It was often enough besieged, once for nearly four years, when the occupants were reduced to eating dogs and rats. It had quite a history (like Scotland!). A Byzantine fort originally, the Lusignan Crusader family who ruled Cyprus for 300 years were the major builders. Their coat of arms is seen above the inner gate. They held off their Genoese rivals on the seas but lost Famagusta to them. Then the Venetians held Cyprus for over 70 years,

Left: Kyrenia Castle's sea defences
Right: Kyrenia Castle

and they made major additions to the castle (and to those of Famagusta and Nicosia). Maritime power being the Venetian preoccupation, the mountain castles of St Hilarion, Buffavento and Kentara were largely dismantled.

The Venetians in turn surrendered to the Ottoman Turks in 1570. (The Admiral who took the castle died soon after and his tomb is in the castle.) Because it was never battered by war means the architecture is well preserved. There is a truly huge inner courtyard enclosed by buildings several storeys high, and on the ramparts the complexity really shows. There are dungeons in plenty and the Venetian battlements are a showpiece of their time. I took a few photos inside but it was the view of the castle that caught the eye. I often sat at the old harbour cafés to read or just watch the world go by, fishing boats chug off and, always, these monstrous walls were leering down. (What building skills through the centuries!) Across the harbour at the end of an arm turning out from the NW corner tower is a tubby tower with a pillar on it, called the Chain Tower, because from it a defensive chain was run across the harbour entrance.

Kyrenia Castle was in useful line of sight and communication with the three mountain castles. We never visited Kentara to the east, but I explored St Hilarion and Buffavento by myself. St Hilarion was a hermit who had to flee the Holy Land when it fell and at one time there was a monastery here, hence the large size of the church that remains. Overgrown, wild as it was, I expected to meet the great god Pan. Far too rough for the Aunts. I was able to explore all the way up – the highest point is 2,400 ft so is quite airy above the summit cliffs. There are three self-contained 'wards' with water cisterns etc, each with walls and a defensive gateway, a huge one leading into the middle ward, then, on high, the royal apartments of the Lusignans who fled here from Nicosia's summer heat – and the Black Death. The best-known feature, which took some reaching in the jungly neglect, was the Queen's Window, which had seats set in the wall's thickness, just like Ravenscraig Castle [on the Forth, by Kirkcaldy]. A kestrel was keeking, a wren reeling, and, low down, I just about jumped when a partridge went off in loud complaint. I had a sort of talk with a beekeeper at some rows of hives. He had very little English.

Buffavento

I also visited Buffavento, perched even higher than St Hilarion (over 3,000 ft) but I've no account written from Deversoir. I suspect some letters with Cyprus notes have not survived. We all visited Famagusta and Salamis, major outings, and I've no note of them either. Just one other site, a castle again, was described for home consumption:

Kolossi Castle just had to be seen as both Aunt Sis and I thought it looked perfect on a Cyprus stamp. We made a detour to see it [5 miles out from Limassol] and were rewarded. Unlike most forts that sprawled, this solitary tower sat four square, clean lined, crenellated and with machicolations over the drawbridge entrance – a copybook castle – built by the Knights Hospitaller, the Knights of St John. Richard the Lionheart captured it. He had met the tyrant Isaac Comnenus there earlier, a man as evil as any but only one of two who ever ruled Cyprus for themselves; otherwise over the millennia Cyprus was always ruled by foreign powers, none of them benign.

Crystalla

* Does any country come out of its past without having been torn apart? When the Turks invaded the north in 1974 they landed on the shore below Aunt Nellie's rented house, which they blew up. She, luckily, had been in Scotland and Ireland and had just died – so was spared this sadness. She died at Aunt Sis's home in Dublin, her will was eventually found in Dunfermline, her home was now in a war zone. Knowing my interest in books, Aunt Nell said I could have her modest collection. This included a 40-volume leather-bound set of the works of Voltaire of all people. She also had a small framed sepia pen and wash sketch by Gainsborough, and its loss I do regret. The international lawyers took some time (and most of her minimal estate) in sorting things out. Just after we finally thought everything was settled, a letter with Cyprus stamps came through the letter box. It was from dear old Crystalla, her maid, whom we all knew and loved and had presumed dead, saying she was alive and well – and, please, could she have her back wages?

Being posted on to Kenya prevented a return to Cyprus and now I don't think I would want to return. I have seen too much of the displacement of peoples in my lifetime, too many treasures smashed, too many sad and hungry faces.

My main historical interest lay in the Lusignan centuries and I'll end this Cyprus rambling by reproducing part of the youthful piece I wrote in Deversoir for the *Dollar Magazine* and which would appear while I was in Kenya. Oddly, I was working on this book when the school magazine mentioned the RAF section of the CCF had been to RAF Akrotiri in Cyprus for two weeks of Easter camp. Ah, to think I might have had my two years there! The editor of the article cut all personal comments, alas, leaving a somewhat dry study.

'*You are welcome, Sir, to Cyprus.*'

Shakespeare: *Othello.*

ISAAC COMNENUS was in a rage. In his harbour lay the ship with Berengaria of Navarre and the Queen Dowager of Sicily on board. All his hypocritical invitations of welcome had been refused. 'Go,' he ordered, 'and bring them.' The armed galleys set off to capture the noble ladies, but in this history of blood occurred an act from a fairy tale: Richard the Lionheart sailed over the horizon at the critical moment. He, too, went into a rage, rescued his bride-to-be, and laid Amathus in ruins before the self-proclaimed Emperor's beaten army. Here, too, he married Berengaria and composed some lyrics, reputed to be of 'no mean quality'. Among his nobles was one Guy de Lusignan.

This, however, is a late event in the long history of the island. People are still finding Neolithic, Bronze Age and Iron Age remains. Five centuries before Christ's birth the Persians conquered Cyprus and two centuries later Ptolemy I had it within his dominion. It is interesting to note that it was in Kition that Zeno, founder of the Stoic Philosophy, was born. Julius Caesar's legions marched across the plains, but Rome did not have much interest in the 'Island of Copper' (hence Cu, cupric, cupreous etc). The Bible tells us of Paul and Barnabas who, with John Mark, landed at Salamis and went on to Paphos, where they left a wondering Sergius Paulus and a blinded Elymas. Cyprus, mentioned many other times in the Acts of the Apostles, became one of the first Christian lands.

The Emperor Hadrian also left his mark on Salamis, and the broken pillars of marble bear testimony to his powers of building. Cyprus entered a period of Byzantine rule after the split of the Roman Empire, and their typical architecture can be seen all over the island, though during the centuries pillage and destruction have taken heavy toll. An aunt of Mohammed fell from her mule in Cyprus and broke her neck. The little boats used to dip their sails on passing her Tomb among the trees. For 300 years the Moslems held sway over the land.

In 1191 King Richard arrived on his way to the Holy Land and made his takeover but, a true Englishman, he needed money, so he sold Cyprus to the Knights Templar. On an insurrection they hastily passed it back to Richard, who, with equal speed, 'rewarded' it to Guy de Lusignan. The Lusignans were to suffer miserably for their 300-year Frankish rule.

To see this period of the Middle Ages and the Lusignan family, Kyrenia Castle is something of an illustrative textbook. It was first besieged in 1220, surrendered, and was again under fire 13 years later. The besieged had taken (as safeguard) a fine harem of noble ladies, including the Queen. She, most inconsiderately, died, and a truce was arranged for her funeral at St Sophia, Nicosia. Later, the remnant defenders were starved out. In 1349 Hugh IV imprisoned his sons, Peter and John, in one of the very unpleasant cells I saw. (The most unwanted guests were treated to a special cell, one that filled at each high tide.) These lads, desirous of seeing the world, ran away with their tutor, who, poor man, had his hands and feet cut off before being dragged to the gallows. Three days later the king died – never mind how – and Peter, succeeding, decided that others should sample the fine dungeons. Into their depths went the Sultan of Cairo's ambassadors. Peter II, at his Coronation, enlivened things by murdering some Genoese merchants, and soon he was behind Kyrenian walls under fire by the Genoese. The Queen, by changing sides at the right moment, saved the situation, and a truce was arranged, neatly broken, and the king tortured to death in Genoa. They rested a few years, cleaning their armour, and then rode forth again, when a Cardinal Lusignan entered upon an orgy of bloodshed, from which he emerged with the blood-splattered crown upon his head. Such was Lusignan history!

Leonardo da Vinci visited Cyprus, and for 70 years the Venetians were rulers. After much brave resistance the Turks drove them out. Nicosia, the capital, held out for 45 long days but ended with the population of 200,000 people being unmercifully slain. Famagusta resisted for a year, but their treaty was violated and their governor, flayed alive and his skin filled with straw, was hung up on display at Istanbul. After the period of Ottoman rule (misrule) the island became British in 1878, and a Crown Colony in 1925. Even today some are not happy and clamour for a new ruler – Greece. (Greece in 1915 had refused an offer of the isle.) But most of the people have not cared: it is not the babbling of politicians that makes a people, but the ageless tillers of the soil.

✳   ✳   ✳

* Alas, it was very much to be the politicians (inept, well-intending or fanatic) who would drive Cyprus's destiny since I wrote that, back in 1954. Bitter years and divisions still mark the island, whose peoples, wherever, remain engagingly hospitable and welcoming. In order to understand the years since I was there, I have written Note *4, a catch-up history from when the Turkish displaced the hated Venetians.

Cyprus had been an unexpectedly vibrant introduction for me to the Mediterranean world (which would be further topped up by the visit to Jerusalem a few months later), a world where compelling ancient histories rose in stone and story to grip the imagination. Cyprus being unreachable, I would later travel to see historic Roman sites along the Turkish coast or seek out the rich paintings in the rock-cut churches in Cappadocia *but* it was in sunny Cyprus I first drank at that spring.

Notes

*1 Aunt Nell's smoking fascinated me, as a boy in South Africa. She chain-smoked Navy Capstan cigarettes, which came in cylindrical tins with labels showing a sailor and lifebuoy – and, important for me, included cigarette cards, at that time on the Flowers and Birds of South Africa. I had the albums for them and as a result became interested in flowers and birds, an interest which has lasted a lifetime.

Then, suddenly, we were going 'home', a place which had never been that. Panic! I was still a few bird cards short (the flowers book was complete). I pestered Aunt Nell to increase production, vainly swopped possessions at school and seriously suggested I was left behind till I found the wanted cards. I could catch a later ship to Scotland.

My spare South African cards held no interest for my new Scottish schoolmates. Those five blanks remained. Why couldn't Aunt Nell have smoked more? Thirty years on, browsing in McNaughton's Bookshop at the head of Leith Walk, I spotted the familiar South African cigarette card albums on a high shelf. They were in a polythene bag with dozens of loose cards. I paid £1 for the lot and, after a rummage, found the five missing cards! My yell of glee might have been heard in Kyrenia.

*2 The earlier part of the Aphrodite myth – mercifully – does not appear in the Botticelli masterpiece (nor in any tourist guidebook). How come then that Aphrodite is riding ashore on a giant scallop shell? Briefly: Kronos (Saturn), master of the cosmos, was responsible (or irresponsible). He would later eat his children to fend off the prophecy that one of them would destroy him as he had his own father, Ouranos. With his mother Gaia's encouragement, Kronos had used a great sickle to castrate Ouranos. He then hurled his grisly trophy far away over the seas. Wherever blood fell in passing, living beings emerged, most of them unpleasant, and when the genitals eventually splashed down into the sea, it was off Cyprus. Out of the resultant turbulence rose this figure of godly beauty, Aphrodite, whom the Romans called Venus.

Temples to Aphrodite were built in various Cyprus locations, most notably at Old Paphos – which was mentioned by Homer in the Odyssey – and Aphrodite, assimilating the earlier cult of Astarte, has inspired more art and sculpture than any other from the Greek pantheon.

*3 Cicadas. These fascinating creatures fall silent on being approached and are difficult to discover. Their life cycle is extraordinary. They only live six weeks at the most but in that time they will have mated and deposited their eggs in the bark of trees. The hatching grubs drop to the ground and burrow down to live off the sap in roots for precisely 13 years, or 17 in some species, when they then erupt, emerging as shelled, six-legged creatures which crawl up the trunks then split open to release the winged, perfect cicadas. How they count the years precisely remains a mystery.

*4 Catch-up history
Ottoman Cyprus, **1571–1878**, was not a very happy place. Although the rulers did abolish serfdom early on, generally they were despotic, corrupt and ineffectual. Oddly, they reinstated the Greek Orthodox Church, which had languished through the Lusignan and Venetian years. The restored archbishopric, however, was as much a temporal as spiritual power, something that would be noted by a later archbishop, one Makarios III. Under the Ottomans, taxation was heavy, life drudgery for most. Through much of the **17th century** there were plagues, drought, famine, earthquakes and locusts, and the population halved.

In **1821** the Greek Cypriots sided with Greece in its War of Independence from Turkey. This rumbled on for a decade but, with the support of Britain, France and Russia, its success seeded ideas in Cyprus that would lead to the wish for Enosis, union with Greece. The island was increasingly becoming drawn into the expansionist interests of the great European powers (the Suez Canal would open in 1869). In **1821** the Turks reacted to Greece's freedom by sending more troops into Cyprus and treacherously executing over 400 leading laymen and clerics. War with Russia and the defeat of Turkey destabilised the balance of power, so in **1878** the Conference of Berlin was called to regulate boundaries and disputed claims. The wily British premier Disraeli secretly had been making his own moves and, a few days before the Berlin gathering, announced Turkey had ceded control of Cyprus to Britain. Britain would be there till 1960.

Britain set about building roads and schools, establishing a postal system and a forestry service, eradicating malaria, and creating general law and order. Enosis was fairly low key. In **1914** Britain annexed Cyprus when Turkey sided with Germany in World War One. For one week in **1915** Britain offered to cede Cyprus to Greece if Greece at once declared for the Allies. The offer was rejected, but not forgotten by the Enosis-minded.

In 1925 Cyprus was made a Crown Colony. The inter-war period was generally peaceful but in 1931 the first serious riots occurred throughout Cyprus. Government House was burnt down, the Legislative Council suspended and rule was by then by decree. In World War Two, **1939–1945**, the Greek faction supported British in the war (without relinquishing Enosis hopes) while the Turks were hoping British rule would continue. A setback for Enosis came when the Greek political factions in Athens began fighting among themselves. The situation became more intense when Archbishop Makarios was elected spiritual – and political – leader and, with support from Greece, aided the Enosis campaign. (A poll of Greek Cypriots showed 96 per cent in favour of union!) There was something of a clandestine triumvirate with Makarios, the Greek premier and the Cyprus-born Greek Colonel George Grivas (the Cyprus Che Guevara) working together. In **1954** the UN turned down Greek demands for Enosis, so more riots followed, these escalating in **1955** with EOKA[42] launched under Grivas, from his base in the Troodos Mountains, his force of a few hundred tying down British forces of 20,000 and 4,500 police. In **1956** Makarios was deported to the Seychelles (almost a norm, surely, in the history of independence struggles?). Britain's Turkish auxiliaries allegedly tortured EOKA captives. A state of emergency (the inevitable next step) was declared and lasted till 1960. In 1958 the Turkish faction was demanding partition, fearing Britain was yielding to Greek demands then, in **1959**, following a meeting in Zurich by Greece and Turkey, a surprising agreement was announced: Cyprus was to be an independent republic with a Greek president and a Turkish vice-president, and a ratio of 7 to 3 was to be applied to a Council of Ministers, the House of Representatives and the Civil Service. Both Enosis and partition were proscribed, and Britain would retain sovereign military bases at Dhekelia and Akrotiri. Each power had the right to military action if the constitution was threatened. Makarios became the first president. This Treaty of Guarantee **1960** was an astonishing outcome.

---

42 Ethniki Organosis Kyprion Agoniston, Cyprus's National Organisation of Warriors.

Such a complex and ideological arrangement soon proved impractical and in **1963** perceived imbalances and conflicting demands made the constitution unworkable in effect, and inter-racial fighting escalated. Britain rushed in troops to Nicosia but eventually the city had to be divided by the 'Green Line' (reputedly officers drew a ceasefire line across Nicosia in green ink). In **1964** a United Nations Peacekeeping Force was created to separate the warring factions. Fighting continued for a decade.

In 1974 the military junta in Greece supported a coup that saw Makarios flee (he was restored as president in 1977). Turkey called on Britain for help (in the terms of the 1960 treaty) but when this failed Turkey invaded the north of Cyprus with 40,000 troops and eventually controlled 37 per cent of the island (for 18 per cent of the population). Talks at the United Nations having failed, a *de facto* border existed, the Green Line extending to 180 km, and something approaching 400,000 people were forced to migrate to one side or the other. UN forces remained as a buffer between the Zones – and are still there today. The situation at the time of writing (2021) bubbles rather than boils, and some crossing of the Green Line is possible for tourists in a way inconceivable a decade ago. The 1983 Turkish Zone, claiming itself an independent state, has not been recognised internationally (except by Turkey) so one can only visit the north via mainland Turkey. Economically the North lags behind the Greek zone, but this has seen the North retain the certain charm I knew. There are no built-up costas. The people are still as friendly and welcoming. Maybe there is time to sun my old bones at a café below the walls of Kyrenia Castle, coffee on a chair beside me, the clack of backgammon players nearby, the quiet harbour mirroring the colour of the sky. Well, I can dream.

4

The Zone, 2: the teenage telephonist:
21 May–19 September 1954

Vampire

During 1953 in the Zone there were 20 fatalities listed as having been caused by terrorist acts (details from the gravestones in the cemeteries at Moascar and Fayid). In the same year there were 36 further such deaths, of which details have never been released, and many were incidents involving two people or more. Will the truth ever be told?

In Ismailia there was one fatality when a police jeep was pushed off the road by an Egyptian lorry. There was one death from a motor accident and two others of own-side deaths (from stupidity). Sadly a pilot officer died piloting a Harvard, and there were seven fatalities in a Hastings crash near RAF Shallufa, on a flight from RAF Fayid (12.1.53). Notorious was a case where a motor cyclist was killed (nearly decapitated) by a wire stretched across a road, a favourite terrorist ploy. This was recorded as a 'road accident'. In April a Greek civilian NAAFI manager was abducted and killed.

None of this is mentioned in my letters home, but then I knew little or none of it – as was intended. In the cemeteries in the Zone there are about 500 named gravestones, of civilians and forces alike, a statistic never publicly acknowledged, but all listed in an appendix in Findlay's book.

Douglas Findlay's service in the Equipment Section at Deversoir ended a couple of months before I started in the Signals Section. We were to meet decades later in the Scottish ranks of the Suez Veterans Association. He recounts a nasty incident one black night on the road along from RAF Deversoir's guard room. He was on guard at the gate when a truck overturned, and by the time help reached the scene it was only to find all the truck personnel dead – strange, if the truck had just flipped from running a wheel off the tarmac. There were eight privates of the East African Pioneer Corps, one British private and one major. That, too, was 'an accident', for 50 years, until it was officially admitted as being the result of a terrorist attack.

Deversoir

21.5.54

I'm back in Deversoir after a jerky journey. We stepped out into a pitiless 110°. What a pile of mail! Writing this in a spell off in the PBX. The electric power has just failed so our wee fan has stopped. It is desperately hot in this tiny black hole (black, as our emergency lighting is also down). I'm already plonked for 24 hours of guard tomorrow. Nothing happened here while I was away, I was told by a bored mate. Oh, how I revelled in the restful bustle of Cyprus with its antique atmosphere, the fantastic exuberance of the flowers and the friendly loom of hills! The Zone is just enervating clockwork life.

Next Thursday I have back pay of 6d a day to the 7th April. Aunt Nell gave me £2 and later £5. I spent £7-15-0 on clothes: sandals £2-0-0, flannels £1-15-0 and a very good blazer for £4.

WANTS s.v.p.[43]

1. A tin of Gibbs.[44] 2. 1 doz clothes pegs (my last two broke). 3. 1 tin boil plasters (gave my last one to a billet casualty). 4. 1 tin Nivea Creme. 5. My Youth Hostel map off study wall (one with routes marked). 6. DDT Powder (our running fight with ANTS!). 7. A wee scrubber for laundry work (I washed 25 garments today). 8. Some plain postcards. 9. 2 pkts envelopes (here out of stock as usual). 10. Economy labels.[45] 11. Sellotape. 12. Books: Seton Gordon's *Highways and Byways in the West Highlands* (lots of legends), the *Albatross Book of Verse* and *The History of Philosophy* (study glass bookcase).

A real pile, but stuck out here, even everyday items are unavailable or beyond our means. I'm very grateful for all the home parcels. Not everyone has such good fortune.

Both Ian and I received endless parcels. I now feel guilty at making such demands. Family life in Dollar or Crail was always hectic, hosting endless family and friends, there were school and church calls, dog and cats, beekeeping, houses and gardens to run. And Gran. Mother's next letter would start:

> writing on the beach rocks, Crail … Gran can't be left alone. I was desperately busy before leaving Dollar. Nikko (Siamese) had four kittens so with animals, messages (shopping), cleaning house for Dad and David and Nellie all arriving at different times, it was

---

43 *S'il vous plaît* (please).
44 Toothpaste.
45 White adhesive labels printed up specifically in order for people to re-use envelopes.

demanding. Gran's bed was a muddle and some pie for me I'd left in the oven vanished. She knew nothing yet the pie dish had been cleaned and put back in the cupboard. She's less of a handful here in Crail.

The beach rocks were just along from the harbour and house, and Mother would sit at a favourite rock, back supported and knees up to make a lectern, and write endless letters, at least once a week to Ian and me, never mind all the relatives and friends – to whom she was something of a rock in another sense. Gran had dementia and could be unpredictable – 'last week I found her dressed, fur coat and all, saying she was off home. A week ago she did get on a bus but they'd the gumption to put her off two stops later: "Here you are, then, dearie," and she toddled back to Devon Lodge.' I recall going into her room, once home, and finding her attacking the ceiling light with a walking stick – she was back in her childhood when a rod was used to switch off/on the gas light fitting.

Hard to see her as the once vivacious lass who travelled through the Suez Canal a reputed 13 times, having married an engineer who was building Siam's railways. Mother

Hamish, a pencil portrait by a billet-mate

had been born in Bangkok in 1904 and, an only child, was swept off her feet by her Billie, a young banker who arrived following World War One, in which he had served at the front, been wounded, sent back again and then captured by the Germans. Ian was born in Dunfermline during leave, I was born in Colombo in 1934 and David in Japan in 1940. The day World War Two broke out our parents climbed Mount Fuji. We had quite an experience escaping the Japanese from Malaya, Father from Singapore as it fell, his ship then bombed … Mother's letters were kept and, with my memories and Father's account, were turned into a book, *East of West, West of East* (2019). Perhaps there lies the genesis for this collection of letters.

31.5.54

Dear Ian

Cyprus was wonderful – a great get out from the prison of Egypt. It is very hot now – although the 90° as I'm writing feels cool to some days when we've gone up to 125°. We even had an outrage of rain. Hard hitting but at least vertical. With the hot weather the PBX is like an oven and the sweat runs down our legs and wets our feet. On the chairs we sit in a puddle. Just heard on the wireless of another chap murdered in Ismailia. It's a bad spot. One shouldn't go wandering alone. Folk disappear or turn up in the Sweet Water Canal after being butchered. Not so much now though.

The food in Cyprus was all one could want, the aunts good fun [Ian would later visit Aunt Nell in Cyprus], the climate kind, the country beautiful and the people friendly. I only wished I could have stayed two months not two weeks. The country is full of interesting old monasteries and smarmy priests.

The next thing to catch me is the Padre going away for six or seven weeks so he has asked me to take two church services here and two in another base called Fayid. I'm rather thrilled – and a bit scared. But I said I'd help him out. Bother! I've to go on another board right now – chap wants off as he's feeling ill. Good news about Roger Bannister getting under the four minutes mile – just! Tell me more about your messing about in Tanks.

In Ismailia I had a wee 'incident' with a local youth, the only time I've ever hit anybody 'with intent'. He was shoving clothes ('very cheap, sur!') into my face, and I wasn't having that. It's a favourite trick, to distract while a hand underneath tries to pick a pocket. I stepped back but saw he had a knife in his hand – so I hit him – and scarpered. I was in a daft place and alone. Not an escapade I've mentioned home. Don't you, please! The supervisor i/c the PBX was not pleased. I could hardly use my right hand properly for days.

31.5.54

Another day of sun assault so as soon as I can I'll be off to the Point. I have not had a swim since coming back – been too busy. I've washed nearly all the things I possess, darned many and made a new collar for my blue Aertex shirt (I'm very proud of that bit of needle-work) and am desperately trying to get immediate letters done. It's quite a job writing with the shirt sticking to your back – and your bottom sticking to the chair. It's been very busy at the switchboard too so I'm just dripping sweat. On Friday the weather began a pattern which we've been following since: bright mornings and by midday extremely hot, then a breeze and then before sunset a good sandstorm followed by a quiet night. Two days ago it rained mud.

Mail just in. I expect a parcel from Cyprus with about a dozen Penguins I bought and Aunt Nell's 'Gunnis' [guide book] without which I can't contemplate writing anything about Cyprus. One chap has just fallen asleep reading a book – and the supervisor is lying flat on the floor trying to cure a 'very bleeding nose'. Time to go on the board – my last half hour for today. I have tomorrow off. I went to the pictures in the end, partly to be cool, and partly to see our F.P. star Jimmy Hayter again, in *A Day to Remember*, a good laugh. Also saw *Moulin Rouge*.

Sis and Nell have left Cyprus. Already it seems years since I was with them. Pass on my best wishes. They rather deserve each other. Let me know when Aunt Nell arrives in Dollar. She fed me wonderfully in Cyprus. Crystalla was amazed at the quantities of bread I consumed: fresh and crisp, lots of kinds too, with home-made marmalade.

8.6.54

I've got my books from Cyprus (let Aunt Nell know please) so I had better start writing properly for the *Dollar Magazine* and for the play for Christmas time: a tragedy we decided, after an argument. I've based it on the Cyprus legend about St Mamas, in Gunnis. I do a great deal of reading but wonder how much I'll remember. Still, it can only improve my own efforts. I find it hard to study, though, with such an irregular lifestyle, other, easier activities, and the enervating climate. (Now there's a word out of the dictionary.)

LATER. Just a wee note to add to yesterday's before I post. Now six in the morning and showing every promise of being 'just another bloomin stinking day'. I expect I shall have to go on guard again tonight. They are coming round once a week now. We need to keep good watch for Ramadan is just two days past and the locals are even more anti-British than usual. What a noise there was coming from the villages on the night of the feast. They fast in the day and then make whoopee all night so it is not surprising everyone's nerves are all to pot by the end of the month.

A note from Mother on this letter sent on to Ian:

Mrs Blake next door was raging about the cat noises and no wonder, we've had a terrible week of yowling and keeping the Siamese inside. They tore umpteen curtains to shreds. Quite glad to escape to Crail! *Very* peaceful. No rest in Dollar with so many of us. Aunt Nellie is so noisy but good fun.

---

* I can't recall us ever not having Siamese cats; the most demanding of friends – but how they talk. And when they raise their voices neighbours will not be unaware of feline romance. Our big Victorian house on the eastern outskirts of Dollar had been turned into two dwellings, the other half the home of George Blake, the novelist of the Clyde. A large, frog-faced man, he was held by us boys in a certain awe, not that we saw much of the family.

9.6.54

I have just come off a crazy hour on the board: so desperately busy I couldn't pick up another call as I had no cords left. On again it will be on the busier position with only a u/t to partner me, but I like challenges. I went on guard Friday night and had the officers' mess to patrol. I met a very nice officer. His father was killed in the Normandy landings ten years ago. However, he was just back from Cyprus so we had plenty of pleasant things to talk about. There were two wee ginger cats which followed me everywhere. They were full of fun and purring fit to burst. (Most cats just bolt if you go near them.) My second shift from 0200 to 0400 was very weary: I could hardly keep my eyes open. Nobody likes the inbetween-ness before dawn: cocks crow and dogs bark on and on, at nothing. Early meal and the sun soon gnaws away at the long shadows. For the rest of the day I was on escorts. I asked the driver where he was going. 'Back and forwards to Abu Sultan for sand.' In a desert, that sounded rather like coals to Newcastle – but it was specially fine sand for making cement he wanted. It was a scorching day and I got burned. Still, it took time for the local workers to shovel the sand on, and in my four trips in the gharry I managed to read two John Galsworthy plays. I was finished by 14.30, did a good wash, handed in my rifle and in the evening saw an uproarious film, *Hobson's Choice*. Broad northern voices, and Charles Laughton is funny any time. I've also seen the excellent film of the play *The Holly and the Ivy*. There are no films I want to see now until the end of the month when there's *Kind Hearts and Coronets*. Reading Rachel Carson's *The Sea Around Us*.

The weather is creeping to 100°. We have a Station Parade on Thursday for the Queen's Official Birthday for which I washed and ironed a uniform yesterday. Washing here is fine – it takes five minutes to dry a vest and only ten for a sheet or a bit of uniform, a contrast to Devon Lodge's wet washing hanging on the pulleys. It was kind of Jessie to send chocolate, but I could have done with a straw to *sook it up*. Another boy had a parcel with chocolate which had run like treacle, and we had a good laugh at the mess it made of the clothes wrapping it. We had communion on Sunday so I missed lunch. I had a plate of chips, egg and peas and a glass of assis in the NAAFI instead. It cost 3/6.

10.6.54

Writing in the billet. This heat could blunt a knife. The sploshes on the page are from the sweat dripping off my forehead. We have all reached the stage where we do not bother to try and keep a dry skin. After lunch I took a couple of salt tablets as I am on guard again tonight. I sometimes put my hands on the *chati* to check coolness really can exist! This morning we had the Queen's Birthday Parade. There was a fly past of the Squadrons too. I don't know why they have parades, for they do not inspect us as it is too hot – and there is such a crowd. Our new Group Captain took the parade and it was all very impressive – for the seated spectators! Work has been very hectic. The last two mornings early I was the only fully trained operator and spent an hour or so of furious work. Just to make it harder, the locals had cut our cables, and the radio links proved very temperamental and often just refused to work.

I have had to discard an Aertex shirt and the one I'm wearing will soon follow suit. They rot in no time. I do a small wash every day. Don't want prickly heat. I bought a big packet of Tide and nearly dropped on finding it was 4/6. I must return some bottles to the NAAFI before they shut, and collect the tuppences for doing so.

* A letter may be missing and/or I was on duty at the switchboard when RAF Deversoir was the venue for the Coronation Aid Display back on the 5th June. Being constantly deafened made it a memorable shift no doubt. I'm indebted to a Mike Knott, RA71 HAA, Fayid at the time, for the account he typed up immediately afterwards. I could never have known all that detail:

Commenced with a flight of Vampire 9s flying past to form the letters E II R. One gave individual aerobatic display – rolls, turns, looping at high speed etc., then a formation of four did the same. A Valetta from Kasfareet flew over and two men parachuted from it. Then came a Meteor 8 doing aerobatics to be followed by four more from Abu Sueir.

These stunted and finished by looping with plumes of coloured smoke gushing from them. A Meteor 13 flew past towing a sleeve bearing the word 'Interval' which was shot down by RAF Regt bofors. Two Proctors circled the airfield shooting down red met balloons with 12-bore shotguns. An air race over a triangular course between a Meteor 13, Proctor, Meteor 8, Vampire 8 and an Auster resulted in a finish in that order at an average speed of 520 mph. A Valetta flew over and dropped six parachutes. 4 Vampires bombed an imitation fort to be followed by a squadron which attacked it with rockets all the time under heavy bofors[46] fire. Then RAF Regt. men plastered it with mortar and small-arms fire and the Infantry doubled in with fixed bayonets and firing from the hip.

Vampires and Meteors gave demonstration of inverted flying, 'Derry' rolls, peeling off and landing 15 on the runway at a time. Display ended with a flypast in arrow formation of 29 mixed Meteors and 24 Vampire 8s.

The Static Exhibition consisted of a Valetta, Vampires, Auster, Beaufighter, Meteor II, Meteor 8 and a glider, all of which could be entered by the public. Heavy Anti-Aircraft Artillery, bombs, guns, rockets, radio, engines, parachutes, radar and anything connected with the RAF were on show.

11.6.54

Walking to the Armoury with the lad who sleeps next to me, I said (after his complaining about 'Circles Guard') 'I hope I never get that guard' – so of course I did; the hottest, dustiest, most lonely, most tiresome patrol of the whole selection. Luckily my mukker (still grumbling) and I managed first shift (6–8 and 12–2, am and pm). The first shift was in daylight and we wandered together (illegal). The second was one particular Orderly Officer's favourite visiting time so we kept strict beats. He came around too, and I just about shot him for pouncing the way he did. He is a very unpopular OO. He inspected the guards before we marched to the guard room. Probably hiding his inadequacy by playing the big man. Another lad in the PBX is getting charged for the crime of missing one of his brass buckles! (Mine were still shining from the parade in the morning.) We did nothing but talk of rugger while together.

LATER. Another nonsense. We are not allowed to swim unless holding an RAF Swimming Certificate. I'm OK but for the poor beginners there will be no fun till they learn – and how do they do that? Cock-eyed.

You seem to be in Crail quite often. Gran is not the only one who likes meals in the Victoria. Are you letting first half of July? £6 a week seems very reasonable, and it ought to be

---

46 An automatic cannon of Swedish manufacture, used a lot in WWII.

fairly easy to find people. Probably end up having the same folk year after year. Was the Burnside dancing for an occasion – or was it *the* occasion?

14.6.54

What a difference an organist can make to a service. In the morning we had three really good Wesley hymns, which were murdered by the slowness, then at Evensong we had similar hymns but in lively fashion. The choir had some boys in it who are David's age. Today we had a dull, wandering sermon through which we sat swotting the inescapable flies. I took my RAF Swimming Prof.[47] on Saturday morning. (I have five now!) Still the trip made a nice break, giving both Saturday and Sunday off. Our supervisor was supposed to be back today but so far has not put in an appearance. We are rather glad: he is extremely crabbit,[48] a married man; we've named him The Cleg.[49]

I have actually started on the Cyprus article but it will take some time. I'm so busy I can never do all I want. Seems to be a failing with one half of the world, while the other half lies about doing nothing and grumbles at the slowness of passing time. Pity we can't buy time off them. I stood on a nasty pointed shell in the Lake and left a blood spoor coming home. Neat TCP and a bandage dealt with it.

LATER. Hoping this will arrive in time to wish you many happy returns, Gran. I can send no present but when I come home in 1955 I hope I shall be able to bring something suitable. I am saving for presents. I have just washed face and ears to rid them of the sticky melon four of us have been eating. We now only have sheets on our beds and often don't bother with them.

18.6.54

Stand Down, so both Saturday and Sunday were free. Unfortunately a lad in the exchange was posted to Aden so I had to go on night bind, hence I slept most of Sunday. I will have next Saturday off to make up. I'll also have to buy another costume. This one has just fallen to pieces. Thanks, too, for the parcel. The wee tin of strawberry had burst and smelt like beer, but luckily never affected anything else. I left the parcel paper on the floor and in ten

47 Proficiency.
48 Grouchy.
49 Horsefly.

minutes columns of ants were marching on it. They get in everything – even cake tins. I think melons are safe – anyway I'm bound to have had a jag for every possible threat some time in the last six months. I've never actually had a *bad* dose of gippy tummy. My boils are OK. I dealt with them myself – used that sulphur ointment as well as others. They healed up twice as quickly as some on another lad here. Foot is fine too.

The RU[50] extra that came yesterday is Murray's *Story of Everest*. They do plenty of travel as the parcel will show. I've read quite a pile of plays lately. Over the weekend I read Eliot's *Cocktail Party*. Two people moved from the billet today so we have a fine lot of room. Enclosing note for Jessie [Godmother] as I can't be sure of her address.

24.6.54

Today I had the morning off so went down to Fayid (down = south). I went to the MMG first with a pile of magazines and had a drink. The dear old ladies wanted me to stay for lunch but I excused myself. Bought the swimming costume (50 akkas) and in the NAAFI Emporium (their motto *Servitor servientum*) purchased two large tins of red plums. (One left now!) We have reached a low ebb in the mess. Trouble began with an order about dress, just what will be worn and what won't. That on top of deteriorating food and filthy service is a bit much – and now the essential – bread – is rationed to two slices. Complaints are pouring in everywhere and I am not surprised. There have been many more cases of real upset tummies lately, so higher authorities must know what is going on. We really shouldn't be treated so badly.

I have just finished reading some Restoration comedies. Remember *She Stoops to Conquer* at school? At Music Circle an officer (the MO) had great *Nutcracker* records. Far from being all sugar plums, it's grand: varied orchestrations with great tides of strings and reefs of brass. I haven't had my desert outpost 'fix' for some time but, wherever, the night belongs to the stars. There are lots of keen sporty types here to balance the 'beer and bints' brigade. Not that anyone is very active in this summer of discontent. The heat is grim: we thole it and when the sun dips we scuttle out like crabs from shelter. Be something to have experienced I suppose – afterwards.

---

* Perhaps the greatest moan was about females, lack of, though I often wondered how much was just macho imaginings. In the early fifties most of the population still regarded

50 Readers' Union.

sex before marriage as wrong. And the reality of sexual or alcoholic excesses would be difficult on £2 a week before stoppages. I don't know if cigarettes were milder then, but I don't think there are many references to smoking in these letters which, as a non-smoker, I'd not have enjoyed. Perhaps we had an enviable tolerance among the ranks. And there was loyalty as well as tolerance; we looked out for each other.

1.7.54

Dear Ian,

I've been reading a great deal just now but if you are having my home letters sent on you will know what I have read. I went to the cinema on Monday to see *Calamity Jane*. The whole camp is whistling the tunes now. This early morning one of the tunes drilled into my head along with the dentist's weapon of torture. I had no injection, and in one of the fillings he went right into the nerve. He put in dressings and turned me loose. I next went to wait for a booked medical jab and after having sat for an hour my tooth began aching. Never have I suffered like it, so right after my jab I staggered back to the dentist and was soon blissfully asleep – the first [and only] time I have had gas. Of course for lunch we had a very solid meal and I kept bleeding the gap.

I bought the complete Cyprus set of stamps when there (still George VI!), as half the places we visited are shown on them. Aunt Sis was genned up on that, being a philatelist. I can keep tabs on stamps, as a pal has *Gibbons' Stamp Monthly* sent out. You will have noted an Egyptian won Wimbledon [the winner, Drobny, in the then longest match ever, was actually Czech by birth], and Bannister's record didn't stand for long, cut by an Aussie – in Finland. Things are pretty quiet just now. Music Circle on Wednesdays. I've a Paul Robson record and hear that the monkey Senator McCarthy has him on his little list. Yanks never do anything in moderation. Well I'd better do my line checks and settle down. Everyone here girns[51] too much. I wonder, do we dislike being here any more than a Roman soldier from the Middle East would have disliked a posting to the dreich Antonine Wall?

PS. Meat at home comes off rationing on 3 July. Bet it makes no change to our endless Corned Beef and POM. I suppose better food is about the biggest gain you have being an officer. Gaudy sunset tonight. I always hope for a 'green flash': remember Carn Dearg?

---

51 Grumbles.

Carn Dearg was a youth hostel on the north-west seaboard of Scotland, where we saw this rare phenomenon on a family cycle tour: at the instant the setting sun dips below the horizon (nearly always a sea horizon) a flash of green shoots along the horizon; our parents often saw it at Colombo.

1.7.54

Greetings! You lucky lot in Crail. I am now on afternoon shift, sitting sweating and drinking gallons of hot, sweet char. I have the fan blowing on me and just feel sticky and not runny. I only rose from my hard mattress this morning at ten as I felt dog tired after a very hectic 5½ hours solo evening shift. To make sleep harder too, there was a bit of concert at the other end of the hut. Ah, another cup arrives – looks vaguely like tea and is strong enough to do a highland fling on. Good old chai swindle.

I suppose you have been hearing quite a lot about this part of the world on the radio. We certainly have! You should hear Cairo! For me, I may stay on here till we close and then return to the UK, or I get posted any day with little warning and go elsewhere in the Middle East (i.e. to one of these: Gibraltar, Malta, Cyprus, Turkey, Amman, Aden, North Africa or Iraq). Much as I would like to return and see you all again, I hope I'll be posted elsewhere rather than go back to England – which is about as unhandy for home as anywhere else.

My book club books arrive at odd times. I highly commend mountaineer Murray's *Conquest of Everest*, a good piece of writing, and thrilling. Now I am on *Gods, Graves and Scholars* which is about archaeology and is, rightly, a best seller – the most fascinating book I have read for months. Read those two if you can. I haven't bothered reading fiction choices. *People of the Deer* is due next month. The sandals came, and once the honey was off them and the toes cut to let sand out they were fine. Have you a photo of Hamid on White Wisp [a local hill] you could let me have? I miss the animals.

---

* The agreement that provided for the Zone's evacuation had been jump-started and we'd begun to withdraw our 65,000 personnel from the Canal Zone. 18,000 King's African Rifles would also be returning home – and to a grimmer sphere of effort. This had all been agreed with Colonel Nasser and his military backers, and obviously Deversoir was going to be an early casualty. The complete Zone evacuation was expected to take until 1956.

At home the rationing introduced during World War Two was finally ending – after a 14-year imposition. The burning of ration books might have been an early indication of the social upheavals ahead. In Egypt, and in Kenya, we scarce questioned, never mind challenged, the status quo. We Broons were a stolid middle-class family but did not have a car, for instance. One still got money back on lemonade bottles. Things had permanence. Not now. The plastic age began in the sixties, the throwaway society that has thrown away all certainties for its mess of pottage. Most people now believe the world started with the Beatles.

If I was constantly pleading for food parcels from home, remember (or visualise) these pre-motorway times, when a generous worker's wage was £10, and holidays abroad were only for the rich. Even the NAAFI had limited use, with something like £2 a week available and books more tempting than chips however empty the stomach. In our wilderness a parcel chit was the herald of manna from heaven.

6.7.54

As I sit writing, I'm in swimming trunks – and with a bandage round my leg just over my right knee; another boil, on the back, so I cannot fix it myself. However the poultice put on this morning has already drawn out some green pus. Yesterday I came off guard and may not go on another at all. My mukker Chris has received a posting (a favourite one) to Iraq. That is the second posting within the month: one to Aden, one to Iraq. It would be really good if another came, sending me to Cyprus. Keep praying! Well, I am taking Chris's place on watch, promotion of a kind as I was preferred before an LAC.

I have just had a letter from Ken in Germany, and he encloses two photos. He is right in the depths of a pine forest and lives in a charming brick and wood building – just like a chalet in Birnam Wood, say. I don't think I'll reciprocate with a photo of our half-buried huts, though the view of ships apparently sailing over the desert with no hint of water is weird enough. I am going to place these two snaps in the album alongside one of my tin hut and the sands. But seeing them just makes me realise how bad it is here. You grow less aware when there is nothing to compare with, and the dulled mind slowly accepts the desert and learns to be happy with it.

I couldn't resist reading out his descriptions, bit by bit, with the billet groaning and jeering in between. No wonder. Billets were stone and timber buildings like alpine chalets. Each held 20 men, two sharing a room/curtains on the windows/

Billets

central heating/hot water always/bottles and showers/LR to take them to meals or work (it was a big airfield)/easy working hours/weekends free/free to leave camp/a station cinema-gym-swimming pool/dining room like a civilian restaurant/NAAFI with games room, reading room etc etc. We had a jolly grumble about Dev (I won't repeat the language) and was told to tell Ken our reality. Not only the Israelites murmured in the wilderness.

NIGHT. I am trying to write this and listen to *The Happy Wanderer* sung by the German Girls' Choir. A Welsh boy in the PBX sang competitively against them in a music festival. (His choir was beaten.) He and I were glued to the prom before tea: a Tchaikovsky programme. It would be nice to have something with a bite – *The Rite* eh? Now I have managed onto watches I may be able to start considering the future. The senior Education Officer (Henderson-Beg) is all but a Padre, and takes all the C of E services just now as the station Padre is away on marriage leave (compassionate grounds?).

What are the plans for D during the summer holidays? Tell David he should be out here with his goggles: there are lovely wee sea horses under the pier – and all sorts of creeping and waving creatures after their kind. The birds too are interesting, from skittering wee wagtails to butcher birds (shrikes) to high-soaring vultures. And the skies at night are the greatest glory. Every star at home is a million here and the moon when full looks ready to burst.

10.7.54

Beginning to get into the run of 'Watches' now. One advantage is an early meals chit. We are all crushed into one half of the mess still and the [RAF] Regiment is pouring back from their desert 'excursion'. Queues are big but we can usually go early. There's a case of typhoid so soft drinks and ices are not to be touched meanwhile.

I went to Fayid yesterday as I needed shorts at once. They took a bit of finding. I nearly got into trouble with two slimy young Egyptians. I had my spec case in my pocket and seeing it they came up and started demanding a fag and finally tried to take what they thought was a packet from my pocket. After a struggle I got them off and they then tried to attack an African (soldier probably). It's these little chaps in European clothes and spiv manners who cause all the trouble.

Nice lift there and back: the breeze the only time I have stopped sweating for days. Constantly hot, even at night, though heavy dew later on, then the dawn pause before it all heats up again. Mealies grow well here and melons are still good. The Mess gives us them at odd times so they must be alright. (And they can't spoil them!) Dates are forming on the palms.

I am getting genned up for my two days of taking services. The RAF is run on signatures – and cups of tea – I've umpteen chits to clear my travels for the Fayid services. I wonder if officers in my congregations will realise I'm just a young sprog. Quite a thought that everyone will be up and down at my behest – which appeals to my sense of the daftness of things. I have put my name down for Cyprus leave for Christmas/New Year; but talking the other day (over our inevitable chai) with the Sqd. Ldr, he said we might well have left Deversoir by then. HQ MEAF[52] are moving to Cyprus 'more or less definitely', and this station is likely to close as a Flying drome.

Had a terrific sand gust yesterday: it burst open the doors and went through the billet like a train in a tunnel. We'll need several days to clear out the sand. The DDT came just at the right moment to meet a new ants invasion. My stores of honey etc are in a tray of water in a circle of DDT. The ants have a habit of creeping along the lines above our beds and dropping on us. They bite!

Early today the post office rang through asking for a few willing hands to help sort the mail. For the second time in the past month a plane had trouble, and was grounded at Malta for 24 hours. Ken, in Germany, has a standing invitation of coming to Scotland. He says that he has sent some reproductions of paintings to Devon Lodge for me. He is the brightest little specimen I have ever met.

The Education Officer is a fully trained reverend but has entered the forces not as a Padre but as an Education Officer and, because of being a *combatant officer*, cannot be a Padre. However, he can stand in, as he has been doing. Our OD Padre is a Methodist. (I don't particularly like him, hence my hobnobbing with the C of E.) I think my cake will arrive in time, but goodness it seems no time since my last birthday (in Crail). I think for the 13th I'll go down to Fayid and have one good meal as a treat. Payday today, and I received my £1-17-6d per week, which has nearly all gone, or is put aside for various things. They call me an old skinflint. You could send some Oxo cubes – anything cheap to remove the chlorine taste from the water. Would you like to send on the National Geographics – if they don't go anywhere already? Would you wish them returned – or passed on with all the other magazines to Fayid hospital?

C of E Padre was back for last Sunday night's service, and was very good. As I write this in our Signals rest room, which we have managed to win after a lengthy struggle, I can see the mealies ripening by the verandah. Across the 'Sports Ground' from here is the MT[53] Section (where that bomb exploded), and the Cinema. All in a dreary waste of grubby sand! Doing no guards now, I miss the star-bright nights and the sounds of distant dogs barking at their own echoes. I miss watching the locals at work: ploughing with oxen and wooden ploughs, threshing the grain on the threshing floor with the poor camel going round and round and round, women picking the melons and loading them in long chains, the docile donkeys under the care of young boys. How meaningless we must be to them.

---

52 Middle East Air Force.
53 Motor Transport.

* Ken did join me, brother David, and Colin Chapman on the VPSC cycle tour after we had been demobbed. Before being called up, cycling had been the only way we could travel to explore Scotland, which we did every holiday. Things usually went well – but once, heading from Perth to Aberdeen via the Devil's Elbow in 1952, I had a puncture halfway to Blairgowrie. I repaired it, but the cycle was Ian's and he'd been touring in France, and the French valve wouldn't take my British pump. I had no option but to walk all the way back to Perth and, in the middle of the night, ask help from the police. They gave me a cell along with the Saturday night drunks.

15.7.54

Dear Ian,

I have a fan on my desk and the PBX room is flyproof. So is our billet (our efforts – not the RAF's), which is a blessing. Flies are far more pestilential than ants: a tactile horror too. Must test all outside lines which takes ten minutes. Cutting our communication links is an occasional locals' game. Our Signals Officer (good bloke), Sqd. Ldr is heading home to Scotland on leave. Lucky man. Our MT Section is on the billet to PBX walking route so I've a few mukkers there. They employ locals to 'help' with repairs. I was told of one local coming out from under the bonnet of a truck, cursing mightily, and then grabbing a sledge hammer, and was about to apply it when luckily the corporal saw him – and saved the engine. I believe both the English and Arabic tongues were expressive! The locals really are klefty wallahs and little good at anything else in our eyes, not even as terrorists. Lose anything and a local source can sell a replacement, probably stolen in the first place. There are a few spiv RAF types, I can

PBX 03.00!

tell you, who make something of a two-way trade. Not long ago I shared a guard with an innocent-looking lad who said before being called up he was a burglar. He gave some useful gen about getting into locked cars! [Thinking of the MT Section, I later heard the story of an RAF mechanic slamming down the bonnet of a lorry with the minimalist judgement, 'the fooking fooker's fooked'.]

One of our Squadrons has now gone to Amman[54] and other Sections have

---

54 The capital of Jordan.

moved elsewhere so, even if Dev doesn't close, there will only be a few folk left, ourselves included. Can't do without telephones! I must read almost a book a day just now, but I never seem to have any fewer books in my orange-box bookcase. In the last week I have written 23 letters too. I must try and settle down for an hour or two of work on my long-promised article about Cyprus. Maybe use the Padre's office. I also earn a few needy akkas writing verse for people (usually amorous poems to be sent home: very yucky but I learn some surprising things about airmen's lives!). I've a nice picture of Dollar from the *Bulletin* stuck on my wall now, as well as reproductions of paintings – Impressionists – giving the impression I'm living in a library-cum-art gallery, at least until you look up at the curve of corrugated iron ceiling. The billet keeps the day's heat, but no sooner does the night flatter us with a glimpse of cool than the sun is back to bully us.

I've come on this torn piece of PBX log which shows how we go from one day to the next, with each entry signed of course. I'm surprised our sneezes are not recorded.

23.59 Diary closing on odd date log.

00.01   Diary opening on even date log.

00.02   Fayid, 205 Group, 9 BAD in order. Ismailia, Moascar ten set links o.o.[55] Duty mechanic informed.

00.32   Ten set links to Moascar, Ismailia in order.

HB at the PBX, RAF Deversoir

Working on the switchboard is all very logical and simple, really. We sit on a stool with adjustable height and don a headset for hearing and speaking (at times we could do with three hands free). We face a board with all sorts of numbers on it, and sticking out is something like a desk with the rows of cords which we plug in to make connections.

So an 'eye' closes. One plugs the cord in with 'Number please', then for an internal call the companion plug is pushed in and the ring key is pressed. As you are doing this you are already saying 'Number please' to the next call. One can end up juggling a dozen calls at once. 'Sorry, no reply, sir,' would be said politely. A call over, the plugs are pulled out and their cords shoot back into place.

A great exercise in coordination. Calls from outside come in on a row of little flaps which fall open as the current triggers a latch. Certain outside lines are directly connected to other stations – as the diary quote above indicates. At busy periods two boards can be in use, both hands of both operators working frantically and words flowing without pause.

55 O.o.= Out of order.

At two o'clock in the morning there is no need to sit at the board all the time. An alarm is switched on which rings when any call comes up.

I once had an unhappy morning with senior officers, accused of sleeping on night duty and not answering an important operational incoming call. The time had been noticed and, luckily, the Orderly Officer had been in the exchange at that time (for chai and a chat no doubt), so could verify I was wide awake. The flap had not dropped, we found, a discovery which should have been made by the other station on a routine check as done in the quoted diary above. Everything is covered by set procedures. You just got on with the work. The 'panics' are welcome, for much of the work – like anybody's anywhere – is just routine but, however boring, still requires concentration.

We hear a great deal of what would be classified, or private, so come to know probably more than is good for us. I don't think we sign the Official Secrets Act but 'work' is never discussed outside the exchange. (Gossip can be another matter.) Army engineers keep the telecommunications in working order, despite what we, the locals or the weather do to the system. Calls to the UK need to be slotted in and booked. Such calls being tricky and expensive, the operator listens in to see nothing cuts them off, or to deal with anything that does. We hear it all: the bad, the glad and the sad. An airman or soldier phoning home is only likely to do so for important family reasons: the joyous arrival of a baby, an engagement – and, too often, losing a parent, wife, or girlfriend. I hate listening in to those calls and each seems to tear out the stitches of life.

There is also a lighter side to operating the switchboard. We are in control after all. Someone being obnoxious, you just apologise, 'I'm sorry, the number is engaged' – again and again – till he goes crazy with impatience. The other day a horrible WO was giving a poor squaddie hell so I removed the plug and left him raging at thin air. It was a while before he noticed and then he was bang, banging the phone to me. 'Oh, sorry, sir, there seems to be a fault on that number.' My 'best' was swopping plugs so this same nasty WO and the detestable, bullying wife of the CO were suddenly, not knowing it, connected to each other instead of whoever they had each been speaking to. They were soon raging at each other to get off the line and calling each other unprintable names. Whenever she is on the line anyway we make it crackle badly so she is soon raging at us about it. 'I'll reconnect you,' I'd say sweetly and then as soon as she'd be yelling at someone again (she never just *spoke*) I'd give a real blast in her ear. We all hoped she'd get apoplexy (just looked that word up in the dictionary). Don't worry! 99.99% of our time we behave ourselves.

Just handed round Polos, which were the 'wrapped around sweets' in one roll of newspapers from home. Subscriptions time it seems. I will certainly renew my SYHA[56] one, even if not going to be hostelling soon. A treat to come. [A life membership would be my 21st birthday present from Gran.]

Sometimes I must give the impression we're a miserable lot. We are anything but: we rag

---

56 Scottish Youth Hostel Association, now Hostelling Scotland.

each other, we talk – heavens, and how! – and we sing even if it ends with The Harlot of Jerusalem or Eskimo Nell. There's lots of laughter. 'Always laugh when you can. It is cheap medicine' (that's from the poet Byron). I can have all the fun I want without tanking up on Stella – the NAAFI beer.

25.7.54

At the PBX this morning I had my first FIRE call. Being genned-up I cleared the dozen places I inform, in just 3 minutes. It was a bush fire, though in such a position that it might well have devoured the pump station. Horror of horrors – Deversoir with no water! My pal Chris phoned me this morning – he is still waiting at El Hamra for a plane to carry him to the Garden, east of Aden, called Habbaniya.[57] Or is it north of Aden? It is on the banks of the Tigris, whatever, and infinitely better than Egypt. Well, between blethering to him and saying cheerio, see you in Scotland, and dealing with the fire-call and answering mail enquiries, I read the Book of Esther, the perfect example of the short story. Oddly, it is the only Bible book that never mentions the word 'God' and has the longest verse in the Bible and has its chief setting in the palace of Xerxes after he had been trounced by the Greeks.

6.8.54

I am on guard! Last time a few stray shots came my way. (Annoying, not dangerous.) I am on a searchlight in a few minutes so this will have to be a hurried note. Thank you for Crail letters. I knew those people would want back again next year – who wouldn't? The other day the OO came out of the guardroom to check on me as I'd been on my hunkers in the open for ages and he was wondering at my sanity. I was just watching a dung beetle. (Probably confirmed his speculations!) He was not at all interested. Some iridescent beetles too, but they tend to give off a pong when handled. This is a most uncomfy bed [in the guardroom] and the springs are digging into my behind so I'm going to go for a walk (and a drink) before I set off with my gun to play soldiers for two hours. Then sweet, sweaty, sleep! I do not mind guards really, it's a change and one is often alone, and, as often as not, looking over the more fertile land outside the wire. First guard at night (two hours) I sang the whole time. (I have a list that takes that time nicely.) The searchlights attract a wonderful and colourful host of flying and creepy-crawly things. They were quite

---

57 Habbaniya was famous for its botanical gardens while the RAF was there, until 1959. At the time of writing it's uncertain that they still exist.

fascinating. There was a huge brown beetle in the PBX the other night and my partner came out in haste looking for the broom. Real squeamish he was when I let it crawl on my hand. Saw a fearsome praying mantis yesterday. It was inches long: green with white spots, a vicious thing too, and wouldn't move over to let me sit down – just put its feelers back and waved at me with its horny limbs. Did you know that when they mate the female then *eats* her partner?

A French Legion troop ship bound for the East passed the other day and before our eyes a fellow dived overboard in full kit. As the boat passed, four others were seen in the water. One was English and had got roped in at Marseilles while drunk (or so he said). You should have seen the crowds and heard the din. The MPs soon arrived and told the locals to *imshi*!

---

* *Imshi* was the much-used Arab equivalent of 'bugger off!', and meeting the word here reminded me of an incident in Tangier in 1975. I was passing a senior school in a prosperous area when pupils were streaming out. Having always found Moroccan teenagers friendly and invariably polite I was a bit worried when surrounded by a group who were being anything but. I was becoming a bit anxious and a deal more angry, and suddenly let rip on them in a barrage of gutter Arabic which could only have been learned in the Zone. They at once looked mortified – I'd understood them! – apologised, and melted away. I was left wondering what on earth I had said, for the words had simply come from unconscious memory – and were forgotten again as quickly, except for '*Imshi*!'.

Troops heading east not infrequently jumped ship somewhere along the canal and were soon picked up by the police, to whom they probably owed their lives. In the Far East, in local hands anything could – and did – happen to people posted there. In July 1954 an agreement had ended the war in Indo-China, dividing it along the 17th Parallel, communist Viet Minh to the north, the south with French support still. Thousands of refugees would be displaced (the Boat People) and nothing really was secured. A decade on, the USA were hopelessly entangled in the Vietnam War.

BAOR 23

8.8.54

(from my brother)

Dear Ham,

Many happy returns. This for the 13th. You'll still be there I take it. It would be good if you came here: RAF stations at Celle, Hanburen and Fassberg (Ken's station!) are all near. I sometimes see a film at the RAF Celle Astra. I keep fit with hockey and swimming and walks and regular Scottish Country Dancing at the Church of Scotland Centre.

Tomorrow is the start of a two-week exercise. We did have a big one in the Hartz Mountains that lasted a month. Exercises are dire if the weather is foul. Tanks and vehicles bogged down. A truck hanging over a bridge is a pleasant problem to deal with. On an exercise a month ago there was a spectacular accident. Going down a hill too fast a truck developed a speed wobble, glanced off one tree, knocked a second out of the ground, jumped a six-foot ditch and ended on its side, having lost front axle and wheels. Driver and co-driver climbed out unharmed. An interesting recovery for my LAD.[58]

We have a new C.O.[59] Of course the departing one threw a party then all his officers took him to dine at the Club. The Sgt's Mess also had a party. So several very late nights. You are the one who escapes much of the bullshit.

Crail must be lively with Gran, David, three cats and a dog in residence. Maybe the attic could be used for sleeping, using the folding ladder for access.

We hear little of your part of the world. What's this of you taking church services? You seem to be making the most of life in pretty grim circumstances, no doubt worse than you tell. At least you have the lake and the canal. Do you ever get shot at?

Dollar sent me a 3,000-word German Vocabulary. It would be nice to have some socialising. Oh, it may surprise you but Anne C ('almost' fiancée) and I have gone our separate ways.

(Hints, there, of the very reasons I did not want to be an officer: Mess life, dressing up, routine, routine, it would have driven me crazy.) Aunt Nell later told me that Ian 'was onto that ghastly uncouth language, German.'

Friday 13.8.54

MORNING. In return, here is my birthday letter. The very welcome £5 came yesterday and the cake is in the post office at the moment. I have no idea how I shall cash your cheque; the Station Adjutant whom I met had no suggestions. I'll try Barclays Bank in

58 Light Aid Detachement.
59 Commanding officer.

Fayid this afternoon. I am looking forward to the services; I can be assured of the largest congregation Deversoir has had, for all of Signals Section are determined to come! Not to barrack, I hope!

Heavens! I miss music but yesterday I heard the Beethoven Prom and was quite delirious. Today I was halfway across the blazing sands after having suffered another apology for food when I heard 'La donna è mobile' being belted out. A programme of Verdi, so I sat to listen, in a dwam,[60] with the stinking sweat running into shoes and shorts.

I long to see hills again. To stand on Ben Cleuch in the mist and rain will be wonderful, in snow and ice even more wonderful. Sand and sky here are dreary in repetitiveness. Scotland, with hills and water, clouds and trees, seems a dream. Every day coming from lunch I look up to search for a cloud. If I see one, we all go and stare at it. When it next rains we are all going to parade outside and get soaked and then march through all the puddles like little children. What we will do is to hold out our mugs and have a drink of natural water – the first for six or seven months. I think some of the lads are so bored because they've not much behind them in the way of memories. I can fill an hour any time by speeding up the Burn of Sorrow in a whirring dipper's flight – in imagination. I know every pool and fall to the springs of Maddy Moss then home by King's Seat and the Valley of Dry Bones to Dollar Hill and the Victory Cairn view of all the world. I have my escapes.

Papers came yesterday and I gorged through 2 *Times*, 2 Broons [*Sunday Post* comic sections], 2 rags, 2 *Blackwood*s, 2 *Chamber*s, 1 *Scottish Field*, 1 *Scots Mag*, 2 *Litt. Supps* and the *Galley*.[61] I almost got thrown out of the billet for sniggering and choking over bits. I'm sometimes asked to 'read out the funny bits' – which sometimes nobody 'gets'. Reading is a black art. Hamid seems to be a little devil. I wonder how daft he will be when I see him again. I know he will remember me, even if, in equivalent dog years, I have been away about 14 years. Pity he fights so. Could you not just let him, and maybe a thrashing from a tougher dog would settle him? Who did he bite because she went near the cats – *his* cats?

You ask about my 'billet buddies'. Seven just now. *Pete*; he is an NCO and a very quiet lad usually, but at times has grousing fits and moods. Seems to do little out of duty hours. *John,* who is going shortly, was very bright when he came (same day as me) but now is very lazy and spends hours each day on letters to his girl. The last few days he has been trying to make a wireless work (his job in civvy life). He never reads, so also grumbles at time passing slowly. *Tom,* with receding hair, spends every minute he can in bed. If he exerts himself he plays Monopoly or sees every movie picture possible. At the moment he corresponds regularly with a Hungarian dancer in Cyprus who can't spell the address correctly. He is quiet too. *Tom* (another) is the guitar player. Reads much and is more contented than most. We swim a lot together. *Oz* is the quietest of them all, and rather mysterious. Not very obstreperous so a good neighbour to have in my corner. Then there

---

60 Trance/daydream.
61 A school publication.

are two noisy ones, *Snap* and *Fred*. Snap is always gay[62] but Fred sems to have great hates for various things and people (like our supervisor).

Now the Section. *Chris,* my great pal, has gone and my other mukker, just out of hospital with a liver complaint, is being invalided home. *Primus* in the exchange, is the Supervisor. *Reg,* whom no one likes, causes endless trouble and is remarkably glaikit. (Jock called him a gormless git – nice alliteration.) Jim: he is the snootiest, rudest, most boorish person *any* of us have met. *Jessop* (another crazy character whom I like) had him up in the gym. It was like two kittens pawing at each other. He knows a great deal about the job and is very nice underneath. I think he is just shy. *Henry* is another good lad at heart who plays the big-boy with the others. He is going to get married soon. *Jock* Gordon is married and is the quiet, thrawn Scot and puts the fear of death in most people. *Jock* Henderson reads good books (so, often skint like me) and has sailed the China seas. From Perth. We walk a lot. *Bernie* is the artist, and nearly very good. No one quite understands him; I like watches with him. *Paul*[63] and *Taff Ginger* are the newcomers. Paul is shy and nervous of yelling at all and sundry on the phone as yet. Would faint before correcting the CO the way I did the other day. Ginger sooks up to Reg – has to as he sleeps next to him and otherwise his life would be a misery. We have long talks on music. He competed once against 'that choir from Germany' (*sic.* the Vienna Boys Choir) who sing 'The Happy Wanderer'. And then there is *Ekins*. That is not his real name even, but it's what he is in the RAF as far as they are concerned. In civvy life he is either a millionaire or a crook I think, and in the RAF a la-di-dah play actor. A right bairn. I like them one and all really.

To add to that, one of those in the billet was something of a professional poker player – and never broke – but had another prowess that earned him the nickname King of Farts!

EVENING. I went to Fayid in an army 3-ton gharry in the afternoon: first to the MMG, then all over the shopping centre. The Bank is only open in the morning so I will see the Accountant Officer about cashing your cheque. I am going to buy a grip, a fairly good clock and a briefcase. All for £5? Yes. The grip is suede leather – £2 (started at £5). I bought some books for a birthday treat too, seeing I had a little back pay, so I'm not exactly short of reading matter, *viz* Dumas: *The Black Tulip,* Flaubert: *Madame Bovary, Aesop's Fables,* a

---

62 Not in the 21st-century sense of the word! Just cheerful.
63 Paul is the only person from this company with whom I'm still in touch. When Dev closed he was posted on to Amman, in Jordan.

book on Buddhism (hard going), *The Aztecs of Mexico* (fascinating, if tragic. You can blame *Gods, Graves and Scholars* for my buying it), Thomas à Kempis: *Imitation of Christ*, Anton Chekhov: *Three Plays* (Cherry Orchard, Three Sisters, Ivanov), Camões: *The Lusiads*, and Dostoyevsky: *The Devils* (all 700 pages of it).

But it is time to have the cake before going to *The Planter's Wife* at the pictures. Could this 'little friend of all the world' please have his copy of *Kim*? Wee one with soft red cover. Also Jim Corbett's *Man-Eaters of Kumaon*, the only film of a book ever to give me nightmares (remember?). Surely it might appeal here.

---

* The Burn of Sorrow and other homesick names were all places up in the Ochils, the hills above Dollar which I knew intimately. Only rarely did I ever meet anyone on the hill; the only adult encountered occasionally was W K Holmes who soon became my gentle mentor, teaching me to love all aspects of our world. Dollar Hill was crowned by a cairn to celebrate the end of World War Two. The Valley of Dry Bones does not appear on a map: it was one of my schoolboy 'convenience' names. We had many; one example: we often met up with friends above the castle (Castle Campbell) at William's Stone, a name we gave it one day for a plooky pal, so I grinned when, years on, a Civic Trust booklet suggested the name could have connections with William the Lion!

Tuesday 13 August was Hitler's *Adlertag*, the Day of the Eagles, when the Germans marked the Battle of Britain as beginning. Like most boys of my age I'd read every book about our wartime pilots and was certainly proud to be in the RAF rather than the army. Fidel Castro seems to be the only notable sharing this birthday.

* There were some more 'over the top' musical comments in this letter which I've cut. The abiding memory is of the Music Circle, which played classical records under the palms by the Bitter Lakes – as romantic a setting as could be found – though occasionally competing with the yowling local music from villages along the shore. Well, Um Khaldum did outsell the Beatles! Fishing boats with their so-different sails seen against the glitter of the lake always delighted. Sometimes in the dusk a man would be thigh-deep, casting out a circular fishing net.

There were those musical times. Father was musical and we'd grown up with a radiogram onto which we'd heap large vinyl records of everything from Bach to Harry Lauder. (What an improvement when a symphony was no longer spread over several records.) We even had Stravinsky's *Rite of Spring* (and loved it) – very progressive at that time.

Since those days I've heard comments about the enmity from regulars towards National Servicemen regulars seeing their status challenged or reduced by being lumbered by those whom they would have to train, only to lose them when competent. This was not something

I experienced. In the PBX we were always so short-handed we all slaved, mukkers together. If our board supervisor was disliked in Deversoir it was by everyone, and for his personal qualities, not his position. I've no memory of who was a regular or who doing NS among those I've described.

17.8.54

Since last writing I have been to Moascar and Fayid, taken the two church services, gone swimming at dawn and at dusk, swum to an island in the Lake, had a heat rash, finished having a boil, seen the temperature going to up 110°/120° every day, drunk eight bottles of coke one day, lost a pal from the billet, and saw that 'Fact-Finding' committee arriving by Hermes and setting off in the staff cars.

The service in Fayid went very well. About 50 present. My transport was supposed to have collected me at 10.15 but came at 11.05 and minus the organist. A Raff snafu[64] for you. I largely made up the service as I went along due to the singing ambush.

I have just found the ring in the birthday cake and yesterday I found a wee silver 3d. (So did one other lad.) I was highly tickled. Going swimming now and then, after tea, darning, and to work a little on the Cyprus article. I overheard myself called 'him with the books' yesterday. There was a certain adjective too. Please could you see if you could find me a book about the canal – the who, how, when etc of its building. It's amazing. And big. [Appendix III outlines the story.] I have vainly been all round the camp trying to find a way of cashing the cheque. Finally I saw the SAO[65] and he said it could not be done, so I will have to return it. You could send a postal order; that would work here. Last night two of us were swimming about with a group of 45 Commando officers who were leaving today. They were just back from Greece where they had an exercise with the Greek Commandos. We still have the Regiment.[66]

I was up at 04.00 and was off to Moascar, near Ismailia, for a training session for the coming Wing Swimming Gala. Ismailia is the Canal Company HQ and is a big town. Lake Timsha on the other hand is small. The name translates as 'crocodile lake'. (Not now though!) From the Lake, Moascar looked just like a home town. There were flats and trees, quays and spires, and over on the other side the impressive 1914–1918 war memorial on its ridge of sand (Jbel Mariam). We arrived at dawn while the white mists were quilted over the flatness of the desert, and everything was quiet. When we were returning from our swimming practice the streets were streaming with jeeps and bullock carts, whites, blacks

---

64 Situation normal, all fucked up.
65 Station Admin Officer.
66 RAF Regiment, eventually posted to RAF Habbaniya, in Iraq.

and Arabs, soldiers and hawkers. Great Nile barges held us up at the lift bridge over the canal. A police lad who looked about 15 directed the traffic.

In camp we walk miles as all the buildings are so scattered about: the PBX, mess, guard room, cinema, NAAFI etc. Yesterday I had to run for it coming off watch to escape a big dust devil. One hit our hut, when the door was open and it took days to tidy up. Keeps happening. There was sand on my toothbrush which had been inside my sponge bag! Guard duty is a bit of a farce. You can't patrol the miles of the whole camp circumference so it's just the vital places like the water filtration plant etc that are pinpointed. (We drink the Sweet Water Canal!) The locals therefore do get in through the wire. A patrol checks the perimeter every day. There's a great story going the rounds about a local working in the workshops who used to wheelbarrow gash bits of wood home now and then. His load was naturally always searched at the guardroom. No contraband. Then the motorbike crowd started on a making track in a far corner (noisy things!) and decided they wanted a barrow. Word went out and this local said he could sell them one: very cheap, very good price etc. When it was bought, one of the bikers actually recognised it. Investigations followed and a search of the local's house found lots of wheelbarrows. *That's* what he'd been stealing.

19.8.54

Fayid is rather nice in its own way and reminds me strongly of those early American towns you see in cowboy films – only everything is built of stone (or mud). All the shops are open in front, some with glass windows and most with half the wares tumbling out into the street in an attempt to lay hold of one. Most of the wares are bright and, with the green trees and the white buildings, are rather pretty. The din is colossal. I saw some fine silver work and carvings in ivory and lots of leather: pouffes of every shape and colour, cases, holdalls. The really good is pricey but you can have a wee bust of Queen Nefertiti for a song, or buy any number of the preferred 'feelthy postcards'. Last time I was there, busloads of be-fezzed Egyptian police poured along, herding all the pedlars and street vendors in front of them. They were all piled into a truck at the point of the gun and trundled off. There are terraces where we sit and drink long, cool drinks (usually assis). Not too many flies either. When any of my pals wants to buy something they beg me to go and do it for them. Surprising how one can battle prices down, and I seem to have more aptitude for this than most – at least so they say. They should see Aunt Nell bargaining! The journey to Fayid is pleasant although somewhat smelly if there is an offshore breeze.

Last night at the Music Circle we sat outside under a sky like shattered glass. At times the palms rustled or a child called in the distance, but most of the time we were carried far, far away. There was a bit of Mozart written when he was 19: younger than me! But what nearly brought tears to my eyes were the pieces from *Madama Butterfly*, rather out of place here. Did you know Verdi wrote *Aida* for the opening ceremony of the Canal? Wonder what the locals made of it. [This was a myth. It had been so intended, but was only written a year later, 1870, and then premiered in Cairo in 1871.]

 Found this in my bed last night. A gecko which can walk up walls or on the ceiling. A welcome visitor as it eats flies. Well, I must start my washing and take my Sunday shirt to be starched. This is the first night of the week that I have not had something to do, so I'll only now start typing up the Cyprus effort. To try and prevent us starving they now give us tea and a bun at 11.00 each morning. It fills one, but so would gabbro. What a place! Deversoir. Our noses are really going to be put to the grindstone. Our Section will be down to five instead of the one-time dozen or so. On the last guard I spent the day escorting the CO and his wife up and down the Zone. I suppose I am the RAF's 24 hours a day! The latest rumour has Dev closing by Christmas, so I could be posted, except they'll need telephones till the end, surely? Wherever we go, it won't be more fly-blown and poochie-infested.

Well done, Ping! I can imagine Gran finding a new-born kitten in her bed! I miss the menagerie. Going to see *Genevieve* next; Ian says he's seen it twice. Is my bike sold? Are the kittens named? Questions, aye questions!

I hope to buy a bottle of orange squash soon to take the chlorine taste out of the gallons of water we have to drink every day – like drinking the Alloa baths. I have not fired a shot at the range here since the week I arrived. I proved a 'first class shot' then, and I like shooting. We renew our chits every 6 months. Everything is being tightened up – except food and sanitation. We are expected to be better while they make things worse.

---

* We didn't go on guard in pixi uniform! This was a family in-joke. As a boy I used to doodle endlessly with these pixi figures, my imaginary friends, creating scenes of their mischief-making. They became well known to the family … … There is something poignant reading about discovering pieces of music which have, now, been known for a lifetime. Only once can they be touched with the magic of serendipity. And what about the thousand books still to be read?

Mother, writing to Ian on the back of my letter, said, 'David enjoyed being out with Old Greenaway in *Seal*, the dinghy with sail and outboard, as well as poling *Hope* [fishing boat]

into harbour. D thinks Crail *even* better than Carrick! He haunts the harbour.' Father added a note saying he'd taken 300 lbs of honey off our hives so far this year. Our Crail neighbours, the Hannahs, kept bees. He had 24 hives up at the water works.

In Egypt, the flies could be bad. We seldom risked eating out. Somewhere, sometime, I heard the story of friends going into a fly-blown street café and when they complained at the abundance of flies at the table they were told, 'No worry, soon we start making mealtime, then all the flies go round to kitchen.'

28.8.54

I am i/c A Watch now. No sooner had I closed the last letter than we changed because the three here being posted began clearing. They go tomorrow which leaves us five people to carry on the work of the PBX. I have my other two services tomorrow (Fayid, Dev) so the night bind I came off yesterday was quite handy. Choosing hymns even takes ages. I've found it quite hopeless painting with watercolours. Even a dollop from a brush dries instantly. Just one sketch of our hut circle, I'll keep as a memento. Had no breakfast today – just couldn't touch it. Even the bread was foostie.[67] Had a mug of soup instead,

My watercolour of our hut circle

---

67 Fusty, mouldy.

then, after cleaning for CO's inspection, on to work: morning and evening today. At least the switchboard concentrates the mind.

LATER. The board is dripping wet and giving shocks. Very heavy dew and the heat has cut off all outside/internal links and half the extensions are PG (Permanent Glow, *i.e.* u/s). It's gradually rectifying itself as the sun rises higher.

Last night we had a wild attack by beetles and cockroaches. The heavy dew drove them indoors. I woke up to feel something crawling over my bare, sweaty chest. I leapt for the light and found a huge four-inch beetle. A beauty! The others sat up, and when they saw it they all rolled down their mosquito nets! Did you know bed bugs can go a year without food, not that they suffer deprivation here? We had a hornet flying about the PBX yesterday.

Boils report: one on knee and a rash of them on an arm, not healing completely: they develop so far, then go, and then resurrect. You could send me a variety of plasters (boils, tin of dressings and long strip) and some cotton wool. I'm completely out and can't replace. Sulphur ointment is excellent and I've still half a bottle of Dettol. I'm the billet boil doctor! Going to stop and darn a stocking. Of course I've read *Kim*. Often. That's why I want it. Going round the billet yesterday asking who wrote *Kidnapped*, only the Scots knew. Suggestions of Dickens, John Buchan and Agatha Christie! Two got *Kim*, the rest never heard of it.

31.8.54

The lad who was doing permanent night binds crocked up (no wonder!) and until a lad comes back from leave in two days' time, I am volunteered for night binds. Working all nights is no fun, for sleep in the day is nigh impossible and, at the best, is like being in a bath. This morning, going to sleep at 08.00, I set the alarm for 11.30 to go and cash my postal orders. Of course the place was shut. I staggered back and went to sleep again and woke up not long after with a bug bite so spent the rest of the time till tiffin covering everything in powder.

Any homes for the new Siamese yet? How much will you charge for them? The dogs that wander about camp are frightened, wild things and will not come near. Some of them are horribly deformed with great bodies or heads and short legs. (A few are adorable.) I'm surprised they are allowed to be kept so freely and in such large numbers. I dread to think of the effect of rabies breaking out. My mates all turned up for the Dev service which was nice of them. They didn't barrack me! Went without any hitches! The Signals gang was larger than the normal congregation! Did you read about the new Lightning fighter? We just have Vampires and prop jobs now. Another hour and then I can have four hours trying to sleep across two chairs. I fell off last break – plonk onto the concrete floor.

8.9.54

Now early afternoon and the buses for the Swimming Gala are about to depart. The PBX can't spare me – so I'm right scunnered at missing out – a pleasant excursion, never mind being in a team with good hopes of winning.

Two days ago a lad in our billet phoned up exchange and asked off escorts as he was feeling sick. I came off night bind. He grew worse all day: vomiting and messing the bed, floor, everything. Being a brave ass he took no advice and by night was unconscious. I phoned then and they took him away in the ambulance. Next day they phoned to ask about his normal behaviour as they reported him to be running amok in the ward *sans* clothes. He is now in Fayid dangerously ill with some sun thing which has gone to his brain, combined with bacterial dysentery. I had emergency calls over it on the board and his next of kin are being informed so it looks bad. If only people would report sick at once instead of trying to be tough guys. None of us really noticed, for in the morning those of us in the billet were sleeping off night work and not awake enough to take anything in. In the afternoon every-one was out dead. So not till evening did the three of us who were in realise he was that ill.

On my desk as I write is the packet for the *Dollar Magazine* – I dealt with it last night bind on a wreck of a typewriter which was suffering from mechanical meningitis. I went over to post it. Post Office closed. That means getting up from sleep tomorrow as I'm on night bind tonight. I'm going to buy a copy of Gunnis (Cyprus guide) for myself. I want to read it thoroughly and also I want to return the Kyrenia-borrowed one. Cooling down now – and one blanket for sleeping.

11.9.54

Unfortunately my hours are very likely to last as they are till we go; probably about the end of December. Well, *maalish* as they say. This station is *definitely* closing down in December; it was in Orders a week back. Who will be on to take the last, 'Number please'?

I am sure Crail is wonderful for David. Kids out here are all mad on swimming – the word 'timid' not in their vocab. I'm good but get beaten often. Some of those in the forces will only swim in the Canal – with the whole lake there! It only became a lake when the canal was built and filled up a swampy hollow, so all the fascinating life in it must have worked [its way] in from the Red Sea.

Could you not just let Gran do more or less as she likes, even if she eats wrong things – it would cut out some skirmishing. But then she would be quite miserable with no one to quarrel with. The cats seem to be real individuals. I can just imagine squitting into the electric fire to make that stink. Ping sounds delightful. Sad she lost the kittens. I wonder if Nikko would adopt Siamese kittens if they kittened at the same time and Ping goes ill again? [Nikko, the tabby, happily shared feeding Ping's kittens later.]

My play was read through last night – and praised! It will cost £3 to have it scripted and two copies made. That will be from my pocket no doubt. I made another few *akkas* writing a poem for a lad, which paid for going to the pictures two nights ago.

14.9.54

Just in case you didn't hear my yell of glee from here. In one of my off-board spells I went over to meet our Padre who is just back from UK leave. In ten minutes my name, and my pal Dave's (the MO), were down to go to Jerusalem in a week's time – probably the last chance, with the Zone now being run down.

↑ To
Nablus

Jerusalem
1954

International
boundary

Israel

No Man's Land

N

Damascus
Gate

Pool of
Bethesda

Herod's
Gate

St. Stephen's
Gate

Church
of the Holy
Sepulchre

via Dolorosa

Mount of Olives

GETHSEMANE
Church of
All Nations

Tomb of
Mary

Kedron Valley

New
Gate

Pool of
Hezekiah

"The
Old
City"

Moslem graves

Golden
Gate

Dome of the Rock

Jordan

Jaffa
Gate

CHRIST
CHURCH

The
Citadel

Wailing Wall

El Aksa
Mosque

Jewish
Cemetery

No Man's Land

Zion
Gate

Valley of
Mt. Ophel

Dung
Gate

Hinnon

Pool of
Siloam

To
Bethany
River Jordan
Amman

Israel

To Bethlehem

5

The joys of Jerusalem: 20–29 September 1954

As with Cyprus there simply was no time to write letters during the visit to Jerusalem. However, once back at Deversoir I periodically wrote about selected Jerusalem experiences in my letters home. I have extracted these vagaries of memory and given them here, with little alteration, in some sort of order. They are, of course, the words of a receptive nineteen-year-old on release from debilitating detention in Deversoir. Like Cyprus, this was life enjoying another 'get out of jail free' card. My friend Ken in Germany went on a similar course at Cologne.

We were fortunate in visiting Jerusalem at a time of relative calm. The city had been divided in 1949 with a no-man's land separating Arabs and Jews. The Old City and most of the Christian sites (and Moslem) were in Jordan, and Christian tourists/pilgrims were a welcome source of income. We found the men of the Arab Legion fascinating, though their leader, Glubb Pasha, an Englishman, would be sacked a couple of years later. Since then there has not been much peace in a city regarded as holy by three of the world's great religions.

This, then, was the situation in late 1954. The vast sprawl of Israeli West Jerusalem (their capital) lay west of the Old City and was naturally out of bounds to us. After the Six-Day War in 1967 Israel annexed the whole city of Jerusalem and, eventually the whole West Bank (of the River Jordan); the unhappy situation today.

A very brief note about the city's history, well, its more modern history, for Jerusalem has endured thousands of years of violent drama. What many people know is how it was captured from the Turks by the British in December 1917, by General Allenby – with the side story of Colonel T E Lawrence, who wanted the Arabs to have their freedoms. But already there had been political duplicity: in 1916 a secret Franco-British agreement had decided that when the Ottoman Empire fell, the area would be divided and ruled by France (Syria) and Britain (Palestine and Mesopotamia). The League of Nations agreed that Britain should have this Palestinian Mandate, a poisoned chalice if ever there was one. In 1917 the Balfour Declaration commented in favour of a national homeland for the Jewish people – and they, naturally, considered Palestine the proper choice. (With the growth of Zionism back in 1903, the British government had suggested that Uganda might serve the purpose!) The British Mandate actually began in September 1923, and what followed was the too-familiar story of demonstrations leading to riots, to curfews and martial law, deportations, bombs and mayhem. Jews were arriving in ever greater numbers. Arabs fought Jews, Jews fought Arabs, and both targeted Britain, whose troops had an impossible task trying to contain the situation. A Royal Commission in 1937 considered the idea of partition, which pleased nobody. (In October that year the Arabs blew up a railway and derailed a train. T E Lawrence had died in 1935, else he might have given a wry smile.) In 1938 a mosque in Jerusalem was blown up. There was some marking time during World War Two, but afterwards the situation steadily became impossible. In 1946 a wing of the King David Hotel in Jerusalem, the HQ of the British Army, was blown up.

Too many soldiers were being killed. In 1947, first the US and then the UN voted for partition. Britain left, and in 1948 the State of Israel came into being. Today, all over the world, as well as in the Middle East, we are seeing the bloody fallout from the arrogance of Victorian/Edwardian Europe when lines were drawn on maps as if it were a game of Divine Rights. The year 1954, then, was not a bad time to be in Jerusalem, where, as ever, the ordinary people were just trying to live their lives in peace. Things would revert to blood and greed again, but in 1954 our unhappy today was, thankfully, the unread future. (Montefiore[68] mentions sniper fire in and around the city in 1954, killing nine people and wounding 54 – not something we were aware of, any more than we were of the atrocities happening in the Zone.)

❈　❈　❈

Jerusalem descriptions abstracted from letters written later in Deversoir

---

We flew from Fayid to Mafraq in Jordan, then went in to Amman – which is a real city – much larger than Old Jerusalem – and is a real mixture of poverty and richness. The King has a residence just over the road, so to speak, from where refugees huddle coldly in their rags under rotting canvas roofs. I shudder to think of the conditions when it rains and I am told that the rain in Jordan, when it rains, is heavy, causing floods and mud and disease. Amman isn't much of a place but at least has some heights in it, slopes dotted with white buildings – and trees. Everyone took photos of trees! The girls of our group and the Padres were in the Continental Hotel. They said King Faisal of Iraq was also there. [He was assassinated in 1958.] Some of the party went round pulling all the w.c chains

<hr/>

68 Simon Sebag Montefiore, *Jerusalem: The Biography*, Phoenix 2012.

for the novelty of doing so! I think the white-robed waiters were flattered by our food consumption: we were smilingly offered second helpings.

Britain has had a fighter base here since 1948 [until 1957, when it was closed], and we are very welcome in the country. The Arabs have little air power compared to the Israeli section of Palestine so they are all for us having Air Stations. Mafraq is not surfaced and is just beaten earthy sand. When a kite moves the dust is something to be seen, and when a jet moves, everything vanishes in a great blanket of dust. Every now and then twisting columns of sand come whirling across the naked plain and can be very unpleasant if you find yourself smothered. We were caught twice. We went by bus from Amman to Jerusalem – after changing into civilian clothes.

Suddenly seeing the ancient city against a glowing western sky was unforgettable: 'Jerusalem the golden' indeed. We were accommodated at Christ Church Hostel in the Old City, near the Citadel of David, a bit overwhelmed by the very names, the sights, the sounds, the smells (a nice change!), and the wonder that we were there at all. There must have been two dozen of us, of all ranks (even females!), for what was a house-party as well as a 'course'. *Moral Leadership Course (No.99)* was an odd title for what was really a thorough series of theological lectures, which were fascinating. In charge was the Canal's OD Staff Chaplain, Douglas Lewis, and Padre Leonard Bridgeman. We were all OD of course, 'other denominations' than C of E (Church of England) – into which everybody was consigned unless RC, Jewish or Moslem. Everyone was categorised on joining up, and unbelievers or anyone else simply had C of E put on their card. (Someone suggested the powers that be were simply trying to make sure we had the right words said over our graves if that eventuality occurred.)

---

* Most of what I wrote home about had nothing to do with the actual course, but as it is now a historic curiosity I'll include the summary I sent home. The lectures were excellent. I've heard poorer in university colleges.

September

Mon. 20   17.00 arrive. 19.00 dinner, 20.00 Instructions. 21.00 prayers.

Tues 21   07.30 breakfast, 08.15 prayers, 09.00 Lecture 'Belief in God'. Tea break, 10.45 Lecture: 'Belief in Jesus Christ', 11.45 'Belief in Holy Spirit', 13.00 Lunch, 14.00 Visit to Bethlehem, etc., 16.30 tea, 17.30 Group Discussions, 19.00 Dinner, 20.00 Group findings. Prayers.

Each day was something similar –

Wed 22	Morning: visit to Temple Area, Dome of the Rock, Solomon's Stables.
	Afternoon: lectures, 'Belief in Holy Catholic church', 'Christian Doctrine of Man', Evening: Discussions etc. Night wanderings!
Thurs 23	Morning: lectures, 'How we got our Bible', 'OT & NT', 'The Holy Sites' (by a Canon Every of C of E Cathedral). Afternoon: visit to Bethany, Mount of Olives, Garden of Gethsemane, tomb of Mary, Chapel of Agony, Church of all Nations, etc. Evening: free for shopping.
Fri 24	Morning: Lectures, 'Meaning of Prayer', 'Modern Challenge to Christianity', 'Marriage and the Family'. Afternoon: discussions etc. Visit Gabbatha, Via Dolorosa and Holy Sepulchre, Calvary.
Sat 25	Morning: Lectures, 'Early History of Church', 'Contributions of PMUB Churches'. Afternoon: Samaria, Jacob's Well, etc.
Sun 26	Morning Service in Gordon's Garden Tomb, Service at Hostel, lecture: 'Leadership in Action'. Quiet Time, Lunch, Questionnaire, Tea, Communion, Dinner, Prayers.
Mon 27	05.00 breakfast. Off 05.30.
Tues 28/Wed 29	Late night fly, after a two-day delay. Deversoir 22.00.

Christ Church, Jerusalem: the hostel yard

* I never worked out the who or the what of the Christ Church facilities we enjoyed in Jerusalem. There were refugees in one corner, a fine old church, and centuries-old buildings surrounding a central courtyard. A modern guide book mentions its guesthouse use still existing. According to Montefiore, back in the days of Victorian evangelical revival and the urge to establish missions, Palmerston ordered the Jerusalem vice-consul, Young, 'to afford protection to Jews generally' at a time when many powers were showing interest in the area. Shaftesbury then persuaded Peel (along with Prussia) to establish a Protestant bishop in the city, their choice a converted Jew. Missionaries then 'created an Anglican compound with a church run by the Jews' Society and British consul' – Christ Church, a Protestant church designed for Jews,

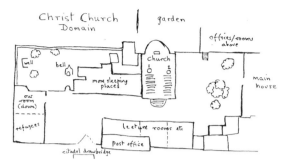

surviving today. The sketch, from a letter home, explains the layout, the site dominated by the Citadel, the drawbridge which was across the road from the entrance to Christ Church.

The Citadel (Tower of David) is a great castle, like any you would find in Britain – it even has that drawbridge round which gather the splendid lads of the Arab Legion. The country is full of their soldiers who wear k.d.[69] and red and white checked headgear that looks like a piece of dishcloth[70] thrown over their heads. However, a little observation shows that everyone has them a special way – like the red gowns at St Andrews. The oldest bits of Citadel go back to Herod the Great, who was really a monster. The Romans saved parts in AD 70 and turned Herod's proud palace into a barracks. Some is Crusader period, but most of what we see now was built by a Turkish Sultan in the 16th Century. Much of the stone in Jerusalem is 'the colour of a lion's pelt'. Nearby too is the Police Station, where the policemen in their spiked helmets change the guards in great style. From the roof of Christ Church we have a breath-taking view of the city – and south to the Israeli side too, across No-man's Land. Fruit was cheap and plentiful – so we all had upset tummies the first night. But, oh! the pleasure of a civilised meal, with decent food, and delightful company. Life, too, without the F word.

There is an Armenian Convent a hundred yards further on from Christ Church, which we popped into one night. It has some beautiful paintings done in light colours, flat, but decorative. All the buildings are interesting: streets noble and clean, arching across the way, balconied and flower-decked, rub alongside lanes which are filthy tunnels off which run little warrens full of half-starved children.

The huge Old City walls are only 1½ miles round, so, as the psalmist says, it is a city 'compactly built together'. Churches everywhere. The streets are narrow and as often as not break into steps and stairs. On the Via Dolorosa there are arches and bits built right over. In many places sunshades turn the streets into tunnels. The shops tumble out onto the streets and sell queer-looking, smelling, sizzling eatables, which few of our gang chose to

---

69 Khaki drill.
70 Tea towel.

try out. They smelt good! Men and women of all nations pass, from veiled Arabs in black to rich, noisy Americans. Porters who carry huge loads from their headbands rub shoulders with proud robed sheiks and beetle-black monks.

Near us was the historic Jaffa Gate, once the main western entrance. Along a bit is the New Gate (1887), both closed, as looking into Israel. The same applies to the Zion Gate on the SW corner. Circling on, anti-clockwise, are the Dung Gate, then, facing East, the closed-up Golden Gate, and St Stephen's (or Lion) Gate, [from which Israeli forces took the city in 1967]. and Herod's Gate (where in 1099 the Crusaders took the city). To the north is the biggest and grandest, the Damascus Gate. These are all in the Arab part, so we saw them all. On all sides there is plenty of pleasing new building, modern in style but sitting comfortably in the landscape. The city is obviously expanding rapidly, but our interest was centred in the Old City.

Outside the hostel gates there was, from the earliest peep of dawn till the golden setting of the sun, an old man with his box of shoe-cleaning materials. He is [sic] always dressed in a ragged old shirt, and he has a great black shaggy hair and a huge glass eye (the right one) which stuck out and gave his face a rather droll effect – rather like white dogs with large black eye-covering patches that make their faces so comic. He is always most polite in saying his good mornings (even if it chances to be evening). He can put a very wonderful shine on shoes and we seriously considered smuggling him back to Egypt where he could easily make a fortune off keen RAF types. Round the corner is the post office, and on the first day their terrified clerks were faced with a gang of philatelists seeking stamps of all designs. One of them has on it an amphitheatre which we saw from the bus in Amman.

Moses, a policeman, was a special friend, and we had marches up and down the only flat street one night. (He had all his excuses ready too, if an officer should come along.) His helmet had a spike on top and a cloth down over his neck at the back. He was a bit of a lad – but so were we, I'm sure, in his eyes. He was huge, had a grin under his moustache, and some of the most fantastic yarns. He was often up our way; almost became a mascot. People were all so interesting.

We came to know one, Abraham, who is 16 and owns a shop in the Chain, a real business, with two pretty sisters, and a young brother who yatters at a fearsome rate in half a dozen languages. We spent many hours in his shop drinking tea and talking (and sometimes buying). He ran the place like an expert, his books all in order. He had had a business course and some day hopes to visit England. He is well educated, and speaks several languages. Many young lads we talked to want to visit England, and I do not think they were just being polite in saying so. The younger lad, when we were saying cheerio, went madly from hand to hand and nearly pumped them off while weeping and talking all his languages at once. As we walked away he kept running after us to say something else. He was a little dynamo – of 12 perhaps.

On Wednesday evening three of us set off on a walk. After looking into another Convent to see more attractive paintings, we went on down by the wall on the south. The Zion Gate was shut and sandbagged, and on the walls were the Legion. We yelled greetings at each other and two of them walked down to the Dung Gate with us. They have ordinary uniforms but wear the head cloth held on by circling cords,[71] which is rather exotic. A bit further on two more joined in, along with the usual pack of kids. I noticed the men had British rifles. They were young and talkative, and we had a comparing of service grouses. After greeting the police-man on the gate – he looked just like Billy Bunter[72] in disguise – we left the soldiers. The boys came on with us though they were supposedly going home. They talked excellent English and were 'glad to have our company in order to improve our speeching'. We walked along a path and joined the Jericho Road by the Kedron (which eventually flows into the Dead Sea). One boy got well prickled by a prickly pear. There were many graves and, being Jewish, many were knocked about. Going on, the walls were huge above us and darkened against the sun-set sky. All Arab graves here. After profuse handshakes at St Stephen's Gate we parted, they to their homes and we into the dark Arab quarter of the city. The Mount of Olives was really golden on that walk, and great streamers of light waved behind the city's outline. Oh, it was so good, so *ordinary*. We don't get the ordinary of life very often in the Zone.

We made two historic excursions, one long drive northwards, one shorter to the south, this latter taking in Bethlehem. From the Mount of Olives our bus with 30 people plunged down into the Valley of the Kedron below where the Hinnon joins, and then in wide curves climbs like a stiff gentleman up on to the summit again. Quiet breath-taking country: great rolling hills, olive brown in the soft sunlight of early afternoon. We passed shepherds on the hills

the entrance to the Church of the Nativity, Bethlehem.

The entrance to the Church of the Nativity, Bethlehem

who waved to us. In the small villages, or even from the small cave dwellings the wee children ran out on bare feet to clap and shout 'Hello', while we, delighted, waved and called back. We drove past Bethlehem (5 miles from Jerusalem) and stopped for a moment at the place where the Shepherds had been tending their flocks by night (believe what you will). Then we visited the town and entered the Church of the Nativity with its tiny entrance. Once the door had been big, but had been bricked up to leave a small door – for obvious reasons of defence – and also nicely symbolic: one has to bow to enter.

Inside is a great hall with massive Corinthian pillars, very old and dim, and very holy. [The construction of the church had started under Constantine the Great in approx. AD 300.] We were shown old Roman mosaic floors under the present one. (Like Dunfermline Abbey: seen through a grille.) There are several altars, some fresh and clean and others with the overwhelming glitzy eastern decoration. We went behind one altar and descended into the stable-room of Christ's birth. There were two small shrines: one marked by a star

---

71 *Keffiyeh* and *agaal*.
72 The bespectacled, rotund, lazy, greedy, ever-15-year-old fictional schoolboy hero of book, films and comics through the first half of the 20th century.

Left: The Christmas Bell, Bethlehem
Right: Bethlehem

at the supposed place of birth and the other where he would have been laid in the manger. Very peaceful.

We also saw the beautiful Church of St Catherine from which the Christmas Service is broadcast each year. A service was taking place and a procession passed. There were monks, some very young and with strikingly handsome faces, and they were followed by young girls singing away. The children were all dressed in red and some of the youngest toddled along at the back looking a bit bewildered with the proceedings. Coming out again we could see the tower with the Christmas bell – still a month or two before it will be ringing out.

On the way back we paused to see Rachael's tomb, which is thousands of years old. The site was very grubby, and much more interesting was watching some masons over the road who sat under a lean-to roof and chipped away at their blocks of stone. We replied to the *ma-salaams* and left again. Dusk by the time we got back. Poised above the City we stopped, and for a few moments stood silent in wonder at the city lying in all the splendour of the evening hour. I was fascinated by the fact that everywhere, as in the Zone, the flocks were being led, not driven. I wonder, is the change from one to the other a marker of progress – or regression – in the story of mankind?

---

* Once, when reading the Jerusalem letters in early 2016, I noticed a small newspaper article mentioning the completion of two years' work to restore the Church of the Nativity to how it might have looked 600 years earlier. New windows let in light and had mosaics

sparkling. The work was carried out by enthusiastic local Palestinians (and President Abbas) who, of course, are all Moslems. And this at a time when the whole Middle East was (as indeed it still is) a cauldron of sectarian hatreds. The item should have had front page headlines.

One day we were given the choice of a trip down to the Dead Sea or visiting historic Samaria – now Sebaste. As the Zone has its own salt sea the choice was easy. The journey to Samaria took several hours each way. Leaving the main road we picked up a policeman for security. The village looked very scruffy but was friendly enough. We noticed an old ruined Byzantine Church [which] had a row of Mecca-facing faithful in action. Women with water pots were no doubt off to a well for water and gossip.

The first place we visited was where John the Baptist was held prisoner. The guide was a bit mixed up with just who was prisoner here and who got executed, for it had also been the residence – a most foul, dark, dank, and smelly one – for the prophets Elisha and Obadiah. After hacking our shins up and down the steps there we trooped round to see the new Roman tomb, tumbling down a steep stair to it. I gave it a careful look, for there were some very attractive, well-preserved carvings. We were told a local had been caught selling curios and pieces he'd been pilfering. He gave himself away by becoming rather noticeably too well-off in the poverty-stricken village.

We went for a circuit of the hill. There are many ruins, but only some are pointed out. We clambered about the basilica where Salome did her dance and asked for the Baptist's head. Tall columns were stark as chimney stacks. Walking through the olives and figs we passed the oldest bit of building, which dates from the time of bad king Omri in 800 BC. Alexander the Great built a tower on top of it in 331 BC. At the far end stood the temple of Augustus – a present from Herod the Jew! Little remains, and we went round to the small church were John (*sans* head) was buried. In the trees below it could be seen one of the pillared walks along which marched the soldiers of 2000 years ago. How destructive we are that so little remains of once fine buildings.

We came over the brow of the hill again and back to the village. Women were filling pots from the well and weary donkeys were drinking. Barefooted boys ran wildly down the road after the bus as we left.

We stopped on the way back near the Holy Mountain, Gerizim, to visit Nablus. It was once 'a city of Samaria, which is called Sychar, near to the parcel of ground that Jacob gave to his son Joseph. Now Jacob's well was there'.[73] The well itself is below today's ground level so we descended steps to reach the chapel, which was all candle-glitter and

---

73 King James bible.

guarded by a white-bearded, black-garbed priest in flowerpot hat. The well was walled, with a windlass, and there was a five seconds silence before the splash of a dropped pebble echoed up. The water was cool and fresh to drink, and it was a bit spooky to think that Jesus had sat at this spot to ask for a drink (John, Chapter 4). There's an uncompleted church at today's ground level, not much more than a curved wall (with an attractive keyhole-shaped cross through it) arching around where an altar would have been – directly above the well.

We had an amazing run, as the road kept to the tops of the hills most of the way but on occasions went twisting wildly down great green valleys so that we held our breath and wondered at the beauty of it all. Coming back, the hills turned from brown and green to dark blue, and finally darkness came down. Everywhere people waved – and shouted 'Hello'. Later, we tired singers were silenced by the sight of the city below us: a glimpse of a fairyland of sparkling lights and faint, speculative sounds. Then we were climbing down and into the Old City by the Damascus Gate. A quick change and we were sitting to a three-course meal and to chatter about the day's events.

Jerusalem can boast two ice-cream parlours – at least that is all we taste-starved theologians found, and Moses, the smiling policeman, did not know of any others. After prayers one night a lad, Graham, old Waggy (later found to be Sqdn Ldr Wagg) and I set off for a post-prayers promenade. We did this most nights, and you'd be surprised where we ended up. Some mothers would have had a fit to see young lads wandering in the dingy unlit streets at night. (Maw, you'd love the place!) Well, this night we met one or two others, and in the end we came on a crowd with the two Padres and Nicem our guide. We formed a gigantic dragon, like a conga, and just followed on, out the Damascus Gate and after ups and downs and a thousand corners found ourselves in a bright café named The Gondola, and 30 ices were called for, to be followed by Turkish coffee (which was like cool velvet) and some novel refreshments. My bill was 1/-, which was for coffee, soda, and the ice-cream, the last a dish piled high in six vivid colours. Tasted just like frozen fondants.

Another night one or two of us took the girls to the other ice-cream place, and after the usual glutinous orgy one boy ended up entertaining us (and half Jordan) with some conjuring tricks. In the end Moses, the girls and the boys were competitively drilling each other up and down. We then all retired to Abraham's shop where we had coffee. We finally headed on by the Street of the Chain, clambered up the steps of David Street, round past the Citadel, and so home.

There was one place I found a bit special. At the back of the shop/factory of Nicem we watched the fascinating making of candles; all done by hand. Every holy site of course glitters with candles (no doubt a good market!). A stout man stood unmoving on his feet the whole time, not daring to even glance aside at the watchers. We were told he'd been doing this work for 16 years. How to describe it?

The candlemaker at work

Imagine a wheel (rather like a cycle wheel) hanging horizontally from the ceiling, attached at the hub, and able to be turned round and round – slowly. From hooks round the rim two thin strands of cotton hang down, the wicks to be. With a deft movement of one hand the hoop is turned and with the other a precise amount of melted wax is poured down the threads. By the time a circle is completed the original pouring has dried, and can be done again. And again. And again, till the desired thickness is obtained. It took three hours of pouring and turning, we were told, to make a set of precise candles half an inch in diameter and about a yard long. Below this setup was a great dish with the heated mix of paraffin wax and beeswax which is used. The basin sat on quite the biggest primus stove I have ever seen. It purred away in familiar fashion. Any excess when pouring just dropped down into the burbling basin.

There was also a cruder version of candle making. Imagine frames set up just as we do with comb foundations ready for bees, only from the top of each frame a row of threads hangs down. These are then periodically dunked into a vat of melted wax. Repeat. Repeat. Fascinating too, but must be excruciatingly boring for the craftsmen.

We, all together for once, explored a street, or a route rather, the Via Dolorosa or the Way of the Cross, which is looked upon as the way Christ took (roughly) on going to Golgotha. [The Via Dolorosa is now known to be mistaken, but is hallowed by centuries of tradition.] But, as has happened to so many sites, the route has been done up, and all the imaginative 'Stations of the Cross' are marked: here Jesus fell (a first time), here He looked broken and the cross was taken by Simon, and so on. We began at the Castle Antonio by the Lion Gate where we walked on the very pavement of His judgement place. We went up and into the Church of the Holy Sepulchre. Our guide was a Canon Every from the English Cathedral who had come to Christ Church and given us a lecture. He was a tubby wee man who wore a queer cap – and badly needed a haircut. He was very pleasant and quite an expert. The Church of the Holy Sepulchre marks where Christ was crucified and entombed, so is the most holy place of all for Christians. About 20 different denominations think so! There is so much squabbling that a Moslem has been appointed as doorman.

Even fatter than Canon Every was one of the ministers with us: Padre Leonard Bridgeman. He was a real Friar-Tuck person, broad and beaming, jovial and an excellent lecturer. Padre Douglas Lewis was even better in the lectures, and is very able. He is extremely slight, on the other hand, and to see the pair walking along together is amusing.

Two of us managed to find Hezekiah's pool, which even Padre Bridgeman had never done, and he is in Jerusalem every other month. We had to go through a hotel to it. I've long

The Dome of the Rock, Jerusalem

forgotten most of the sites we found. In the Temple Mount though is the amazing gold-domed glittery, tile-covered building of the Dome of the Rock (Haram-al-Sherif, built 687–691), which is 'on top of Moriah, where Abraham had to offer up Isaac' – and from which rock the Prophet Mohammed ascended into heaven. This and the neighbouring Mosque El Aksa are the Moslem holy sites, Jerusalem second only to Mecca and Medina in their esteem. Here was where the original Temple of Solomon stood, and where the second temple (Herod's) was destroyed by the Romans in AD 70. Part of a wall from Herod's time survives, and is the Wailing Wall where Jews come to lament the loss of the Temple. The Dome recycled Roman and Byzantine stonework, and the mosque is unusual because it is a 'converted' Crusader Church. With all the destruction and rebuilding, sites older than AD 70 are 50 feet underground now.

HB at the Pool of Bethesda

Once Graham and I and one other went off to find the Pool of Bethesda instead of returning for the usual tea. We went in Herod's Gate and with my bump of Scottish direction, twisted through the streets of the Arab Quarter to St Anne's by St Stephen's Gate. There the great monastery rose high and cleanly shining in the sun. We found it was a Greek Catholic place run by Frenchmen. A tiny boy opened the big door with the big brass knocker and the big brass plate. As we entered a man in flowing robes of black and white disappeared round the corner. No one came, and the boy spoke no English. French worked better and his bright Arab features beamed when I spoke. He gave a gesture across the square. We went over past the colourful garden that bloomed in its centre. There were bees buzzing. (A tricolour flew above in the breeze.) The gardener came smiling out and led us to the far corner where in the passage was a notice board bearing the appropriate bit of scripture (John, Ch. 5) in 112 languages, including Gaelic.

We crossed a multitude of ruins and went down into their depths to have a dekko. There lay the pool, or a mere bit of it, for once it had been a noble structure. A flight of steps led down to it. Whoever was first went clump, clump, clump down the steps then splash! Splash! Splash! We took photos of each other and of the church which is traditionally the place of the 'virgin's mother's birthplace'! The gardener showed us a museum. The most striking thing was a model of the city patiently built by one of the Monks. This covered a whole wall and on the one opposite was a model of Rome and the Vatican. It was so quiet and peaceful in there, but then we had to head off under the arches, open the door and brave the busy chatter and bustle of the city.

Early on Sunday morning I slipped down by myself to the Church of the Holy Sepulchre, which is rather an ugly place propped up by scaffolding and very dark, dingy and dirty. There

The Church of the Holy Sepulchre, Jerusalem

are about six different groups active in the site, including Armenian, RC, Greek Orthodox, Abyssinian. As I went in a man ahead of me prostrated himself to kiss the stone on which they laid Jesus when he was taken down from the cross. It looked just like a tomb, and had a covering canopy and in the corners great candles reaching up into the gloom. I turned up the stairs into the Chapel of Calvary. This was like fairyland, for all the lamps were lit and every one reflected the sparkling silver of its neighbour. There were jewels (coloured glass?) on the crosses on the several altars, all among flickering candles. To the British mind it is perhaps rather tawdry, but for a brief spell I was held enchanted. (A child would gasp and clap hands: 'Pretty. Pretty.') I placed a few coppers in the tray and picked up two candles. (A quick-moving monk instantly had my money in his box.)

I went down the stairs again and heard the wild sort of wailing singing coming from the chapel in the very centre of the building. I skirted round it to the sepulchre. At the back a service was being held: Armenian I think. I entered the tomb for a while, which also glittered with dancing lights. On the tomb little children had laid fresh flowers and green leaves. I left a candle there.

The dome above was peeling, and all the interior is held up by great timbered scaffolding. The service behind was still going on, and two men, each with a staff, came out banging them on the floor. They were followed by two young men in fawn and purple robes who in turn were followed by the chief priest and several others dressed in black, wearing chimney pot hats. The principal man was attired in gorgeous robes and swung an incense-burner. He swung it at each of the officers, then at the tomb's sides and then at all of us who stood curiously or reverently at the side. We bowed our heads (and held our noses). He did the same on the other side of the tomb.

By the entrance two Franciscan monks had knelt and after muttering prayers sat back with their lips moving and fingers busy with the rosary. I was struck by their young faces, striking in the pale, moon-like light. I wandered round the other side of the central chapel and seeing a door open I looked in. Inside reminded me of a film I saw of the catacombs of Rome where early Christians had gathered. The air was thick with incense and smoke, and as I watched a priest was swinging the clanking burner back and forwards while the whole room joined in a universal wail. The room was packed with monks (or the equivalent in the Greek Church) and ordinary people and children who all stood round on various levels looking down on the brightly-dressed chief priests. All the pomp and pageant of the east was in the service, and I stepped back with almost a sense of awe.

In the RC side there was more peace as a few monks and visitors knelt silently before a clean and tidy altar. There were many impressive paintings lost in the darkness of the lonely passages. I would lift my feeble candle light and find it glowing over the delicately-painted face of a forgotten saint, with, below, a tiny altar with an unlit lamp left by some pilgrim perhaps years ago. I withdrew my light and the iconic face receded back into the dark.

An altar in the Church of the Sepulchre

I still heard the powerful rise and fall of the distant voices, strange but melodious. I began to descend the steps to the oldest bit of the earlier buildings when I came upon a lady, bent and shrivelled, and muttering, so each step must have been an agony. One hand trailed, clutching at the dank wall. I took the other, and we crossed the floor to go down the steeper steps into the old cistern where they found remains of crucifixes and claimed them as those of Calvary's tale. We went on down into the gloom having been joined by an old man who obviously knew the old lady, for he kept shouting to her in what seemed a harsh manner. We walked across the floor to the altar where the spot is marked and the old lady slipped from our hands onto her knees – where she wept and prayed and kissed the stones. It was pitch dark apart from my candle and the old man took it and led me round the cave, lifting or lowering it here and there, to show me pictures and inscriptions. We left the lady and went up the stairs to the old chapel above; its dome lets in light as it has glass partitions. There were beautiful oil paintings of Christ and saints all the way round and it was clean and fresh compared to the cave below or the church above. I took my leave of the old man who had shown me these things. He knew no English and on trying French I was immediately hailed by two talkative French people who had just entered. They wandered round chatting and profusely crossing themselves before vanishing into the gloom. The old man pointed to the cell and in an awed voice said, 'Finnish.' Finland! The old lady!

I returned to the Calvary Chapel to leave my candle on the stand at the altar but found a service on – very like the others. I again received blessings and another measure of incense from the priest. They all had great, deep and powerful voices which rose and fell, stopped and swelled like an organ thundering out. At another altar knelt several European RCs while over a bit again huddled another old lady who did nothing but cross herself at a terrific rate. When I went out into the sun my mind was in a whirl and I thought myself rather lucky to be just plain Presbyterian.

* The situation in the Church of the Holy Sepulchre today can be scandalous with patriarchs and priests sometimes coming to blows as they defend their patches during ceremonial seasons like Easter or the Holy Fire festival – the latter a belief that on the Saturday before Easter God descends in the shape of a flame spontaneously ignited inside the tomb of Christ. In 2002 a tussle ensured over the rights of precedence, and the holy fire (lit by cigarette lighter) was fought over in the tiny shrine. Not that this is a recent phenomenon. Mark Twain in 1869 recorded that 'the priests and the members of the Greek and Latin Churches cannot come by the same corridor to kneel in the sacred place of the Redeemer, but they are compelled to approach and retire by different avenues, lest they quarrel and fight on this holiest ground on earth'. In fact, there never was a time through the centuries without such behaviour, but periodically brawl could become riots, blood was shed, there were even shoot-outs. Today, well-armed police have the unhappy posting to try and keep apart these factions of Christ's church on earth.

I think my feeling will be well enough summed up by the traveller/artist Marianne North in 1866. Of the Church of the Holy Sepulchre she commented, 'Such a fair outside but so rubbishy within though full of picturesque bits.' In contrast she called the Dome of the Rock 'that exquisite building, the most elegant in the world'.

Sunday was the last full day we had in Jerusalem and a memorable day it was. Bell at 06.45, Breakfast at 07.30 and then at 08.30 we went to hold a service at Gordon's Garden Tomb, an attractive setting. We were not converted to believing it to be the authentic site of Calvary and the tomb. (This was a wild idea of General Gordon, he who died at Khartoum.) We found it very pleasant to be shaded under trees. I read one of the scriptural passages – and not till I finished did I notice a tape recorder in front of me. Two Americans who are tramping the world and collecting various audible memories had thought us worth capturing. Rather amused us. There was a German visitor and one or two others who joined us in worship. I liked that.

Back in Christ Church we had our last lecture given as a sermon during a service: 'Leadership in Action' – the gathering in and sending us forth now with the benefit of the knowledge, discussions and lectures of the week, the 'Go ye' in contrast to the original 'Come ye apart'. After that for an hour there was a time of Quiet and we prepared for the Communion to follow, at 17.30. (Methodist-style as the Senior Padre was one.) Dinner at 19.00, tea and chatting, speeches in lounge till 20.00 prayers.

Monday, 05.40, and we were off at cockcrow. We felt quite sad as the Golden City was lost to view behind Olivet. We twisted down 25 miles from Jerusalem's c.2500 feet to something like minus 1,000 feet, as the Dead Sea was not very far away. A very barren landscape with a few shaggy black goats and dust-coloured sheep the only life. The temperature shot up as we went down. We sang. We crossed over Jordan singing the appropriate Negro spiritual. So, you two may have been higher [Mount Fuji, 3,776 metres (12,390 feet) – on the day World War Two broke out] but I have been lowest!' [The Dead Sea is about 392 metres (1,286 feet) below sea level, but thanks to evaporation and major irrigation schemes up river, is shrinking by up to a metre (horizontally) a year, leaving old harbours and resorts high and dry. Its level is clearly lowering as well.]

We were faced with delays at Amman, then flew back at about 6,000 feet most of the way: two hours over rugged mountains and wavy sands. (Why on earth did Moses and Co. spend *40 years* wandering about a deserted landscape, like Robert Service's 'great alone', only sand, not snow.) We were almost glad to cross the Red Sea, and for Dave and me, 'home to 'Good old Dev!'

A DREAM OF JERUSALEM

O, for the shock of the Arab world
With the sting of the sand in the air,
For the dusty road and the camel path
And the play of the sun in the hair.
O, for the smell of the sweet-meat stalls,
The busy shops in The Chain,
The clatter of a thousand tongues –
Like Pentecost again!
O, for the night on the rooftops there
With the stories running wild,
Or the sight of the city at dawn
And the smile of a passing child,
For the tramp of the Legion men at dusk
And their wild cry from the wall
And the last farewell on the Bethany road
Where the cypress stand so tall.

6

The Zone, 3: Deversoir dying:
30 September–18 December 1954

Meteor

In 1954, the year I was at RAF Deversoir, 48 servicemen are listed, (from gravestones at Fayid and Moascar cemeteries) as having been killed by terrorist acts in the Canal Zone. Not included in that figure is a sapper in the Royal Engineers whose body the Egyptian police found in a railway wagon, with a head injury and two gunshot wounds. On 11 March a pilot officer I knew was killed in a Vampire crash and a Valetta crash in April killed three. There were also fatalities on the roads. Never released by authorities to this day are details of 13 other servicemen (usually in pairs) who were also killed by terrorist acts.

As late as 2000 Dr Lewis Moonie MP, a government minister, stated that only 40 had been killed, and 75 injured, in all the Zone years – an astonishing continuation of obfuscation by the government, and an illustration of its lack of any humane feelings. What innocent cannon fodder we were, and are, for manipulative politicians. I'm surprised at the number of deaths in 1954 from terrorism; after all, we were starting to leave. Things were more niggling than nasty for me at Deversoir. We certainly were not told of incidents of torture, mutilation and murder.

Some remnants of the imperial past are hard to credit. For instance El Qantara railway station had ten toilets built, but this apparent abundance was not quite what it seemed: notices indicated that three were for officers only (one each for European, Asiatic and Coloured officers), three were for warrant officers and sergeants (on the same racist division) and three were for the rest of us. Oh, and one was for women – rank and race unspecified.

One tragedy that was still being talked about in my Dev days happened two years earlier when a Sister Anthony was shot dead in a convent in Ismailia – because she was teaching British children. Other nuns were ignored, as the assassins purposely went 'to get her'. You might ask, 'How could anyone ...?' Just look about the world today.

Somewhere I came on the following list of euphemisms the British government would use in its desperate attempt not to use the word 'war'. If war was admitted then one was morally – and legally – bound to the code of the Geneva Convention. So, instead, in Palestine, the Canal Zone, Cyprus, Kenya and elsewhere we had disturbances, troubles, conflicts, risings, emergencies, rebellions, disputes, discord, engagements, agitations, contentions, problems, difficulties, complications ...

Deversoir
29.9.54

Back in the 'fleshpots of Egypt' again after a concentratedly wonderful week. We were delayed 36 hours with the kite[74] having engine trouble. I arrived late last night and immediately start a week of night binds.

Found 8 letters, 4 parcels and 5 lots of papers waiting. I have 4 parcels of books ready to send, then there are 2 addressed to *me*. Please just put them away as they may well be presents which I don't want opened yet. Jerusalem was full of cheap fruit and the hostel perfect – down to changing for dinner every night. I must unpack, and once more start to tholl[75] the dreary reality and the appalling inefficiency of the cooks.

2.10.54

I have just risen from some Egyptian PT (i.e. lying on my pit and sleeping). Three nights in a row done now. I have volunteered to stay on over the week or until I become too run down. The watch is one nobody likes but will leave days free, so if there is something I really want to go to, I can. I'll get to Church regularly for a while. I did enjoy taking those four services in August. Still very warm and no swaddling blankets needed on the night shift yet. Chewing Crail toffees. Yesterday I had the same meal three times – corned beef and POM. During cycle tours I quite liked the stuff but we can smell it miles away from the mess – would make a concrete substitute. I used some of your soups last night.

I took four of our billet's 'guests'[76] out in our boat this afternoon and they were greatly thrilled. One of them had no costume but after a while did join us in his underpants. Coming back I let him steer, so he was sitting perched between the two hulls in his ragged pants. When we were about ten yards from the shore I said, 'Steer for the young lady.' There

---

74 Aircraft.
75 Endure, put up with.
76 Temporary workers, mostly deconstructing.

was a yell and the lad was crouching down trying to hide while we all roared (there was no lady). The water is cooling and is delightfully fresh.

3.10.54

Dear Ian

I had to go and ask someone to find out what day it was. My memory is not wandering, but ever since I came back from Jerusalem I have been doing night binds the whole time. I met one of my old Deversoir pals in Mafraq (Jordan) and as our kite kept having engine trouble and we were delayed 36 hours, I spent several hours with him. He would like to know the address of the firm who makes those wooden-mounted crests like the St Andrews University one you have in your bedroom at home. Could you send the gen[77] to me – if you know it? Also the price; I'm sure you'll recall that! [Ian, once home, duly obliged.]

I had a hugely enjoyable week in Jerusalem. It was really satisfying to be a civilian for a week, with immaculate bogs, having to change for dinner, to sit in a comfortable lounge, to have beds made for us and shoes shined etc. At late supper tonight the conditions were the usual poor food, shortage of plates, not enough room and so on. I normally go to the more civilized early meals, but four of us were out in our boat and were caught out by a rising current and wind. The journey from the island (where we had been swimming) usually took ten minutes sailing back to the Club, but yesterday it took over an hour of desperate rowing to reach the shore and we were then about three furlongs down from the Club. Great fun! We all had our belongings soaked as we sprung two bad leaks – which were stuffed by various articles of clothing! The boat is home-made but sails beautifully.

Conditions here deteriorate steadily. We have five visitors in our billet just now who are dismantling the ATC tower and Ops, and we lose JAPIC[78] this week along with all the front-line servicing people. Then the Regiment goes, and so on. Telephonists will no doubt stay till the Egyptians come and take over our little PBX (and the best of luck to them – they'll find it somewhat temperamental). There used to be 2000 folk stationed at Dev. I'm beginning to get sentimental over the dump.

Deversoir is unusually quiet, seeing our Vampires and Meteors have gone. [These two classics would be replaced by Venoms and Sabres, then, by 1956, Hunters and Javelins. Could Zone pilots ever imagine a Concorde? Yet the papers were once full of a man who had seen the Wright brothers' first flight and who was able to fly in Concorde.] I'd a sneaking feeling for Vampires as our boat's panels came from them. They first flew back in 1943 and were the first to exceed 500 mph. The Meteors also came in before the end of the War. (It

---

77 Information.
78 Air Traffic Control, Operations, Joint Aeronautical Photographic Intelligence Centre.

"We saw a cloud yesterday !"

pushed the record to 606 mph.) It was famous for being faster than Hitler's V rockets, and could shoot them down or get a wing tip under one and tip it over so it would crash long before its target.

If you are ever visiting an Art Gallery please try and get me some reproductions (postcard size) of paintings. Here I manage to find quite a few repros as I see a large selection of magazines. The smudges on this letter are squashed mosquitoes. I must stop and copy out the last of my Jerusalem Course's lectures: each took 1¾ hours to deliver so you can imagine what my rough notes look like. Hey! We saw a cloud yesterday, like a stain on the uniform blue. This is being written at two in the morning and I have another hour to do before my companion takes over the switchboard. If you count England and Scotland I have been in seven countries with the RAF: Scotland, England, Malta, Egypt, Cyprus, Iraq, Jordan. Not at all bad for a year – five interesting plane hops too. [The final total, adding Sudan, Aden, Somaliland, Kenya, Uganda and Tanganyika, was to reach 13.]

10.10.54

Dawn has just broken and the desert is chill and clear with a yellow sky glowing behind the clouds like a cottage window in winter. An hour or two before our relief comes. As I wrote the date I remember it is Hamid's birthday, the tenth of the tenth. Hard to realise he is now five years old. I do miss him, my companion on every hill day at home.

I spent two hours last night on lesson one of touch typing, being tutored by one of the teleprinter lads on the printers which are next door to the PBX and from where an eye can be kept on the board through a hatch and there's an alarm goes off when a call comes up.

Yesterday afternoon was our All-Zone Church Rally in Fayid. There were between 200 and 300 packed into the church, where we had an excellent service. It was conducted by a Group Captain Potts and the sermon was by the visiting Staff Chaplain from the Air Ministry, a Gp Capt Appleyard, a Queen's Chaplain. After the service we went round to the YMCA for a small 'tea and natter'. All but four of the Jerusalem party were there, and everyone had photos to show, and the girls had on their Jerusalem mother-of-pearl earrings and bracelets. Both Jerusalem Padres were present, and the show ended very happily in some speeches and a blessing. Several children were present, including two of ours. Today, after morning service, I am being given a lift down to Fayid by Sqd/Ldr Horner, our Signals man, for a luncheon party. I will probably spend the afternoon there with various friends and come back in time for Evensong.

12.10.54

Awakened this morning to find our billet's visitors hurriedly packing. Strangely quiet in the evening. I spent the afternoon piling all the furniture back how it was before the invasion. Dark early now – usually in wonderful sunsets, as we actually have proper clouds for sunset to paint with extravagant colours.

I went to the pictures tonight and saw *Elephant Walk*. Nothing very wonderful but filmed in Ceylon with plenty of elephants, a glimpse of Polonnaruwa, etc. You may like to see it for that. [In the thirties, Father had filmed the many elephants and excavations of Ceylon's great ruins.]

There is a steady splatter outside and for a moment I was sure it was rain! I dashed outside but the sand was still dry and the cold moon had gone behind the clouds. All it was is the dew, such a dew that it drips off the roof as noisily and in quantity as rain might. So far, at work, it has caused eight PG's (permanent glows) and as many numbers u/s. A letter from Aunt Nell yesterday. She seems to have enjoyed her stay with you. I must write back. She says everyone seems to be out to fleece the officers posted from here and looking to live in Kyrenia. The Killinglies are going off for a year, *living* on the rental of their house let to someone in the RAF.

14.10.54

I do always make sure of at least seven hours sleep a day, and swim whenever I can, or go out in the boat. So night bind was all right. I am glad to be off it all the same. From today I happily take over the place of our Cpl. Supervisor, who is going home – not that I'll get a corporal's pay! I'd a pleasant row with him the other day. He yelled at me to 'get my finger out' with checks when I had already done them, as the log would have shown. I try to just shrug – *tedapah*[79] – but we'd had our fill of his puerility.

This is being written in the reading room. I relished sleeping in my bed last night, the first time for three weeks. Now I have to be up early to work, and it's somewhat *chilly* then, and this last few days we've had a dank fog that tasted of desert and which one felt able to swim in. Year almost up. My turn to tell others to 'Get some in!' Last time in the open cinema we saw a very bright shooting star which burst into a million twinkling fragments like a flare and then all was dark again. Cinema will be indoors now. Last Music Circle joy was Grieg's Piano Concerto, a different sort of northern sharpness compared to our silver-plated moonscape here. [Oddly, I've since heard this Grieg performed (live) in Scotland, Rabat and Lima!] There are sails out on the lake usually, and voices drift over. The palms rustle at any breath of wind, which also brings the inimitable night scent of desert. I try to imagine a soft wind at home among real trees.

20.10.54

I feel a bit more active now after being asleep all day but for two short excursions over to the Mess. I took a dose of salt and aspirin and have been dead-oh. Woke up to find a letter from you by my pillow. Two lads returned to the PBX so I will have another on the board with me. Last night bind was killing though I did get a wee snooze by letting my friend the Police dog-handler work the exchange; he quite likes coming in and has an attractive dog. He can manage extra rations and I always cook stuff for the three of us – he, dog and me. A good chai swindle here always. I'll be in bed after this is scrawled, and get a ten-hour stretch. Strange to think of you all sitting round a fire. I have not seen a fire since I left home. Nearly forgot, last night we had a wonderful electric storm: there was silence the whole time yet every second the sky lit up in a flickering sheet of light upon which were cast fantastic cloud shapes. It flickered all along the horizon, strange and beautiful. The lake and the night sky all sing of freedom while life is made prison by barbed wire. A camel train passed on the skyline when I was last on guard patrolling the wire. I should have reported it for investigation, instead I joined it in imagination and went over the lost horizons.

The Padre (C of E) has told us to expect the church to have an 'Un-dedication Service' soon, with a lot of brass present and most of the close associates of the church. C of E and OD will officiate. I have been given the pleasant Presbyterian position of carrying out the Bible. After that there are only one or two services before we move from camp to live else-where, with travelling here each day to work till Dev closes.

---

79 Never mind.

12.10.54

Sorry about the smudges. I dashed off to shut doors and windows, but even so this sheet is gritty with dust and I can't see 50 yards for the flying sand – our bold autumn weather with gusty winds (and sand) and erratic temperatures. Everyone is catching colds. I felt thoroughly muzzy when I woke at four this morning to do my half of the night bind, but it was only the result of an hour or two in a stormy lake this afternoon. Almost too bracing to swim these days, cold, but once in I never want to come out.

Today I can say I have done a year, so just one more to do. I wonder where? A Jerusalem letter I covered in stamps and sent to myself here had all the stamps removed. I wonder where the theft took place. Glad my parcels of books are arriving safely. Have either of you read *Gods, Graves and Scholars* yet? I found it fascinating: a history of archaeology. Reads like a thriller. Oh, you were mentioning rain: this afternoon a party of us were in the hut and I was laying forth about Jerusalem when suddenly there was a patter on the roof. We were out in a flash and were soon dancing about in the first drops since February. A scene from Charlie Chaplin, however, for it lasted two minutes and merely left a pretty pattern of dots on the sand. We returned to our chai and chat.

Work can be quite social in the PBX at 0300, with up to four in for tea and discussion – on such varied topics. Even at night, late, you will find two operators, one lad from Signals next door, one from the army, one dog-handler, and anyone who can't sleep. Bit like a club. Tonight I am all alone, as my partner is on guard and, being 11 o'clock, I have eight hours non-stop ahead of me which will make 24 hours *sans* sleep. Last post being played – always sounds so sad. After this I'll read till my eyes feel tired and then I shall write up some Jerusalem notes – and by then I hope it will be near dawn and I can start cleaning up. Oxo before anything! Nights would be improved by having calls to deal with instead of only a few checks.

* On 26 October Colonel Nasser escaped an assassination attempt in Alexandria, at a mass demonstration over the Agreement of Britain's withdrawal from the Canal Zone. He took drastic revenge on the culprits, the Moslem (now Muslim) Brotherhood – a name not unknown today!

29.10.54

I wish this dock strike at home would clear up and let us have our sea mail: now three weeks since we had any. [The month-long strike ended on that very day, the 29th.] Have I mentioned Suez, Ismailia and Port Saïd are *in bounds* again? Some day I might manage a tour and see some sights. I can't afford to go on an eating spree, and anyway the food has improved a bit. (Fewer of us to feed?) I hope *Lord of the Flies* film comes before I flit elsewhere. I am now LAC (Leading aircraftsman), which is as far as I can go in this 'trade' doing National Service. Sixty per cent of our various Signals blokes are due for immediate posting. I feel quite glad to be among the 'essential personnel' – feelings I can't even explain, for any posting would be a dream and better.

Now 03.30. I have just taken over from my partner and will be here till seven. I should have been on from 22.30 but I have trained this lad from the printers next door and he was delighted to do half a night bind. Only woken once, when the Fire Section phone went out of order. A very sleepy Army Signals Mechanic had to be roused. Our whole Signals Section is falling to pieces and in a day or two there will be only the ten of us left (five telephonists). I am senior operator in what are the rags of time remaining. I am also in the midst of a dispiriting nose cold, but a mixture of Vick, hot drinks, Aspirin, Nivea (for red nose!) and sleep – every minute possible – is, I think, having an effect. Two pals, back from Jerusalem, looked in yesterday; thrilled with their visit – definitely the very last from the Zone to go there. [Jerusalem all too soon was to be out of bounds.]

---

* With its central position by Lake Timsha, Ismailia was very much where officers had their clubs and creature comforts, and was in and out of bounds for the rest of us depending on the political situation. Some of Ismailia's colonial architecture still remains, with Frenchified tree-lined avenues and the lake's beaches giving the air of a spa. With Port Saïd and Suez both shoddily reconstructed after the Six-Day War, Ismailia is now proclaimed by Egypt as the 'Queen of the Canal towns'.

The incongruous RC cathedral at Ismalia (Dave Lee the figure)

8.11.54

This overleaf [a fire report now lost] – is what happened this afternoon not long after I came on. All over in a couple of minutes with guard room, sick quarters and Fire Section doing their stuff – and Abu Sultan standing by in case they were needed. A 'panic' is a welcome distraction. 'Pity the fire didn't burn down the adjectival kitchen' is the most expressed sentiment. I've been madly busy, especially with packing off our Section. Now we are on minimum staff. Everyone has to be genned up.

I have been shipwrecked! I am quite serious – desert island and all! Six of us were out in our boat, which looks a mixture of Kon Tiki and real jet-plane parts, and were cruising behind the island (the one I swam round) to enjoy a swishing see-saw from the wakes of passing ships. We had our sails up and everything was fine. Then a liner came out at a speed far above the normal – or legal – and after it had passed the sea absolutely surged in, boiling round the point. We turned to face it as usual, thinking it would give a good series of dunts.

I was sitting in the bows reading, and merely paused to lift my clothes in case any water splashed in. I went on reading. Then *Wham!* – the finish of all our voyaging. The liner had sucked the water off the coast and, though we were 30 yards away, we grounded and swung round just as a most amazingly huge wave reared above us. The next thing I knew was being wheeched away and tumbled about like a rag in a washing machine, to come up far away with water-filled lungs – and then having a right pounding in what felt like surf. I still had my book held tight. It was called *The Undersea Adventure* (!!). I saw wave after wave smashing down on the boat and its occupants, and then gradually all was still again. We dragged her a bit higher up the beach – she was on the island in the end – and took stock. Our pride lay smashed beyond repair. We were a pretty bedraggled sight when we eventually entered camp. We were very lucky: there could have been serious injury. As it is, all the loss is to personal property: clothes, shoes, watches, etc ruined. My watch has had it. Och well, it got rid of my cold.

---

* I still have Philippe Diolé's *The Undersea Adventure* with its saltwater stains. Sadly, our boat never sailed again. The culprit was Union Castle's *Durban Castle* – which, ironically, I would board later on in Mombasa. So I did some research on the culprit. She had been built in Belfast in 1938 as a liner (205 1st- and 335 2nd-class passengers) but was turned into a troopship during World War Two. In 1947 she made headlines when a cabin steward was found guilty of murdering an actress, Gay Gibson, and stuffing her body through a porthole. The *Durban Castle* was sold for scrap in 1962.

9.11.54

Not another disaster – but we now have no church! I rather enjoyed the somewhat ceremonious 'un-dedication' after a service of thanksgiving and praise. Here's a description (C of E lingo). The procession formed up outside on the verandah – in all 18 people – from Gp Capt down to mere airmen, and a super abundance of dog collars. Led by the crucifer and his two taperers, we entered the church in procession. We filed down to the front, hands clasped before, in slow and measured step, gave a nod (called a simple obeisance) and turned off onto the planned rows of seats. There then followed the service, a very exultant service with impressive singing, and after a few moments' silence the organ began playing 'We love thy … O Lord' (for each appropriate position).

The crucifer and taperers went to the back of the church followed by two servers and the STAFF CHAPLAINS, C of E and OD, and the Station Padre. There they un-dedicated the font bowl and bell. Drawing level again at the front, the crucifer turned and the servers went behind the lectern/pulpit by which I was standing. Padre then un-dedicated the Bible, and I received it and joined the servers. After another verse the pulpit itself was un-dedicated (they

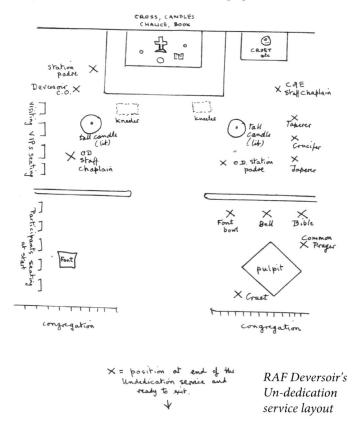

RAF Deversoir's
Un-dedication
service layout

The Procession

could hardly carry *it* out!). They swung across the aisle and the Book of Common Prayer was un-dedicated. That server joined us and then the crucifer, followed by his minions, entered the sanctuary where the altar book, the cruets etc, the cross and candles, and chalice, were given to the appropriate servers, who came forward for them. The last Padre Parry took himself.

The church and altar were un-dedicated, the congre-gation blessed and sang 'Rise up Church of God, go forth from this place'. We did, still in the slow, rather moving manner, the sacred items in our hands. We went out, the doors were shut, and we went right round the building to the singing of 'Onward Christian Soldiers'. I'll draw the order of our going.

Following on were the Station Commander (now Wing Cdr Walker, RAF Regt) and wife, Sqd Ldr Henderson-Beg and wife (he the stand-in Padre) and the rest of the con-gregation. Coming back to the door a final blessing is given and then *finis* to Deversoir Church. We plebs had a short singsong and sat in the once holy place eating and drinking and smoking before going off.

I was given a great pile of papers and magazines today and spent most of the afternoon sorting them out for the hospital. After tea I read Oscar Wilde's *Florentine Tragedy*. I like his work, though my copy is in a slightly worse state after having been in the shipwreck. My own play has been read twice now in company, as well as privately, and has proved quite pleasing to all types. It took two hours with people reading parts. Pity it won't now be performed; *c'est trop tard*. [This piece of juvenilia has not survived.]

We go into 'blue' again soon (stiff collars – yeuch!), and blankets are being issued. I have got the typewriter from the office so will put away my fountain pen. I have to practise on it as the teleprinters have all gone. I've covered the keyboard so every mistake shows; but considering it is only my second letter I don't think I'm too bad.

---

* One of the good points about Egypt, and Kenya later, was the informality of wearing khaki shorts and open-necked shirts. 'Blues' meant shirts with stiffish detachable collars, a pain in the neck all too literally – more so for a Dollar boy whose schooldays uniform was an open-neck shirt, summer or winter. A few years after demob when I'd heard no more from the RAF, I sewed the collars on and wore – and wore out – the shirts happily enough. Eventually I outgrew the mothball-smelling uniform which I came across now and then at the back of the wardrobe. Out of uniform I was probably dressed in smarter fashion than I have ever been since: a tie of course, and sometimes even cufflinks, the ties always kept under control with a characterful tiepin. Hair was not short back and sides. but always tidy. Most of us went in for the 'poor man's Brylcreem' (water) rather than the smelly real thing.

13.11.54

Dear Ian,

This is only the third time at typing a letter so you will have to bear with all my mistakes. My teacher won't allow keeking at the keyboard. It's an old crock and does queer things without my assistance. I hear, via Dollar, that you have been to Berlin; was it for pleasure or on duty? Out here we now have the dubious pleasure of Ismailia, Suez and Port Saïd being 'in bounds'. I doubt I'll see either Suez or Port Saïd. There is an angry growl at the NAAFI just now as the price of cigarettes is going to be almost doubled. I don't smoke, as you know.

Neither did Ian. When he went East to work he asked Father if it would be a good idea to start smoking; offering cigarettes would be a good way of breaking ice with visitors. Father was scornful and pointed out he would impress more as a non-smoker, with a clean, non-smelly office pointing to someone efficient. He suggested having an interesting chair for a visitor – an excellent conversation starter.

LATER: Life is much better now, with a three-pint pot of coffee made and a pile of toast dripping with Aunt Nell's apricot jam. There is really very little news from this dead end of the globe – only I might as well put my typing to practical use.

Last week we did have one thrill when our boat got wrecked in the wash of a liner and dumped on the island. I got washed overboard before I knew what was happening. I was busy reading and when I came up I still held my book, called? *The Under Sea Adventure.* (I kid you not!) I had had no intention of swimming that morning either, as I had a stinking cold.

Going to the pictures is aye a bit of a treat as it was, till recently, outdoors, under the stars. Not quite the Bug House in Tilli.[80] Some of the films I've seen here were *Moulin Rouge**, *A Day to Remember**, *The Holly and the Ivy**, *The Good Die Young*, *Hobson's Choice** (fun!), *Kind Hearts and Coronets** (more fun!), *O'Rorke* [sic] *of the Mountains*, *Calamity Jane**, *The Planter's Wife**, *Genevieve**, *Escape from Fort Bravo*, *The Seekers*, *Gentlemen Prefer Blondes* (Well, if they were like these!), *Salomé*, *Elephant Walk*, *Hondo*. The good ones I've marked, several were a waste of time, others I've forgotten. I go to about one in six showings.

On Tuesday last the Station Church was un-dedicated. There was a lot of pomp and pop-ery, and as it was a mixed-use Church we got roped in too. I had to go trooping round with the Bible in my arms. I came in for quite a lot of OD teasing and a good time was had by all. Everything went without a hitch. (I was just dying for someone to drop the big brass font-bowl.) Now for Church yours truly gets a Land Rover to bump him over the sand to Abu Sultan, which is the desolation of desolations of a base, in the desert east of Dev.

Looks like I'll be here till the middle of January. Do you not get demobbed about then? [Ian's discharge was 3 February.] But I must get down to my line and security checks. Routine is all.

16.11.54

Well, here goes for another bash on the machine – about letter No.7 of touch typing. This exchange is rapidly becoming a Literary and Theological Society. Last night there were more than a dozen in; from the Duty Officer to two Abu Sultan lads. We had a great time talking and drinking [non-alcoholic]. In that time I consumed eight pints – oxo, coffee, chai and cocoa – and guzzled piles of toast dripping with syrup and raspberry jam. On Sunday I went out for church, and for so doing a Vanguard, driver and escort were placed at my disposal! Our OD Padre, Horner, we were told, was in hospital but we had a good stand-in, Wright, who had a deep, resonant voice we could have listened to all day. I enjoyed my doing Evensong again. Easier than taking services.

We are now without church or padres of course. My own OD Padre I do not miss, for he had some very strange notions, but the Station Padre, Padre Perry, the C of E Chaplain, is very much missed. He was more than just a Sunday figure, he became an everyday friend and counsellor, and the centre of the camp's Fellowship. Norman and Chris were sacristans and servers in the C of E ceremonials. He is in Abu Suweir now, and rather 'down' away from Dev and still with some weeks before his overseas tour ends. We might go and give him a surprise Dev invasion. He was never bossy, but influenced all who came in contact with him. The teapot was aye ready in his office. How we loved to leave work for a few minutes of a morning to slip round to the office for a bit of chai and chat. We won't forget his ghost story telling either, in his soft Welsh tones. I hope I'm as lucky in my next station.

---

80 Tillicoultry, 3 miles west of Dollar.

In a week you should have a spool from me. In it are photos of Mafraq and our kite that wouldn't go. There are shots of myself by the Church and one of my pal Chris, now in Iraq, where I met him – and consumed large quantities of *assis* and spam sandwiches (with a sprinkling of sand).

20.11.54

Half an hour ago I wrapped a towel round me and ran and slid through the rain and thunder to the wash house. It was completely empty, no lights worked yet, marvellous, there was plenty of boiling water. How typical. So now I'm shaved and clean for going to our Fanara [south of Fayid] Church party. We've had a fearful storm which has turned the sand into disgusting mud. First real rain since February. Caused chaos on the PBX.

LATER. Our wash house, after my early visit, nearly burnt down. Chaps found the hot water not just hot but boiling (as I did), but the water was by then rusty red in colour. They broke down the door into the boiler room to find it in flames. Now there is no hot water.

Tomorrow I'll post off two parcels of books I've read plus a now full photo album. The books are *Secret Tibet, Undersea Adventure* (with its salt stains!), *B W Fish in Persia,* the Penguin *Selected Essays,* the *Pleasures of Music* anthology, and J B Phillips *Gospels* and *Letters to Young Churches.* I've added one or two empty honey pots; should be alright as they were well boiled. I'm busy with Christmas letter writing as Christmas cards are impossible to find. About my typing: every time I pause for a second more than I should I get a clout on the head from my instructor. He assures me that it is for my good. I'm going to suggest a tea break. which may give me a respite from my hard-hearted/hard-handed teacher – one of the ex-Signals teleprinter operators. They seem to have forgotten to post him on.

We are now into 'blue', the Padre has gone, there's no longer guard duties, and Dev seems near empty of people. There's a distinctly end-of-term atmosphere. This has been written on a gash roll of teleprinter paper.

26.11.54

Last night I went and saw the film *Father Brown.* I'm sure Chesterton would have approved. Tonight I am going to see *The Caine Mutiny,* which will be the last film to be screened at the Dev Astra. Its closure will be one more telephone number extinct. (We are quite sad seeing our board's extensions closing one by one; so much of life and people lay in them.) I walked round the wire the other day and there were several dead pi dogs. Stinking. They are all being shot; very sad. Even the lovely police dogs will go, as it would be impossible to repatriate all there are in the Zone, what with quarantine and so on. The dog-handler has just been in here for his 02.00 cup of chai; he is a good mucker. He still doesn't know his dog's fate.

It is cloudy tonight and I miss my bright moon shining in over my shoulder as it always does on night binds. The gloomier weather somewhat reflects our gloomy Deversoir closing. We girn, but it has come to be 'home', and we feel sad that it is writing itself into the past tense. I'd a letter from Ken who has been moved to RAF Bückeberg. He still works in the control tower – looking over a snowy forested hill landscape. Very regular work so he does various study courses. The enclosed short story was done the other night when we [the night gathering] had a ploy whereby we all wrote a Christmas story – and drew lots as to what type of story to tell: happy, sad, a murder, exotic, religious, odd location, etc. As you see, mine had to be a *sad* tale. I'll try and send you John's *funny* story. It was hilarious. [The stories have not survived.]

30.11.54

Queer services on Sunday in Abu Sultan. In the evening it was taken by a lanky young lad who had a horrible habit of every now and then diving under his robes and scratching violently. In the OD morning service the MO (Dave) gave me a lift in the infamous old ambulance as we are the only church-going ODs left in Dev. He's quite a good friend; we went to Jerusalem together.

On 15 December a hundred from military ranks and airmen will live at Abu Sultan and travel to work here. I expect to be one. On that date our PBX closes and we go into a mobile X.[81] As it is, we have now removed half our positions and cut down to 50 extensions, on just one switchboard. Everyone has a new telephone number so there is great fun connecting everyone wrongly as nobody seems to have collected the new directories – as ordered. When a bloke gets the Labour Office instead of the Officers' Mess it's quite comic listening in. People get quite ratty on the phone at times, but we stick to 'a soft answer turneth away wrath'. We're not the only ones overworked.

Been down to Fayid and bought some sugar and jam for the night watches and took more magazines (which people give me as well as yours). I'm yawning over a re-reading of *Prester John*. Can't wait for bed; it's 24 hours since I was in it. Sleep is relished in these inclement days but, oh, I'm missing exercise. Ian sent me £1; the most sensible of Christmas presents.

Did I mention Jock (billet pal, and PBX) has had leave cancelled at the last minute? We are all now 'essential personnel' and nobody can be spared, which of course is the result of having cut our numbers to a crazy level. We're all mad of course – wanting to stay here – but it's our PBX, the centre of our lives. Ours! But then, the whole show is really neither here nor there in the big scale of time.

81 Exchange.

2.12.54

Rush! Rush! Seems to be the norm now. Latest rumour is that half the Signals Section may go, but I want to stay as we're a good friendly bunch. Hard to read seriously, but Trevor-Roper on *Hitler* and *I Confess* were serious enough, about such dreadful things. The *Kon Tiki* sequel was sad in parts. I've been covering my Christmas notes with sketches. The sphinx can be given quite a range of expressions! Shocking weather here – just like home – except that everything is cloying MUD. People who girned at the heat now girn that it's unfair: 'this is meant to be desert!' Can't do much outside, but I keep as active as I can and I'm about the only person free from cold. I hope all yours clear up.

Just came on for another night duty. I expected another lad to be on too, but he is absent, so off-duty blankets carried up will not be needed. With one lad returning to the UK he has to take over that watch instead of helping out night work. Och well – I've plenty of tea – from a nice *brown* teapot which used to belong to our Fellowship. I'm going to send it to you, Maw, when we close; it is what you have said you have always wanted. [A letter to me two months later from home said, 'Your big brown teapot is too heavy for Gran to use but was there for yesterday, for welcoming Ian home from his army days.'] There is perfectly delightful music on (for a change!). Earlier some good jazz. My 'acquired' armchair and tea and no calls at present really make the PBX quite pleasant. Now and then a mosquito buzzes in.

When I return home (like Orpheus from the underworld) I want to have a mighty soak of ballet, opera, concerts and drama. I seem to be in the minority over so many things: classical music and literature, a liking of exercise, church going, trying to be disciplined and reasonably ethical! (A proper prig!?) But so many just do not care and exist in what seems a living sleep. Suggestions to get off their pits are not welcomed. 'Give me the fruit, but please, oh please, don't make me climb the tree for it.' Dave says that many of the officers are just as bad. They at least should have more sense. But no, on a Saturday night they end drunkenly round the bar, flirting with each other's wives.

Dave and I had a very pleasant day in Ismailia last Saturday. Our day can be summed up in three activities: window-shopping, dining/talking, and church-visiting. Window-shopping in a proper town (not just a bazaar) was not up to expectations, and prices are scandalously high as may be expected just now with the big places of the Zone newly 'in bounds'. I think the chatting over and after tiffin and tea was the most pleasant and relaxing part of the day. To sit in a place ('Officers only'!) clean and neat, waited on by willing people (who suffered our French happily enough), to eat food that is not flung at us, and to talk without rushing – it was just what we needed, and cheered us up a great deal. We managed to see a lovely church (RC) from which a wedding came forth, and then several Orthodox (Greek, Coptic) buildings. One was mostly a school and we unknowingly walked into a class! No services on anywhere but it was just nice to see beautiful things – a change from the utter dullness behind the wire.

Dave was moved to Abu Sueir. He had enjoyed being Rover Scout leader of the station crew. One Rover, Tom Smith, had been with us in Jerusalem. Despite opposition Dave, on demob, went to college to become a priest. Lucky man: he managed to visit Cairo.

Aunt Nell has sent a parcel as she 'knows my appetite'. Good of her. At the moment I'm being showered with Xmas cards and books. I have written one or two letters a night for the past month. I didn't realise I knew so many people. Dave tried to send parcels home but they all came back. You can't send anything bulky now. Books are OK. I am spending more on food – have to! Today's fiasco was no hot water for three meals in a row. Just imagine our plates, thick in grease, cold and clinging and impossible to wash. One boy in my billet has been spending all his pay in the NAAFI. It shuts on the 13th, even though we come to work each day. ('What! No Stella?') Then by mid-January this place will be no more. That's the theory anyway. Today the Station Sick Quarters packed up and seven more phones became 'ceased lines'.

8.12.54

I was in Fayid today and, with a move coming, bought myself a very big case. 'Oh very good case, *unfundie*![82] See: real leather.' (And the man thuds it on the toughest spot.) 'See very strong: How much you pay? No, no, don't go, sir. For you I make special price …' One of these 'beautiful cases of pure leather' that I had looked at outside had a big gash in it. I had no sooner noticed this than I was bundled into the shop to see the others. I played along for a while and then led him back to the one outside. Holding it up I asked how the case was all 'best leather' when it had cardboard 'guts' for all to see. I did buy one in the end, for they are good enough and having one will solve my travel 'diffetis'.[83] Strange to hear of Crail with snow while I'm lying on the beach. I don't expect I'll see snow till back home – unless sent to Cyprus.

The Last Guard Duty

---

82 His rendering of the Arabic *Effendi*, Honourable Sir.
83 His rendering of 'difficulties'.

9.12.54

I had my last walk round camp this afternoon. I went over past the cookhouse to the perimeter track where the great grasses wave 10 feet into the air and are singing in a chill north breeze. I paused by the old pump-house where the dirty water from the canal is pulled into the pipes (our drinking water, once doctored). There lay the old dog and the puppy that had in the spring so amused us. The house opposite still has a date palm growing out of the roof – and the dates hang there rotting. The usual ragged orphans run about, and the egrets still perch on the cows and donkeys. I saw a hoopoe. Remember them in South Africa? (That is three times I have seen them in Egypt.) I wandered on by the searchlight tower. Nobody up it any more at night.

I very determinedly walked some miles round the wire and came back to the Sweet Water Canal side. I found a hole and slipped through to have a quick dekko. I had to be quick, for a gang of labourers was coming along. I had no wish to risk a confrontation. Hurrying back, there was a robed man on a camel. Anyone on a camel looks rather grand. A boy bouncing along on a donkey was comic. Everything is growing at a great rate. Wild flowers are in blossom and I took a bright one for a buttonhole. Don't know their names. Once more we are round to seeing peanuts cultivated, as when I arrived. A winter crop of wheat is pushing up strongly. All is green where there is the slightest bit of water. When the rains are over it will all dry up again. I won't see it.

10.12.54

By the end of the month, I'm now told, I'll be in a new country: Aden. And immediately moving to RAF El Hamra (well down the Bitter Lake) where all the flying to other countries goes from. (Where we landed 5.2.54). I'm very happy to be staying abroad rather than returning to the UK but, thankfully, not in the Far East. Many National Service lads can tell you exactly how many days they have to go till demob and a few actually strike off days on some sort of calendar: all they live for. Aden sounds a place that should have swimming and a big, civilised town. Roll on, Aden! I've sent another book parcel of ones I've read and don't want to carry from here: *New Poems, 1954* (some shockers), C S Lewis: *Mere Christianity*, the Buchan, Munthe: *Memories and Vagaries* and two vols of *Notebooks of Leonardo da Vinci* which a pal sold to me.

RAF El Hamra

15.12.54

This will just be a wee note as I've been challenged to a game of darts and the lads are all waiting. We left Dev this morning and are well settled in here. I, now, can expect to move in a few days as extra kites are being laid on to cope with the greatly increasing numbers. Been highly extravagant in the food line – for a change. Now 18.30 in El Hamra's Church Club room. I'll probably next write from eagerly awaited Aden, the surprise posting – which may only be a staging post, however. Well, that's me moving on – and Ian will soon be out. He was always keen Army at school while I was RAF.

RAF El Hamra

17.12.54

One week to Christmas and tomorrow I leave Egypt (DV,[84] *Insh'Allah*, etc). The days waiting here in limbo were dreary but the prospect brightens. Another mucker from Dev is coming to Aden as well. I've made my last salaams to the Great Bitter Lake. I'll write when I arrive. I'll be leaving with mist clinging round the camp at dawn. I've ended my last (mobile exchange) shift, and my last anything in Egypt. Sob. Sob.

* Not quite the last anything. At El Hamra I'd been laying in Stella for the occasion, including several empties, these latter scattered about my bedspace while I poured most of one over myself, so was sitting looking like a Buddha and apparently very much the worse for wear when everyone (mostly my billet mates) came back from the NAAFI. I saluted them in slurred tones and had a hilarious time seeing their reactions. 'Ma Goad, it's wir Hamish, fuckin fu! … Really, I'd fucking thought better of him … Listen to that fucking language!' I went into helpless laughter at their serious concern: 'Fuck! He's got a plane to catch … Here, give me a hand with him …' I resisted being put to bed and a glorious mêlée ensued, and when my hiccups subsided a night of hilarity followed. Quite a few of *them* were the worse for wear in the morning. I left, sober – and feeling quite fucking doleful.

---

84 *Deo volente*, God willing; the once-popular Christian equivalent of the Muslim In*sh'Allah*.

Aden *en passant*

18 - 23 December 1954

RAF Khormaksar

Aden

19.12.54

Arrived late last night; a very uncomfy journey, from dawn to dusk with one wee break at fly-ridden Port Sudan on the Red Sea. The kite was a Viking. I admit Aden is not quite what I hoped for but well up on Egypt. This is being written *on bed* on a third-storey balcony! I wrote a letter before but in the wind overnight it has flown off. No address yet for you. Aden is like the Canal Zone for admin vagueness. We are just in Transit here, we now know. It's marvellous to be in a place with some *verticalities*. Views *down* as well as around. Not a pretty place. All concrete. It is freshly hot, and sleeping out, as it were, is a treat. (Some girn of course.) When I reach my final destination I'll let you know *eck dum*.[85] Bubbling inside to know what's to come.

20.12.54

Another night about to fall. From my bed I spent ten minutes doing the drawing till my pen ran dry. This is a place with interests and I could have enjoyed it fine. But oh, I have never seen such a dead crowd of lads. Their attitude is infectious and with the heat it must be very tough in the summer. But I will be in decent summery weather again by the weekend for I'm being posted to Kenya. Nairobi. Couldn't be better – and there for the Christmas break.

Beyond the camp, camel carts are racing along the road and further off are piles of salt and windmills turning in the evening breeze. Lights are coming on and the distant harbour winks in rainbow colours. It is deliciously cool up here on my balcony doss. I saw the Signals building today. It is underground, air conditioned, and soundproof, right by the airstrip. A compact camp. At a Carol Service last night I saw our old Deversoir CO who is now here. Steamer Point is the aim tomorrow. And some swimming! I'd love to scramble on the rocks. Wonder if there's a climbing club. There are possibilities here – yet Kenya sounds way better. Spacious. RAF Eastleigh there is being made HQME Signals[86] and our lads are pouring in. I know folk there, and pals here too. Pleasant to have well-cooked food and full liberty to come and go. Gone to the heads of some from the Zone – literally, too! Daft! Mail is all being held in Dev till an exact forwarding address is known. So I'll probably get the Christmas mail for Easter! I did bring a letter with me from Aunt Sis (she

---

85 Straight away.
86 HQ Middle East Signals.

sends *The Sphere* regularly) telling of her garden flooded and trains from Dun Laoghaire to Dublin cancelled because the sea was over the line at Blackrock. A bridge swept away also meant no trains to Dublin. But I liked this: horses being led out from flooded stables had one of them with a mouse riding on it.

Radio now telling of troubles in Cyprus with British bars bombed and riots in Limassol. EOKA hauling down a jack to hoist a Greek flag, and Turks smashing Greek shop windows, soldiers stoned. It is bound to escalate. Luckily Kyrenia is in the Turkish north so Aunt Nell will be OK. [A year later she was reporting bombs in Kyrenia; one in the Matthews' garden.]

21.12.54

Off tomorrow at dawn. Just back from town and a rush to be packing. At Steamer Point had a non-buying look at the gift shops. There is a new branch of your bank, Paw. A young-looking lad (his third tour, though) is manager. He knew of your name. His name was Ward. At Crater the Chartered Bank boss is a Mr Dixon. Lunch and tea were enjoyed in the Crescent Hotel – only good place – where we ran into a poetry session of all things. Swimming at Steamer Point was inside nets because of the danger of sharks. Been a very pleasant intermission and Kenya an exciting prospect. [Britain had been involved in Aden since 1839, but it was another colony to disappear in the decade after this; in 1967.]

From the Clouds over Africa
22.12.54

My ears are full of the din of engines and my stomach vibrates to the shaking of the plane while the countless miles of barren Africa roll below. My mind is far away, as I have been reading a mixture of the works and lives of Edward Lear and Francis Thompson and as a result plunge from sorrow to nonsense and back again in a giddy sort of way that fits being up in the sky. Thank goodness it is a steady flight and I can read.

An hour ago we left Hargeisa (in British Somaliland) [now the northern part of Somalia] and there was a great sweeping horizon and unlimited sky. Cooped up in Egypt on Active Service was a strain – and now here am I going off to what can only be better.

Time for lunch – a box full of little cartons and packets, an orange, some Smarties, and wooden cutlery. I give away the salad cream. I eat the fruit and another hundred miles has gone. More hilly but still scrubby. We cross the equator and also go back an hour in time.

I hope I can be well settled at RAF Eastleigh; so often at Deversoir I made a friend and then he left. At the end Dave Lee and I were much together. He's rather High Church but we had lots in common. Egypt was fun all told – I would be a sorry one if it were not so. I may be depressed at times, I may be up at others, but I tick along inside fairly steadily. I'm afraid I'm growing up!

PS. Arrived Eastleigh OK. It's wonderful! Wonderful!

7

Black and White in Kenya:
23 December 1954–16 October 1955

The motto on the RAF Eastleigh crest translates as 'Firm and Strong'.

The flight from Aden via Hargeisa in the then British Somaliland touched down in an ambushing world of green at Nairobi's RAF Eastleigh. That night I was in the camp swimming pool with the surrounding jacaranda trees blue and the hibiscus hedges bright. 'Wow!' I reported. Letters home were euphoric, the sordidness of the Zone dismissed, Kenya's lushness embraced and new friends and experiences soon overflowing the cup of life. I was writing home as a nineteen-year-old on a high.

I'll try and recall those first days as best I can for, alas, the letters are lost. In 2018 I had only just, found a stash of letters from this time in the RAF. In Kirkcaldy I went into Costa for a coffee and then settled to skim through these rediscovered RAF letters, ones which told of arriving in Kenya the day before Christmas Eve, 1954. Their wild exuberance had me smiling; yes, this was a story to tell. I then made a visit to the Gents, picked up my heavy rucksack of shopping, and walked to the bus stop at the end of the High Street. And there I realised I'd left the file of letters behind in the loo. Old men do this sort of thing; on previous occasions I'd left a spec case and woolly bunnet in Costa so, even before checking the loo, I asked the girls at the counter if they'd been handed a black plastic file. They hadn't – and it had gone from where I'd left it.

The contents were just my pocket diary and these letters, so would have been of no value to the thief. They'd simply be dumped. I even checked nearby bins on the High Street, but the thief would have hurried off as he'd surely have expected me to return. That was that, then.

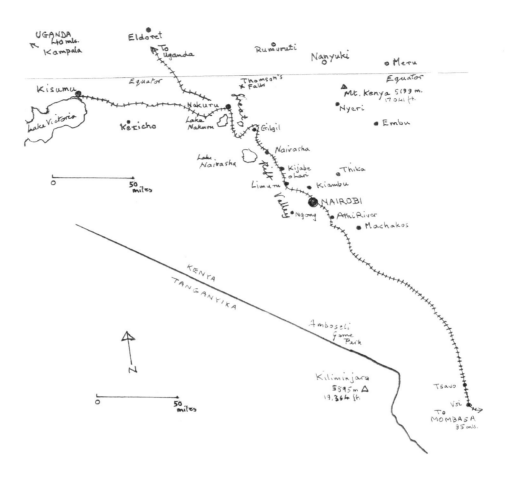

The local weekly *Fife Free Press* splashed the story and it went 'viral' in a local way, but it turned out that the letters had irretrievably gone. For weeks afterwards I was being asked, often by strangers, if my letters had turned up. When I realised my letters home were gone for good I jotted down what I could recall of my doings, but there is no way for me to recapture the excitement, to reproduce the exultant words I'd poured out in writing home.

✻   ✻   ✻

The day after landing and going through the bureaucratic mill of being settled in was Christmas Eve, which meant I was to enjoy several days of freedom before being put to work again in the Signals section. So it was into town as soon as possible for a meal the like of which we had never known in the Zone; side tables with roasts and loads of exotic fruits and fresh vegetables. (I still have the New Stanley Hotel menu: eight courses and all the trimmings.) This was as well, as the food in RAF Eastleigh was – inexcusably – to prove little better than in RAF Deversoir.

I went to the 'English' (Episcopal) carol service, and my Scripture Union badge was spotted. The young minister, Dicky Smart, at once put me in touch with others there from RAF Eastleigh and took me up to 'Bwana Jarvis's', which would soon become a home from home. He was a surgeon, but the family kept open house for servicemen and provided Christian fellowship without denominational ties, which would soon play a vital part in a Billy Graham-style campaign. That night I and others left full of food and having listened to a fascinating lecture on astronomy; we were given a lift back to camp.

We returned to camp to find a scene of, to us, disgusting drunken partying. We couldn't face the billet (an aircraft hangar!) so walked and talked in the moonlight by the pool or sat under the flaming bougainvillea and blue jacaranda trees till two o'clock on Christmas Day. We went back to a morning service at the cathedral, a traditional 'lessons and carols' with the lessons read by the governor ('eagle nose over the lectern'), the city mayor and two cherubic children. Afterwards, we dined in the New Stanley Hotel ('officers only' supposedly, and 'whites only' very definitely). There was a nativity play at some point, and I recall us three from camp being put to work at Bwana Jarvis's helping to build a hut in the garden, a large garden with shady trees and explosions of colourful flowers, a natural feast after the sterile Zone. On Boxing Day we were taken to a nearby game park, where we saw Thomson's gazelles, warthogs, giraffes, lions, crocodiles, hippos (with oxpeckers on their backs) and exotic birds I'd never seen before. We had a picnic while watching rhinos, and there were baboons and lots of flat-topped acacia trees. Homing, in a flaming sunset, we saw a lion sprawled on a knoll, silhouetted against the red sky.

The first lion(ess)

No wonder my letters home in those early days were so enthusiastic. Not that we were unaware of a contrasting seriousness. We were there because of the Mau Mau, and would soon, sometimes, be working long hours and there were rules and bureaucracy aplenty in RAF Eastleigh. There was a 'flap' almost at once following a Kikuyu being hacked to death by pangas,[87] and I was placing calls to every police and military posts the length of the country, to names which were to become familiar: Naivasha, Limuru, Nyeri, Nanyuki, Nakuru. The RAF was engaged in bombing

---

87 Machetes, near enough; standard farming equipment in Kenya.

raids in the Aberdare Mountains, using 61 Squadron's Lincoln bombers, the successor to the famed Lancaster. If much less RAF work is mentioned hereafter it is simply because there was so little to report home. Routine is hardly noteworthy – as it is, I suspect, in most people's working experiences.

Kenya I came to regard as one of the most beautiful countries in Africa, a greedily accepted bliss after the Canal Zone and even more formative for the years ahead. A Christian crusade and abundant off-camp life had me considering a future as a minister in the Scottish kirk. After demob however I could not buckle down to studying Latin and the like, which was deemed of vital importance for visiting the old and sick and insane, consoling the parents of a drowned boy, conducting funerals during the Asian flu epidemic and taking Sunday services – all things I would do in a lay appointment as missionary assistant at Martyrs Memorial Church in Paisley. I didn't read of the scaly fishermen who became Jesus's disciples needing those educational qualifications! Bullshit wasn't a services' monopoly.

The religious enthusiasm of Kenya days I now find vaguely disquieting but, to keep the record fair, cannot alter at this remove. And no doubt there are comments which would be deemed politically incorrect today. My own views have changed about many things over 60 years but, like it or lump it, this was me in 1955, at least the me of letters home, which tempered some extravagances and omitted some of the grim realities. We were technically on active service and on leaving had a medal to prove it – not that an Eastleigh telephonist faced much danger. There would be few mentions of what lay behind our remarkably free and easy life. I marvel at the innocence of those days, but it was a chosen innocence, that of the aspiring Christian life. We could hardly *not* be aware of other worlds, other lifestyles, other faiths (or lack of them), but they could run off us like soap suds from a shower. God led us – which is splendid for the believer! This is what he/I wrote, and I've had to be very firm about not commenting and arguing with what this young erk proclaimed. Goodness knows what my parents thought sometimes. They were ordinary Church of Scotland members, regular churchgoers, Father an elder; but religion was never a 'big thing' at home. Belief was a private matter.

Whenever any faith becomes militant the result is disastrous yet all the 'Religions of the Books' are urged to proselytise. The Mau Mau was simply another faith/ideology taken to bloody extremes. When in history do we not have such examples? (We hardly lack examples today.) So here are my letters home, warts and all.

With better living conditions, a cleaner climate and better food there were no more boils, something that had plagued my year in Egypt. Camp food would be a source of protest (as will be seen) but there was abundant fruit, and eating out was cheap and excellent. Dinner in the top rank Norfolk Hotel was 5/- (6/- on Christmas Day) and this was for as many courses as one cared to consume. I tended to stick when reaching the curry. One ploy later on was to shoot a tommy (a Thomson's gazelle, not some poor squaddie!) and take it to an Indian restaurant, to be given a full menu for four in exchange. Wildlife was casually abundant still. One morning, Sunday service at St Andrew's Church of Scotland was postponed because a big male lion was sprawled across the entrance – and zebra crossings often had an unnervingly literal reality! There was still a touch of *Out of Africa* in the life of whites (and therefore blacks), but beyond Mau Mau would be Uhuru – Independence – and the long growing up of a new world into today. In 1955 we were still trailing the pioneers with guns and Bible. You could say I was wielding both!

RAF Eastleigh was conveniently just outside Nairobi, 5,496 feet above sea level and only about 50 miles south of the equator. We were always amused at seeing newcomers rush across the airport tarmac to greet waiting relatives or friends and suddenly stop, gasping, in the rarefied air. There was something odd in a landscape which was all higher than Ben Nevis. I once betrayed my background when the rosy snows of Kilimanjaro rose above a morning mist and I let out, 'What a hill!' Someone turned and asked, 'Are you Scottish?' When I said yes he added, 'Thought so. Anyone else would have called that a mountain.'

Accommodation was in a hangar, till – eventually – we had comfortable rooms in large blocks with good facilities (like ready hot showers). There was a kindlier climate, and

much more to do in our free time. The working hours were regular – no guard duties and scarcely onerous – and we were even paid an overseas allowance for living in a country where the cost of living was considerably lower than at home. Pay, however, for rankers, (especially those doing NS) was still a pittance. Of course the background was still the macho posturing which most seemed to need, the continuous effing this and effing that which was both monotonous and boring. There was a certain irony too in all that talk of 'booze and bints' – more imagined than practised, we felt, for this was where we won. We met plenty of nice girls socially, which didn't mean we had designs on going to bed with them. It was strange to be so much in the loutish world of the forces and also so out of it.

HB with his roomy bed-space in the hanger, RAF Eastleigh

Three of us ganged up – the Terrible Three as our Hangar No 3 muckers called us – the other two being John Cates (on the same flight from Aden), and Tony Judd. We also came to have good friends outwith the camp, two in particular whom we called our *civilian attachés*, Ian Buist and Wim Schot. John was a fresh-faced lad with a sweep of unruly hair across his forehead (which would only

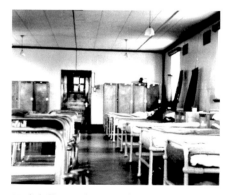

HB's billet, a change after seven months in the hangar

141

'The Terrible Three': Hamish, Tony and John

have been permitted in the RAF), a rather large nose and a passion for *Lorna Doone*, a book he read over and over again. He became a steward for BOAC later, so had many, albeit brief, visits again to Kenya. Tony was taller and dark, with a long, lugubrious face. We must have been a sore trial for the 'doon-sitting hens' of our hangar, the majority who found so little to interest them in or out of the camp. Ian was a tall, gangly colonial official we called Bwana Mkubwi (big boss) and Wim a banker from the Netherlands, just two of many civilians who befriended lads in the forces. We were still in touch 50 years later. A score of other names of fellow servicemen appear in letters and in my photo albums – friends for a while, then postings would whisk them away. These I have largely omitted. The first letter to have survived was in February 1955 – already into the throes of the big Campaign.

2590848 LAC BROWN, H M
Signals PBX, RAF Eastleigh
PO Box 4030
NAIROBI
Kenya
East Africa
4.2.55

Just a short note – written early morning in the caravan in the Jarvis's domain. Many people staying as well as the team itself. This is the third day of the Crusade [it ran 2–13 February] and already there has been great reward. Very busy indeed so don't expect much news from me for the next two weeks, especially as I'm going to take leave to work for the Crusade.

* The campaign had its headquarters in Portal House, with meetings being held in the Rahimtulla and the Memorial Halls in Delamere Avenue. The evangelist was Ken Terhoven, with Roger Voke and Norman Norris completing the team. A Mr Hollanbeck was choir leader (and he also played the violin), a lively character we came to know well.

For Such A Time as this
GOD HAS THE ANSWER

Come
and hear
Ken Terhoven
RECENTLY ASSOCIATED WITH
BILLY GRAHAM
IN THE
GREATER LONDON CRUSADE

Rahimtulla Hall Feb. 2-5   5.30 and 8.30 p.m.
Memorial Hall   ,,   7-13 - 5.30 and 8.30 p.m.
ADMISSION FREE   ALL WELCOME

WATCH for BILLY GRAHAM
in his film Mr. TEXAS

One of the campaign posters that were spread all over Nairobi in 1955

He taught at the American Rift Valley Academy, Kijabe. Headed notepaper and leaflets had the campaign slogan 'For such a time as this GOD HAS THE ANSWER', and posters were displayed everywhere from shop windows to the side of double-decker buses. Perhaps it was as well I was too busy to write much at the time. The crusade began with a service attended by the governor (Sir Evelyn Baring) and the mayor. There had been a preview of the campaign film for the mayor the day before.

7.2.55

Such a lot always on here. I had a huge pile of letters from home today – including the one you baptised in the North Sea at Crail! Is someone going to have the house for July? [Yes.]

It is now 01.30. Night bind. I had a pleasant evening with a Koen Valkoff who is Dutch but fluent in German, French and English, a bit of an intellectual but is nice, a keen hosteller, so we had a hostel-like meal in the huge kitchen of the French house he occupies. Yesterday was day off and in the evening at Ian's we had a hamburger party, which John and I prepared; a great success and the food and games all went with a swing. Ian's brother, Bob, was passing through and goes off tomorrow but I have to sleep (off night bind) so can't join the gang seeing him off.

I received a swimming certificate; no bother at all. I was baking all day Tuesday: éclairs (surprisingly simple). Did I tell you in a Housewife Exhibition here I won a prize for guessing the weight of a cake? On Sunday we saw *Mr Texas* [the campaign film], as there was a big crowd at Bwana's. Friday last was John's birthday. No Crusader Class this Sunday. On Monday our Camp Fellowship is going to have films. I do not know what I could do without these night duties. They let me write letters and study. Letter from Billy Blakey, with whom I went through Square Bashing. He is now married. What is the bee news? How old is the latest Siamese? The Jarvis cat had five kittens – they are much played with by all the forces people.

* Koen was a friend of Ian's but frequently of our expanded company, much of which revolved round Bwana's – Dr Jarvis. The reference to baking came with the need to feed scores of boys at the Sunday Crusader class, boys from the posh schools of the Prince of Wales and

the Duke of York. That became a regular Tuesday challange, if free: turning out hundreds of meringues, éclairs, cakes and the like. All these contacts and activities were an extraordinary contrast to camp life and the PBX work, but we changed from one to the other without any constraint, and this is something which has remained with me ever since: the ability to be whole-heartedly involved with widely different matters at any time. We learned to use every minute, and could never understand most of our fellows on camp. They cursed us, argued with us, and joined in games and swimming pool hours, but few came to life outside camp. Understandable in the Zone – but here, with all Africa at the door?

9.2.55

Last night was a wonderful night. Ken spoke a very quiet, ordinary message yet about 60 people remained behind. His sermons are so full of common sense and plain logic that the appeal must be great. Ken is a tallish man with an intense face well-tanned by the sun. He has had some odd experiences: in the SAAF[88] in the war, and was once a famed dance-leader. His wife, Win, is very sweet. She used to be a nurse – and gives the team their inoculations. Roger Voke is small, moustached, and a bit of a character. The children adore him. Norman I know best, as I work with him in the office. He has an incurable disease (cancer?) but is a great chap, still in his early twenties. I worked on designing two possible posters for the campaign film *Mr Texas*.

Just finishing this off as I want to return the postal order. I am sick of trekking from banks and post offices; they all say it is hopeless, especially as it is made out to PO Deversoir which does not even exist. Can you please change it?

Two Asian lads (17 and 19) have been murdered by Mau Mau just along the road – their wrists slashed and tongues cut out. One yearns for this land. How wonderful, wonderful the world, and yet how terribly man fails it.

---

* At this time the population breakdown for Kenya was 42,000 whites, 131,000 Asian, c. 6 million African. Our gang in the RAF were probably more genned up than most about Mau Mau, but much of what we saw and heard was from official sources, the term for government propaganda, so a bit of background history may be useful.

Most people will have heard of Jomo Kenyatta. In 1927 he became Secretary of KCA (Kenya Central Association), the latest in a line of associations going back to the twenties

---

88 South African Air Force.

hoping to forward some reforms for native people. Failing to get the Legislative Council to listen to grievances he went to lobby in London in 1929 and then remained in London, 1931–1946. In 1932–1934, however, a Land Commission justified the whites' land expropriations. But then, following World War Two, thousands of returning soldiers were not prepared to tolerate the harsh bias of white supremacy. (At home a similar effect after World War One led to the Land Raids in the Highlands and the Hebrides.) Kenyatta became president of KAU (Kenya African Union), the trusted voice for the dispossessed, yet another body in a succession of those promptly banned by the British government. Many tribes were involved, but the Kikuyu were most affected so were dominant.

The main issue was over land (where is it not?) and with some justification: in 1948 about 1.25 million Kikuyu alone were restricted (forced) into 2,000 square miles while 30,000 settlers had 12,000 square miles of land – and that, the best. The labour for the settlers of course came from the dispossessed, who faced endless discriminations: political parties banned, their travels controlled, having to carry identity cards and passbooks, facing forced labour and forbidden to grow coffee … Thousands migrated to Nairobi, where rampant unemployment, poverty and social segregation was the perfect hotbed for trouble. The moderate Kenyatta was sidelined, opening the way for Mau Mau with its turn to violence and the horrors of oath-taking.

In 1950 Kenyatta and six others were arrested and sentenced to seven years' imprisonment. Mau Mau was outlawed. (In 1951 the Gold Coast gained its independence. In South Africa, apartheid was settled official policy.) In 1952 a state of emergency was declared in Kenya. The Lancashire Fusiliers were flown in from the Canal Zone, Sir Evelyn Baring became governor. 1953 saw the establishment of an African Home Guard. Mau Mau attacked white farms, the most notorious in early 1953 being a couple in their early thirties, Ruck, and their six-year-old son, who were hacked to death with pangas, the work of outsider Mau Mau and staff/locals who had been 'oathed'. And in March there was the notorious Lari Massacre. In June General Erskine was flown in and more troops arrived – 11 battalions at one stage. 1954 would see Operation Anvil, which cleared Nairobi of Mau Mau but led to thousands of innocents being arrested, tortured and imprisoned, and whole populations forced into unnatural prison-like villages (villagisation) – draconian actions one would have thought of in line with Stalinistic pogroms. But Anvil broke the back of Mau Mau, which henceforth was mainly restricted to the Aberdare Mountains and Mount Kenya areas. In December 1954 one in eight Kikuyu were being held, with over 71,000 Mau Mau (of whom 8,000 were female). Over the emergency period one in four Kikuyu would have been 'detained' at some time; 1,090 were sent to the gallows. Death statistics (generally reckoned) were: 32 white settlers, 2,000 African civilians, 3,000 African police and soldiers, 50 British troops and a minimum estimate of 50,000 Mau Mau.

Early in 1955, not long after I'd arrived and was rejoicing in the change from the Zone, an amnesty was declared, which even caught Kenya's white population by surprise. Just why it came then is worth noting here. The unlawful killings, collective punishments, property seizures and human rights abuses of the British would only become more generally known half a century later.

The amnesty offered terms to the Mau Mau that if they surrendered they would not be hanged, though possibly detained, and the amnesty also saved security forces from probable prosecution. The offer caused a furore among whites. Humphrey Slade, leader of the *moderate* group in the Legislative Council, wrote, 'This means that men who have killed inoffensive civilians by panga slashing, men who have disembowelled babies before their mothers' eyes, men who have eaten the brains of their human victims, will not even be prosecuted'. Governor Baring would always be looking over his shoulder for settler hotheads, and made some poor decisions as a result.

That was very much what we would read in the papers, but in 1954 there had been a trial for the murder of two Kikuyu farmers which might well show up the incumbent unscrupulous behaviour of the Kenya establishment. The case was brought before Acting Justice Cram, who had presided over many trials and had been the magistrate after the Lari Massacre. He is described as meticulous, moral and non-racist. The two farmers had been taken to the Ruthagathi Home Guard Post (near Nyeri), really an 'interrogation' centre where beatings and torture were used to obtain 'confessions' of Mau Mau connections, the 'guilty' then taken to the local, African, Karatina court where the local chief would pass sentence – usually hefty fines in what Cram described as an elaborate 'extortion racket', to which the British turned a blind eye. In the dock were Muriu Wamai, from the Home Guard post, and five others. Wamai was regarded by the authorities as a stalwart loyalist. The sorry story began on the evening of 18 July 1954.

Shots were heard near the Ruthagathi Home Guard Post, and when the European police officer and DO arrived they heard how Wamai and his men had detected a Mau Mau gang and, in an exchange of fire, had killed two of them. They were congratulated for their effort. But then a different story began to emerge. The two victims were well-known locals with no Mau Mau connections, and they had been detained several days before their deaths. The local schoolmaster explained that, at this time, he too had been beaten up and was aware of these two in the next cell. All the evidence pointed to there having been no battle. The case was handed to the CID, seeing the Kenya police were always desperate not to be seen condemning the Home Guard, something condoned by authority. However a new commissioner of police, Arthur Young, had been appointed by the Colonial Office to tackle the seeming impunity of police and Home Guard actions where the most brutal acts, including killings, were simply being airbrushed away. The Wamai case would be the first brought to court. Before Cram, in December 1954.

The true nature of how suspect Mau Mau were being treated in custody was being exposed but European witnesses (DOs with the Home Guard, the DC, various police officers) all staunchly defended Wamai and his story. Wamai was also accused of faking logbook entries and, when directly accused of murder, broke down. Cram called a recess. Then the true story came out. The two farmers, having refused to confess Mau Mau oath-taking over three days of torture, were simply taken out into the bush and shot by Wamai. His patrol then fired off shots to simulate a clash with Mau Mau.

In his defence, he produced the well-known 'I was just doing what I was told' plea; the chief and the British officers were all part of the system. He had told the chief and local DO (Richmond) what had happened but had been ordered to cover up the truth and to forge the log book entries. One chief and five British officers were apparently complicit in misleading the court. Cram's judgement (32 pages of it) was stern, perhaps intemperate, and he found all the accused guilty, Wamai to be hanged, the others given prison terms, with hard labour.

The governor, Baring, was shocked. Not by the truth, but at the damage the criticism would do. An embargo was placed on the judgement, for Cram had, in effect, accused the administration of being complicit in illegal detentions, torture and extortion. Young resigned in disgust that officialdom (right to the top) condoned such matters, his letter reporting to London too explosive to be made public. Baring then used the excuse of the amnesty to pardon Wamai's convictions telling London it was 'necessary for the morale of the African security forces' (and their white overlords who were in danger of being shown up). An enquiry into the Karatina court – and others – was set up, which dragged on and did little in the end. Efforts were made to blacken Cram's reputation. But that is how these things are done. I'm sure Cram was only too pleased to move on to a seven-year stint as a judge in today's Malawi and then retire to Scotland. Much of this grim history I would only learn a lifetime later.[89] There was an odd personal connection, described later.

In 2009 five octogenarian survivors of the camps brought a claim against the British government. They had all suffered sexual abuse, two had been castrated and one had been beaten unconscious at the notorious Hola camp in an incident when 11 others *died* from their beatings (60 others were injured), simply for refusing to work. The report on this reached the UK Parliament, and there were strong words from Labour's Barbara Castle – and the Tory Enoch Powell! Eventually, in 2012, the British government would pay out reparations of £20 million to be divided among the, by then, 5,000 survivors. Did anyone even notice?

By one of those odd coincidences, while I was reading these letters in 2004 I saw a *Scotsman* obituary of Paul Ngei, one of so-called Magnificent Six Mau Mau who with Kenyatta, freed from detention, would go on to help govern independent Kenya. He 'accumulated' thereafter a handsome Nairobi property, a 3,000-hectare ranch and a seaside home at Malindi; entered Parliament by having its rules changed so he could; became immensely rich (he boasted of having 30 Savile Row suits); and was a noted philanderer who would leave five wives and unknown numbers of children. In 1971 he took a Mercedes for a test drive, and it was still outside his house 30 years on, not paid for and the company too afraid to reclaim it.

God save Africa.

---

89 With the publication of David Anderson's *Histories of the Hanged*, 2005.

10.2.55

Just a hurried note before the evening meetings begin. I had a rest from the Campaign Office this afternoon and spent most of the time baking cream cones and other tasty things. Life is very full. These last few days have taught me a lot. Our theme song is 'God has the answer'; a catchy tune and the city is humming it everywhere. Ken Terhoven has put me in charge of the Campaign Office now, so that Norman can concentrate fully on his job in the team. This is a big responsibility [I was not yet 20], as it entails quite a lot of arranging things and seeing to all that crops up. I work from eight till four and then change into white shirt and tie which is the choir's dress. Ken takes the meeting at 5.30pm and we have singing, solos etc. Yesterday the Bishop of Mombasa was there, giving his help; two nights ago the C of S Moderator came. At the end of his address Ken makes an appeal, and those of us who have been trained to do so talk to those who respond.

I feel RAF Eastleigh needs a new Camp Fellowship. I have had some talks with the Padre, whose name is Must, but he says that he only has nine months to do and doesn't feel up to starting anything! But nevertheless to go ahead. Without that permission I would not do anything, but it does seem a bit odd that he whose job is the Spiritual welfare of the Camp, should be so seldom seen on it.

To continue the programme, though, the next meeting is at 8.30pm and is the showing of the Billy Graham film *Mr Texas* (colour). He is amazing to our ideas of a preacher. I begin to like him now that I have seen him about twice a night for a week. He was nothing like that in London, but there, there, Americans … ! The choir leader is American. He's a scream. Teaches the children of the American missionaries. Last night we were amazed to see the result of the film; it was the hard-headed business men who answered its appeal.

The weather has been very wet and quite wrong for the driest month of the year, but is now warm and sunny and so beautiful. Our hangar floods! A lot of discontents. Two admitted, well, boasted, they were Teddy Boys so I wrote a skit, the 'Teddy Boys' Picnic', and we serenaded them. Got a laugh.

17.2.55

The main bit of the Campaign is over but now comes the hardest bit of all perhaps – the follow-up and, here, the beginning of the Camp Fellowship. Our final Rally in the Services Stadium was packed out, with over 2,000 people there, the papers said. I think one of the greatest talks I have ever heard was one given by a Dr (Divinity) Bob Pearce who is an

American – but speaks very good English! At the Rally Ken mentioned that he was here and would be willing to address the keen Christians of town and forces. For such short notice they chose Bwana's house as everyone knows where it is. The hut was packed and many sat outside the doors and windows to hear. He spoke for over an hour and a half and nobody was left untouched. He spoke about the Christian Church in Korea which has been his care and love since the turn of the century. It was tragic in some ways and in many ways akin to the troubles that we have here. Would we had more men with his behaving belief …

Since I last wrote I have had an experience of the bloodiness of beliefs – Mau Mau – which will be a memory for ever. At the Athi River Detention Camp we stood before a thousand of them – and what an overpowering feeling of hatred! The atmosphere was nearly overwhelming but the result was many of them weeping openly. The team is to have another weekend there. It made a great impression on the police people; in fact all through the Campaign there has been a steady stream of them seeking to know that 'God has the answer'. Albert Schweitzer's words at Oslo still ring in my head, and Ken's messages have had a very similar ring. We must be right with ourselves before we try to help the rest of the world. [I would visit the Athi River camp once again – see letter of 11.7.55.]

The second experience was a look through the 'secret' photos the government have of Mau Mau victims. I felt sick, and Ken says he will never look at them again. They were really heart-rending: there was one of a little trike and by it lay a five-year old Kikuyu child as though asleep. The photo looked all right until you looked closer and saw that the pretty young child had no head. There was another of a baby which had been cut in half and lay in indescribable horror. Enough! How can man do such things? It is no excuse to say they are just a lot of savages. They are not. There are some very fine Kikuyu – I can think of three in Sally's! [A sally of my own: Sally's was St Salvator's, the residential hall of St Andrews University which brother Ian had occupied.] Maybe what I once said [as a ten-year-old refugee in South Africa] about wanting to be a 'man who stops wars' when I grew up is to be nearer than I thought. Perhaps, in a small way, I can do my piece towards peace.

Thank you very much for the breeches. They were waiting for me when I came back off leave the other day. I went right back on watch and am now almost senior operator again. We hope for four more operators soon. Quite a complicated job here but not bad, and plenty of free time and few parades, no guards and none of the usual binds of the Airman. Shows how really awful the Zone was.

This is Thursday. In the afternoon I went shopping for many things, including stuff for my Sunday School Class. Tomorrow I have a Children's Guild to talk to and after that a Committee Meeting of our New Camp Fellowship, which is now my responsibility. You need the wisdom of Solomon all right. We had a good beginning on Monday. Padre was there, which was a change. Let's hope that he is going to come to life. I like him. Tomorrow I have a washing in the morning and an afternoon in the Campaign Office in town. Saturday evening I am out, and then on the switchboard all night. Sunday I'm to take the Camp children's Church as Padre is on leave, and then dash in to Nairobi Chapel, then lunch with the Jarvis crowd and Crusader class. Tea. Cathedral at six to meet a young lad from the Campaign. Singsong and bed. I actually work Monday! Tuesday I have my first driving lesson with my Dutch pal Wim. So it goes on. Last weekend I met Laurie Campbell from the African Alliance High School at Kikuyu – whom I knew at home. He also welcomes forces folk to his home. A good friend.

---

* This may have been the time when a selection of photos of Mau Mau victims, along with a copy of their oaths and ceremonies, was compiled and sent to every Member of Parliament at Westminster. There had been a certain amount of critical questioning in the House. I was to see the photos of another murderous attack at Lari back in March 1953, and helped a friend in the photography department with his printing. I even managed a flight where photography was the reason for the exercise – not, alas, over the summit of Kilimanjaro when the shots of the crater were taken which end this book.

Most Kikuyu had no sympathy for the Mau Mau, and were the main sufferers as a result: nearly 2,000 of them would be panga-ed, disembowelled, buried alive … Captured Mau Mau would sometimes be brutally treated in return. Perhaps understandably – but there were many other factors at work, from tribal displacements to protection rackets, poverty and bribery, all creating a picture the white authorities could hardly untangle, far less control. When Operation Anvil in 1954 finally broke Mau Mau in the city this was done with a heavy hammer, and court proceedings of a questionable nature followed (for example, an accusation alone, without evidence, could see people hang.)

The Christian churches were to see many devoted servants swept up and wrongly classified as hardcore Mau Mau. The Scottish minister, the Revd David Steel, shocked his congregation by revealing the glaring shortcomings and injustices. The majority of whites didn't want to know, and the vociferous were for hanging on every possible opportunity. Possession of a firearm held a death sentence – how easy to plant some ammunition on a rival or one resisting oath-taking, shop them, and see them hanged.

Lari, unsurprisingly, is the most remembered atrocity, used almost as a shorthand to picture Mau Mau. Lari was a scatter of 15 *shambas*[90] built of mud and wattle, set among mealie fields (pyrethrum the main cash crop), about 30 miles north of Nairobi, with many trading and commercial enterprises. Many people had been evicted from Tigoni on government orders and settled in Lari. Many, including the two leading statesmen, Makimei and Wakahangare, were Catholics, but the Episcopal Church Missionary Society and the Africa Inland Mission were also present, the area perhaps 40 per cent Christian.

---

90 Homesteads, small farms.

Ramifications ran through the whole complex loyalties of society; there were many squatters evicted from white farms; many dispossessed; something of a not-always-benevolent Mafia and also riddled with secret oathers and Mau Mau sympathisers. What happened showed an action planned in detail, the killing not indiscriminate but aimed at the chiefs and committed loyalists.

Immediately beforehand, a party of 83 Mau Mau had raided the police post at Naivasha (down in the Rift Valley) to release 173 Mau Mau detainees and go off with a large quantity of weapons and ammunition, which drew away certain Home Guard forces. The day before, too, a platoon of the Kenya African Rifles (KAR) had been withdrawn from the Lari area. Some have suggested these movements were planned by the Mau Mau, but most likely they were handed helpful coincidences. What was no coincidence, however, was the Lari Home Guard being lured away at night following the discovery of the mutilated body of a local loyalist nailed to a tree by a busy path. Reaching this crime scene in an hour, the guards then became aware of the sky alight with flames behind them – from Lari. Something like 1,000 Mau Mau in large gangs (some up to 100) had attacked the scattered settlement, with the homes of specific victims picked out. Homesteads were bound round with ropes and the thatch roofs set on fire. Those who managed to fight their way out were butchered by pangas, other thrown back into the flames. All the cattle were hamstrung. Over 80 people, mostly women and children, were killed and 50 left horribly wounded. Chief Makimei's home was protected by a palisade and attackers were held off. Chief Wakahangari was not so lucky: a 200-strong party targeted his home and he tried to fight, but was hacked to pieces, the pieces carried off for unmentionable rituals and only a bloody torso left. Another chief's youngest wife watched her infant decapitated and the blade then licked. Many Home Guard homes were also attacked. By the time the Home Guard returned, the perpetrators were taking off, so were immediately pursued by the enraged guard and other Home Guards, the police, Kenya Police Reserve and some under the supervision of European commanders. What followed was a second, largely indiscriminate, massacre, vengeance gone mad. Anyone suspected of Mau Mau sympathies was shot or killed, and not a few local scores were settled. About 200 were killed. It took days to gather the bodies.

Suspects of the Lari attack were rounded up and held in an overcrowded, rapidly constructed barbed-wire enclosure with little food and no sanitation, where they were subjected to systematic beatings and abuse in attempts to obtain confessions. Some of the wounded, traumatised women were pressured into naming their attackers – as if they could. Cram, brought in to attest these extra-judicial statements, found evidence of witnesses being severely mistreated. Eventually, over 300 suspects gave confessions of guilt, often after brutal treatment and 'evidence' from unreliable witnesses. The coercion, mistreatment and disregard for lawful procedures was not mentioned at the 19 trials that over the months would lead to 72 being hanged. The government made sure the second vicious massacre at Lari was hushed up. Lari was good for propaganda.

18.2.55

How is Gran keeping? It must have made her sad to lose her old pal Mrs Green. She was a nice old biddie. All these people dying, alterations at home and changes in town and school – I'll hardly know Dollar when I see it again. I've quite a few friends at St Andrews University. One of my girl friends here goes up to St Andrews soon to study medicine. Her name is Alison – a Mackay. Her father is a doctor and the three of us rag anyone from south of the border. Lots of bonnie lasses here. Jarvis girls too.

25.2.55

You and your snow. In all my RAF travels I will now only have one wet season (no cold ones at all) – and that comes in a month or so. It rained last night and then we had those very heavy rains at the start of the Campaign. So locals say it is a remarkably *green* year. I find the heat here suits me fine and the altitude makes life quite bracing. And the great open spaces: hills and plains, sky and freedom, they are all so big and open and wonder-full.

What is so good about all this travelling is that I learn to appreciate so many different kinds of country, yet I become more and more Scottish – especially when another lad, nicknamed 'Haggis', and Alison and I are confronted by a couple of dozen Sassenachs up at Bwana's. We, for the sake of argument, become vocal nationalists. The last baking day I wrote a large E I R in icing on one of my chocolate sponges. Eggs for Bwana's, by the way, are bought by the 30 dozen, and 500 small cakes a week are produced as well as innumerable big ones and all kinds of goodies. The two dogs are great pals of mine, ditto cats, seven kittens, budgies, chickens, tortoise, doves, chameleon, stick-insects and other creepy-crawly things. Just like home, only more so. Luckily no *dudus* (poochies)[91] in our beds now. That was a Zone horror. My typewriter is needed so must stop. Time for a *kahawa* (coffee).

LATER. Did you hear of that bomber crash on the news? I was on duty at the time so was the first on camp to hear of it in all its horror. Really tragic. A pal of mine (Photographic Section) was nearly on it! Funeral tonight. Made for a very hectic shift on the board.

When I came on duty this afternoon the first thing that happened was the crash of another of our kites: a wee one which flew bang into the side of the Rift Valley. The plane was completely burnt out but both men were lucky and are alive, though with broken bones.

---

91 *Dudu* was the local word for any creepy-crawly. In the family we used the more Eastern *poochie*. Fleacht is Scots for flea. All good onomatopoeic words.

That big crash was a real tragedy – not only were six crew killed but several women and children on the ground were hit or burnt to death in their huts.

A while ago Wim and I were up in the Ngong[92] Hills seeing two friends of his, and had a very pleasant night chatting on art, religion and music. They are in a cottage (just like Wim's) and there is a big view of the hills and forests. We left in great spirits with a call to return soon, then this morning Wim phoned to say that one of the two had gone into town last night, had too much to drink and had shot himself in the head. Now I have just had another call to say that he is conscious but that if he lives he will be blind. Neville Price. Sad. You can imagine how we feel. Koen, his pal, is quite bewildered. Bwana Jarvis is the Surgeon, so that is a good thing.

Thank you very much for the cheque. I'll try and cash it tomorrow. On Wednesday I am out to lunch with a lad who was at the Southend VPS Camp in 1952; he had my address from a mutual friend. He is in Nairobi for a Vet Conference and lives up at Nanyuki. Time is just flying by. Kenya is winning my heart away! Ian is going East is he? I'm glad it is not right away.

---

* The crash – of a Lincoln bomber – hit the corner of the Githunguri police post, destroying several huts (and killing the crew). My photographic friend later gave me the photo taken from the air.

1.3.55

The Githinguri Police Post, with the wrecked huts (top right) from the Lincoln crash

Yesterday morning we saw Ken Terhoven off to Durban from the Airport on the other side of the drome, then Tony and I were given a lift into town where I went and paid for a Provisional Licence. We spent the afternoon in the big [MacMillan] library after a very nice lunch. At five we collected Wim from his bank, then picked up a pal of his who has just come out – Karl – and then I drove out to the Game Park. I drove for three hours and we went right down to the place where we saw hippos and crocs. Coming back it was dark, which was a bigger thrill. I would often

92 Pron. ung-*gong.*

pull to a frantic stop in the middle of a herd of zebra or wildebeest or gazelles which had been blinded by the lights. So we saw them as close as to touch.

A rushed dinner at Wim's and then to Camp for the Fellowship. The Committee is a good choice and I feel we can do something now. Tomorrow I will tell the Padre the news; he is quite happy – as long as he is not asked to do anything! (I wonder what our Deversoir Padre would say to that.) He is a very pleasant man, though. I have had some official swimming. I was in the water for an hour, and it is really pleasant without Egypt's salt to choke one. But I miss the lake, the Zone's one touch of magic. I'd saved a dead snake (28 inches long) to show everyone in the hangar, but it was not really appreciated: only one or two would actually touch it and a couple made a quick exit. People!

<hr />

7.3.55

Yesterday was one of those days that will never be forgotten. We went on safari (7 of us in two cars) to the Rift Valley Academy at Kijabe. It is part of the Africa Inland Mission area (they have 2,000 acres all told) and the school is 90% American. A nicer lot of folk you will never meet anywhere. Mr Hollanbeck looked after us. The school looks over one of the most stunning views in the world: nearly 8,000 feet up and, below, the great Rift Valley, and away on the other side a steep wall of hills. As the evening shadows and mists were falling I could see it as Scotland, only more so. One feels a trespasser. Yet two hours' walk away were the Lari Massacres, and down at the far end an old chief was butchered. The school is miles off the main road along a narrow track. We felt a bit nervous going back in the dark – especially as we were unarmed. The school and mission has had no trouble and there are 2,000 Africans in the various schools. They are doing a fine bit of work. The American President, Roosevelt, visited Kijabe in 1909. (That's a bit of a non-sequitur!)

Asante sana[93] for the regular letters – very welcome. Glad to hear the various ailments are being defeated. My driving is coming along. A very pleasant evening with friends, just doing nothing but listening to wonderful music. Thanks for snowdrops update. No; singles don't sometimes turn into doubles. David could do a scientific test on some down the path banks to check! Stamps here are for Kenya, Uganda and Tanganyika, pictorial ones like Cyprus, so I'll send D a set. Are there any very African things that I can bring home for presents? If fragile I can carry something in the Baby. [a big briefcase]. I keep some of my books in the PBX to save lugging them about in the Baby – and they are seldom looked at by others, even on night binds. But now all the camp is phoning to book Cinema seats so I must help my mucker on the board.

<hr />

93 Thank you very much.

* St Andrew's Church of Scotland was a large, newish granite building with a bold tower and arcades, and reached by a flight of steps up to a porch. A few elders stood in the porch and handed out hymn books as the congregation filed in. We had with us my big briefcase, the Baby, and one Sunday, as we passed this solemn group, Tony turned to me and asked, all too audibly, 'Did you remember to put the Baby in the boot, Hamish?' We received some very odd looks.

10.3.55

Today has been a day off and a happy one. From early morning till the sun set we were at the pool – a big one with high diving boards. I can now swim a length under water; first time was by mistake and I was so surprised I did it again just to 'mak siccar'. I got sunburnt so I'm a pinker Brown. At 8.15pm a group of us sat down to a Bible Reading. Some left, some came, but five sat for the whole two hours that we spent reading – right through the gospel of John. We all found it quite thrilling.

NEXT DAY. I have just come for night duty and had better get this finished and posted. Been out all evening with Wim and dined at his abode with all the other Dutch lads from his Bank. They are a refreshing lot and good company. We spent most of the time just talking and looking at books and photos and playing good records. That was after I had had a lesson by driving away into the beautiful Ngong Hills again, a green and crumpled landscape that reminded me of the Eildons. We stopped on top of a ridge and there below

The Ngong Hills

us we saw Kenya fall asleep in the deep, singing dusk. Some deer came out and wandered cautiously by. You could see their eyes glinting in the last splashes of the sun. My driving is good enough to pass, Wim says.

Our pal Neville is to be out of hospital next week and will go the UK – but he wants to return. Kenya is like that. He will be blind, but he and his wife are together again, so good came out of the sad.

---

* On one occasion, walking in what must have been the Ngong Hills, I'd left the others at a picnic briefly and was following a rake along a scrubby crest when a lion stepped out not far ahead. I was away in a daydream and the situation didn't dawn on me at once so I kept on walking. The lion plunged into the bushes and was gone. That woke me! I then scarpered back pdq[94] the way I'd come. Had I stopped at once on seeing him, the lion might have behaved differently, but the encounter certainly registered. (Years later I came over the hills from Ballachulish and, entering forest, suddenly heard the sharp sort of grunting cough a lion made when strolling along. The hairs on my neck stood on end! Then I laughed. There were no free-range lions in Argyll. Just roe deer.) The Ngong Hills would become one of our best-loved places, and visited frequently. Don't just take my word for its allure. The renowned Danish author Karen Blixen said the hills 'are among the most beautiful in the world'.

One or two lads in the hangar never left camp and seldom went further than the NAAFI. There were unimagined dangers out there! ('Lions and all that.') One night we three were discussing going for a dander in the moonlight before turning in when a voice from a neighbouring bed-space said, 'You wouldn't fucking get me going fucking out at night. I mean, a fucking lion might jump you.'

16.3.55

I seem to write on every night duty. Do send on the *Dollar Magazine* with my Cyprus article. I am glad it has appeared. There was another prang here this morning, and it was another miracle of life preserved. A civvy Dakota (Italian) took off, developed engine trouble, and limped back, could not quite make it and came down short of the runway. The plane was badly smashed yet there were only minor injuries to the passengers. There were

---

94 Pretty damn quick.

many VIPs aboard. Oh boy! The fun we had on the boards trying to deal with the Italians who could not speak English.

A pal, Dennis Bedson, and I went up to the Jarvis's house. Mrs was out, but Alison Mackay was there. We baked all morning and then after a cold lunch I had to dash off for work. Dennis did not come back till *chakula*[95] time, and had had the time of his life playing the piano for the Mem Sahib. Tomorrow I am off nights and shall sleep the morning then after tea Wim is taking me to Bahati where he has started a weekly Bible Study with the Africans, some truly fine people. (Not that we forget the Mau Mau! They broke into the Cathedral the other night.)

Yesterday I drove Dennis and Wim in Wim's car to the Park, the Royal Nairobi Game Park in full. He had a remarkable first trip: 41 giraffe, hippos, croc, zebra, all the 'beests and gazelles and a pride of *simba*[96] (male, female and six almost full-grown cubs). One of the cubs had a good chew at the front mudguard and the other made a snarling lunge once. We also ended up (on foot) in the middle of a moving crowd of baboons. That scared us. They have short tempers and poisonous teeth. We had dinner with Wim and then home – if you can call this hangar that. We found one lad in tears. They keep telling us their woes so, with what I hear when monitoring calls to Britain, I feel like I'm sometimes in a confessional. Some pathetic lads are given a hard time.

Bill Blakey is now in Co. Antrim, an auxiliary squadron, so most flying is done at weekends, so he has 'heathenish weekends' on Tuesdays/Wednesdays. There are two Meteors and ten Vampires, all 'flogged to death'. His technical rank is Junior Technician. Fits wireless on planes.

---

* Night duty was just that – overnight – so it was an excellent time to write letters, to study, read, brew-up, and prepare for our many activities. The world fell blessedly quiet then, too, unlike in the hangar, with its cross-section of humanity. The lad in tears was 'super-homesick' and was to be sent back to the UK. Most hated being abroad and seemed unable to seize its opportunities. 'Abroad' panicked some and drove far too many to drink, and our exuberant group of Christians were often enough to hear private woes and be of help. To us, that *was* Christianity working; belief behaving.

---

95 Meal.
96 Lion.

03.00, 19.3.55

Dear Ian,

Jambo! So you are now planning to abscond overseas again. You should come out here – I have seen nowhere like this country: *mzuri sana* (very good) as I was told by an experienced colonist of five! It really is, though, and there is no place I would more readily settle down in – if I ever settle down. Maw says you will go off whenever there is a job gap. You seem to have enjoyed your National Service days. It's a bit what you make of it. This is a mess as it is my thirteenth letter tonight and my poor fingers and eyes are on strike. I'd better stop typing and make a cup of tea. I'm off at eight. My days of so-called 'rest' are every two days now – the other days I work for the RAF! Kenya is great fun, a marvellous freedom after the Zone prison.

I can now drive a car with a reasonable amount of safety for everyone. There have been some trips up country. Once a crowd of us got stuck in the Mau Mau forests when the front car went on fire. On a one-track road. Only a mile or two from the Lari Massacre area. With a 2,000-foot drop on one side. With no arms. We were quite glad to move again. That was not reported home! Actually the Mau Mau risk is becoming slight now. I get a medal for being here, you know. But still Maw always ends letters by saying to 'keep away from the Mau Mau', or now it's 'Please drive carefully'. It's as well she does not see the roads here. They have one or two actually tarred in the city, the rest are *murram*: murderous, hard dirt tracks. Now I must stop and have a drink. The last call was about three hours ago, but there has to be someone on the exchange I suppose.

---

* Ian was eventually posted to Hong Kong and worked there all his days for ICI. He also kept up his army interests in the local volunteer force. He and his wife Valerie had two boys. David eventually returned to teach out his days at Dollar, and once his three boys were away his wife Marina became a reverend! The five nephews started off as engineer, piano tuner, trainee theatre director, fencing coach, and nautical man (at the time of writing, crossing the Atlantic under sail).

A great deal was done to try and restore some of the Mau Mau activists – who, after all, had been thoroughly intimidated and brainwashed into that evil. Slowly the tide turned. But in many areas the unaffected Kikuyu had had to move to huge defended encampments (villagization) as the risk on solitary farms was too great. One token of how things were

The interior of the Rift Valley church built by Italian prisoners in World War Two

changing were notices beside the small Italian chapel on the escarpment road of the Rift Valley. I'd photographed the notice soon after arriving in Kenya: 'WARNING. It is most dangerous to picnic in this area because of terrorist gangs.' A later photograph declared: 'Terrorists. Beware armed persons sightseeing.'

The Kirk last Sunday morning had another Christening Service – half a dozen bairns and a nice quiet lot (last time, *five* yelled the whole time). Wim and I then went up to Kikuyu to the C of S Mission.

MacPherson couple. Oldish and not too active, as the Church is well founded and run by African Pastors. They are in Revival at this present time. We came at the end of the Morning Service, at which Norman Norris of the Campaign had been preaching – for one hour – to 3,000 people. They were all streaming out as we rolled up in the wee car. Norman gave me a great welcome and I was delighted to see him too. We had a very pleasant lunch together. After an hour it was to the Church again. The Church of the Torch it is called, and its name has gone all round the world. We saw why. They do not go home after Morning Service – if they had come a dozen miles they cannot, they picnic and then go back to church and the whole afternoon is there spent in singing and prayer and many of them speak – speak with real power. It was all in Kikuyu and run by one of the Pastors. People just kept coming and coming in an endless stream. The young chief came with his armed escort, and in doing so runs real risk. This is Mau Mau land. It is also some of the most beautiful of all. The hills go rolling to the cloudy horizons. 'Rains soon' the constant talk.

Our Neville Price who shot himself goes home soon. Doug [Calcott, a doctor who lived at Bwana's] was going to see him last night. Had a very cheerful supper where I sat with a chap who is going out to Singapore to the CIM[97] Language School. I was able to give him an address in Aden, where he has a weekend. I found a copy of H V Morton's *In the Steps of the Master* in town. I'd browsed through it in Jerusalem, and it's a very readable 'historical geography'. It was published the year I was born! I don't know what I'd do without the night hours. I think a laze by the pool is called for this afternoon. I'm an excellent brown Brown now, having taken it *polé polé* (slowly).

PS. The Rains began last night. A thunder plump. My bed is surrounded by water as a result.

---

97 China Inland Mission.

4.4.55

Enclosed is another cutting. It's a great old fuss, and I hope the ringleaders cut it out. I don't want any restrictions and had nothing to do with it, though the complaint about food is justified and all the usual channels of complaint failed to produce much improvement. The shindig affects me little as we have *chakula* out with friends half the time. Kenya overflows with good produce. So why doesn't the RAF shop local? Real potatoes must cost less than shipping out the dehydrated POM. Daft!

Yesterday at Evensong, and Dinner at Bwana's. Roger Voke and wife Zena came and he gave another terrific talk after the usual sing song. Tonight I will hear the first of four talks on the Bible in the CMS[98] House Chapel. Church House is the tallest building in Nairobi. Sleep tomorrow morning and then Wim is picking me up at 5, and the whole evening will be spent listening to the Matthew Passion. Looking ahead, we've an invitation to Mombasa by a Scots minister based there. Five of us to go. Is D still keen on stamps? If so I could send a set on an envelope for him, as I did from Aden. Heavy rain twice a day but hot and fresh.

---

* The cutting in the *East African Standard* read, '800 RAF men boycott meals at Eastleigh. Second protest in six months … they attended breakfast because it is an offence to miss the Queen's First Parade, but they ate their midday and evening meals in the NAAFI.' An earlier strike in October had coincided with the visit to Nairobi of the colonial secretary, Lennox-Boyd, which had a similar slogan to this one painted along the Mess balcony wall. After Christmas food deteriorated again. The RAF police confiscated a spool of film showing the notice. 'Many of the airmen are National Servicemen who complain it costs 4/- a day to eat in the NAAFI, "a big hole" in their pay. They described the food as "stuff you would not serve to dogs" – watery eggs, lumpy porridge, stale meat, corned beef and dehydrated potato, which they claimed was their main diet … The matter is being investigated.' The first of April seemed the appropriate day for 'WE WANT FOOD FIT TO EAT' to appear on the Mess wall. I successfully photographed it. There were complaints too about some of us being accommodated in a hangar – which, with the floor often flooded and the noise of aircraft movements just outside, were equally valid.

---

98 Church Missionary Society.

8.4.55

We have been to the Hotel up at Limuru, which is 7,374 feet above sea level; we motored from the Rift Valley. The Brackenhurst is a wonderful old timber-ceilinged building with a view of hundreds of miles of falling hills and endless plains. A perfect evening. John and I went as the guests of an actor chap, Kenneth Mason, wartime RAF. And now Ian Buist, who is in the Kirk choir, has invited Tony and I to a safari to Machakos. None of us have been there, so a new direction and a new tribe.

The *Matthew Passion* thrilled me. I was a wee bit apprehensive about hours of solid music (sitting on a brass coal-scuttle) after having been on the go for 30 hours, but it was a great joy and I loved every note. The German Consul thought I did, too, for he asked Wim who the young lad was who looked so happy at the music. The Germans were a very pleasant little crowd. When they left they all lined up, shaking hands – and bowed. Wim drove me home at 5 to 12. Liberty expires at midnight! Now it is Good Friday, and I am at work. And Sunday too! And there is no compensation to watch-keepers as to others. We just miss the holiday.

The *Dollar Magazine* came. Mixed feelings on the Article. The more personal touches have all been left out and just the dry history left. A pity. And the title, from *Othello,* was not mentioned as such.

Father, in his usual brief note in a Mother's letter, mentioned many people thinking my effort 'first class', including Hughes, the minister and Bell, the school rector, Mrs Jones and 'Miss Wilson (the lame one) who stopped me in the street'. She had been my friendly, inspiring teacher in the junior school, and we still kept in touch. I had sent her a collection of pressed flowers from Cyprus. The magazine was edited by 'Tec' Cordiner, my one-time English teacher. I quite like a set work, and could romp through it and then get up to mischief. He, spotting this likelihood, would come and place an open book on my desk with 'Read that.' I can still recall one particular thrill when coming on Byron's stanzas beginning 'The Isles of Greece! The Isles of Greece …' Mrs Jones was mother of my Dollar girl friend of long standing, and our two families had become friendly. She also wrote to me periodically.

Interesting to hear old Warhorse Churchill has resigned as PM. Eden looks a droopy sort of dog compared to the Bulldog. [Little could we have foreseen his Suez invasion a year on.]

LATER. Easter here has been a non-event for me. The hangar is a mess, with most of the lads on a spree. Thank goodness I have been at the PBX most of the time. Earlier, I had one long day – we were on safari, the biggest run yet: to the Rift Valley and down 2,000 feet to the plain below. Some rift of a valley! In the middle is an old volcano, Mt Longonot, which looks like the Buachaille as you cross the Moor of Rannoch. We drove up to the shoulder, and then far below was Lake Naivasha. The Aberdares were in the distance, and on the other side the wall of the Rift was hung with dark clouds. Our safari was round the lake. In the long grass the air became full of bright butterflies – blossoms on a breeze. We saw spoonbills.

We stopped on the way home, and watched the sunset at the Brackenhurst Hotel. We had drinks by a wood fire, a homely touch. We had dinner at Ian Buist's flat; a classics and music man. [Winchester and Oxford.] He calls his car Fabius – a Consul. Ooh! Another pun: Why are the bees going on strike? For shorter flowers and more honey. Ian's is a perfect bachelor's flat, and we passed a pleasant evening. Looked at each other's photo albums and books, and ended on a philosophical discussion which Tony avoided by reading *Don Camillo* and John by reading music. Exchange of books on loan followed at the hangar. I like the hangar. My bed, a chair, and a huge cupboard is all I have. All I need, as I find it easy to manage. Still dry, has been for a spell so that even the Game Park has reopened. In the rains the roads are impassable, quite impossible: with mud, *earth* mud, unlike the Zone's.

---

* On puns, I think my favourite has to be the play upon the words 'Here's looking at you, kid' from the film *Casablanca*. One Alex Bellos wrote a history of early geometry and titled it *Here's Looking at Euclid*.

Ian Buist rather deserved our 'civilian attaché' moniker as he was a Civil Servant seconded to Kenya for a couple of years. He was often called Lofty as he was well over six foot. Ian played the organ regularly, went to Scottish country dancing and of course moved in the colonial admin circles far removed from our humble lives. He had CHG, OBE after his name. Following a game park visit he'd be donning dinner jacket and bow tie for some classy 'do' while we returned to graft for the RAF. When he drove into camp the police at the gate jumped to attention and saluted – amusing us when we happened to be on board.

Ian wrote letters home, of course, and many of these from Kenya days survived; the civil service training no doubt. He has looked out those where we did things together so I'll quote these periodically. In one letter he mentioned trying to set up a Classical Association. He therefore took an advert, in Latin, to the local newspaper, the *East African Standard*, where it was rejected as they did 'not allow adverts in French'! In a later letter, with the association meeting regularly, Ian was to write home:

During the evening of the Classical Association we constituted ourselves properly and elected Humphrey Slade as President – he is a lawyer and member of Leg. Co. (Legislative Council) – a very nice chap – and Michael Blundell's chief political opponent. At the moment we are an 'unlawful society' and as such liable to seven years' imprisonment – so have to get ourselves registered.

Ian's servant had not returned from leave: 'He was a police secret agent and had recently been rewarded. Of course they [Mau Mau] may have got him by now.' Ian, too, was about to vacate his flat, which involved all of us helping the move. The same letter, with this mix of the serious and the light-hearted, told of an Old Wykehamist dinner and, the governor being absent, Ian had to, in the course of the meal, write a poem in Latin regretting his absence. Also absent was a Kenya timber baron, Colonel Ewart Grogan, whom Ian noted was 'now 80, and in 1900 had walked the 4,500 miles from Cape to Cairo, the first to do so'. Apparently, the main reason for this feat was to impress the father of the girl he hoped to marry!

16.4.55

I sent off a photo last night to show my domain in the hangar. I have since moved to be with pals John and Tony. Tony had slept next to me but was moved to a proper dorm in a block – and hated it! – so came back. The other night John, Ian Buist and I went to a great modern Indian Cinema and saw the French prize-winning *Monsieur Hulot's Holiday*. We laughed the whole time. The night before, Ken Mason, of the Donovan Moule Players, kept theatre seats for five of us and we saw, and enjoyed Agatha Christie's *The Mousetrap*. (Opened in London 25.11.52 and still running!). Tiny theatre, like the Byre in St Andrews, and a very lively

Sourd-sellers at the market at Machakos

performance. Ian, Wim, Tony, John and I were the party. We went there after a hilarious pancake party at Ian's – the last one tossed landed right in the bin. Earlier, we had the run to the Wakamba area and the huge, exciting Machakos market. We dropped in on a cousin of Ian's at Thika. There were waterfalls there [Chania and Thika falls] – a most unusual sight! We caught a big snake and fed it frogs. We also fed ourselves, dogs, kitten and mongoose! We saw bustards and an ugly marabou stork. Argued on philosophy again over supper in the flat, and had a very pleasant time. Left him some of my more provoking writings for when we next meet. Enclosed here a photo of the Ngong Hills and one of a lion I took.

---

* Ken Mason was the suspicious Italian, Paravicini, in *The Mousetrap*. This performance forgotten, years later I decided to see the play at The Ambassadors in London – about its 'Umpteenth Thrilling Year' – and five minutes into the play knew the story line, but it took a while to work out why. Ken was later to climb Kilimanjaro.

At Nairobi YMCA: John, Ian, Bill and Ken Mason, who was appearing in The Mousetrap. *The 'Baby' in foreground*

The Machakos run, I noticed, had a pause to photograph a 'peculiar house' – the Earl of Errol's. That was as near to the scandalous 'Happy Valley' self-indulgent set we ever got – or wished. Errol had caused a scandal after World War One by eloping with a woman twice married and eight years older. They set up here in 1924 and soon there were stories of orgies, drugs, wife-swopping, lots of loose living and nasty dying – all manna for the gossip columns. The clique couldn't have done Kenya's reputation any good. Errol tried it on once too often and was shot, leaving an unresolved Whodunit?

Kyrenia

8.4.55

(from Aunt Nellie)

Don't you go criticising policy. You don't know half what goes on. [Precisely!] I've been dishing out clothes for the Red Cross. I hate good works. Baxter sent me six bottles of sherry for Xmas which comes from my darning socks. I'm reading Steven Runciman's history of the Crusades. What a lot of bloody savages they were. You might like to meet a Col. Brind, I think in command of 5th KAR[99]. His wife is closing their house here to join him. She, Mary, is a dear, but he is an odd chap. Mary was a great friend and they had this house when I was home in '51. She can knock back the gins all right, and he, poor soul, was badly knocked about in the 1914 war and is blotto half the time. Mary is a great sport and he, if you get him sober, is very nice. You seem to have plenty of social life, anyway, without these antiques. You'll have your eyes opened in Kenya. I think people are even more hard boiled than the planters in Malaya.

I've been on tour (is safari the word?) with Mrs Grove, as she is heading home and then settling in the south of France. She wanted to revisit all her favourite places. You saw most of them. I nearly froze in the Troodos It snowed in the night. John [her late husband] and I used to tour like that. At Paphos they were very welcoming. Enosis, my foot!

Puppy went with us. She was nearly killed three weeks ago – hit by a taxi, but came rolling out between the back wheels, a very scared wee dog and a bit oily, but that was all. For this year's dance we booked the RAF Central Band from the Zone. [The dance made £157.] I'll wear a dress I last wore 23 years ago so it will be seen as so very fashionable! Yes, D.V., I hope to be home next year, I have enough for my fare now. I have been right round the world, you know. Been lucky. So are you. I think you have the grandest parents anyone could have, and don't ever forget it. Your mother is so welcoming, and I assure you that matters a lot. She writes so often, most recently from Crail.

Well, enough from me. You're an opinionated devil, which I quite like. Enjoy life. You'll find the C of E not at all popish, though I think saying prayers over and over is rather nagging the almighty (But the words are very fine). Heaven keeps us from the Wee Frees with 45-minute sermons and voices like carrot graters. Your Gran is proving an old terror to people visiting. Hence 'she's to Crail' a lot. Write soon.

Nellie

---

99 King's African Rifles; a 'native' regiment.

* A later letter mentioned Mrs Grove's journey as eventful:

An explosion in the engine room just before Gib, hit a minesweeper in a fog and had to tow it into Newcastle, and the night arriving in Leith the skipper had a heart attack and went off in an ambulance at 2am. Then, because of the rail strike, Mrs G. waited for coal to be off loaded and went on to London by sea. She was collected from the dock by car.

20.4.55

Time flies here. I expect Crail days are all too short, too. Why not stay on more often and let D manage with Gran? We have leave to Mombasa sure now – a 300-mile train run. We are to stay with a very pleasant missionary whom I met at the Campaign Office two months ago. He has an American/Fife voice! We accepted to go on the condition that there is plenty to do for the Mission: Tony, John and I so far: the Terrible Three! By the time we go the worst of the rains should be over. This is a 'dry year' and most of the rain falls at night. When it rains rivers can rise and fall seven feet in an hour or two. We had quite a safari to Kikuyu one dark night.

This weekend I am staying at Kiambu. Considering I have been here a few months only, I know more of Kenya than some do after years. The African people are nice – if you want – and the land has vast opportunities for young people. There are problems, and they are legion, but that adds to the chances, I feel. Ian Buist is becoming a good friend and as he is in Government work I hear quite a bit of the things that go on. The Governor is going to transfer him to Kenya Affairs, which has thrilled him as he loves the land too. Oh, for more like him, and Wim, and Laurie Campbell, and the Jarvis family.

23.4.55

I bought a collar to replace the frayed one. I often need a tie at night. A letter from Aunt Nell just in. Last night Tony, John and I went to the house of Dicky Smart (Cathedral minister friend): all denominations each Thursday for an informal and very helpful Bible Study. (And a welcome meal too!) Had a swim today and yesterday. Land of delights. At the Bwana's on Wednesday we had a talk on acute anterior poliomyelitis. Sounds grim but was fascinating. The choice was that or games, and we all chose the talk. Tomorrow morning Erskine is saying goodbye to the RAF in the hangar next door. [General Sir George Erskine, C in C, Kenya, who was replaced in May by General Lathbury.]

Have you heard of the two young English schoolboys – murdered and left naked by a gang up from here? One of them was in our Sunday Crusader Class. Dicky had the service for their funeral the day before last. So much for the amnesty. [Controversially introduced in January but withdrawn in June.] Kenya is so wonderful it all seems so unreal. We, of course, don't see all the poverty of displaced peoples and the way the White Highlanders have all the best land. 'Might is white' out here. Even we are of the privileged.

Kiambu all Saturday, and it was wonderful just to sleep in a bed with a soft mattress, to wash in a clean bathroom, to have a bath, and to have a roof only 12 feet overhead and not 50 … The day before was spent in exploring the coffee estate – one of the most modern in this heart of the quality coffee area. We inspected new tanks, which are fed from an artesian well. All the buildings are roofed with tiles, and there was a kiln to produce them. The coffee-planted slopes look like deep-pile carpeting. A thorn bush had beetles impaled on it – the store of a butcher bird.[100] We picked pawpaws. The guard dog – a soppy boxer – is called Rommel. Geoff Howarth's a nice bloke. A Mau Mau gang were hiding rather close recently. [Yet a few months later it was deemed safe enough to take RAF Deversoir's Sunday School there for an outing.]

A year later, writing to me at home, Geoff told of the CID there, unearthing skeletons of Kikuyu loyalists who had been murdered by the Mau Mau. There were over 200: 'I went into the man's bedroom and saw 20 sacks of skeletons.' On a happier note, he said he had been up Point Lenana on Mount Kenya – out of bounds for us in 1955.

Last night we had to leave Wim's car after it got bogged down. (Near a house so all right.) The mud is tropical. Wim and I (John could not come due to the floods) had the early evening with a chap Samuel, son of a Kikuyu chief. He was telling all that he could about Mau Mau and how he had so many narrow escapes and was forced to take the oath, then how he used that to find out all he could before spouting. Having done so makes him a marked man. A very fine chap and a good Christian. We recorded his experiences.

100 Shrike.

We met another Kikuyu, whose brother and sister were murdered for refusing to take the oath and deny Christ. The night before, Wim recorded the story of the African pastor – Bwana Elija – who is now working in the prisons. The big job is to come – replacing something better in their hearts than Mau Mau. I like the Kikuyu very much, and then the Kamba tribe, the Masai,[101] are too proud but it is thought there won't be any true Masai in another generation.

28.4.55

Dear Ian,

Jambo! There was a letter in the PBX when I came on, so thought I might reply now. I come off at 18.00 and have the night in town, Cathedral minister first, then dinner and a Gilbert and Sullivan – *Yeoman*. Back to work all night. Last night we were put to it to eat a huge dinner in the Norfolk Hotel. Twenty hunks of cold meat on the side table. Curry did for us. The hotel dates to 1904. We then went to see the Billy Graham film *Oil Town*: far better than *Mr Texas*. Will you be going to hear Dr Graham when he goes to Glasgow soon?

Hamish in the Norfolk Hotel, Nairobi

Just now it rains most nights, and terrific rain at that. Last weekend we were up-country and had a wonderful stay on a farm. We chased possible Mau Mau and did quite a lot of strenuous things! I am very lucky having all these friends. I would not mind returning to Kenya; so full of opportunities. Please continue to keep my home letters. What do you actually do in your London job just now? Doesn't sound very chemical! [Ian was with ICI.] I hope, in the year after demob, to just 'look around', perhaps then think of reversing my collar. I hope to spend some time with a chap, Laurie Campbell, up at Kikuyu who is ex-Edinburgh and is going to leave his teaching job to become a minister. I knew him before at SU[102] camps. He's held in great esteem as headmaster. This is being typed erratically as I cannot leave the board. When do you expect to be sent East? What do you think of Eden as PM? And Churchill gone?

Enjoy London, *Kwaheri*.

---

101 The then British spelling of Maasai.
102 Scripture Union.

* A decade after Kenya I was teaching at Braehead School in Buckhaven on the Fife coast, pioneering what came to be 'Outdoor Education'. In those early days we often used Glen Coe youth hostel, being run up and collected at start and finish by another teacher driving the school bus – a popular outing, giving a day off school. One teacher doing so was a Laurie Campbell. I'd known Kenya Laurie even before National Service days. I didn't even connect the names being the same. And there's a Scottish photographer of that name too.

Braehead's Laurie Campbell had been appointed head of English. He was a good teacher, popular with pupils (teaching them how to bet on horses!) and a great yarner on those runs. What I did note, however, was some variety in the telling of his life story, and simply put him down as a likeable bullshitter. He'd escaped from the Congo wars destitute not long before, and such escapades do improve in the telling. Returning from one trek we found he had been arrested! Typewriters had disappeared, at Braehead and at his previous school so, with a connection made, the police had raided his house. The finds were interesting. A variety of stolen goods. And two wives. And a stolen identity. He was not Laurie Campbell. The story of his Congo escape, in what he stood up in, without even a passport, was a complete fiction. He had been a National Serviceman in Kenya (we might even have met!) and, befriended by Laurie Campbell at Kikuyu, had seized the opportunities to go through his host's papers and note the details that allowed this scam. Any checks made on his claims of course tallied. He moved into teaching. With hindsight I was annoyed not to have connected the two names. I could so easily have said, 'Oh, I knew a Laurie Campbell in Kenya.' We felt a bit sorry for the prison which would inherit this inventive genius. He probably ended up running it.

6.5.55

Yesterday John and I went to Wim's Boss's house for dinner [the Tillings]. We left a frantic Children's Guild party here and went in at seven, had drinks, and then a very pleasant Dutch meal. I like Dutch cooking: plain yet tasty. After a chat we played a very amateurish Mahjong, which was quite amusing. I won both times.

The usual rush back to camp and on duty after collecting a fried egg sandwich from the Mess. Have no qualms of my not having enough sleep. Some of my spells sound daft, very likely – but I have plenty of time to make up. I spent all this morning in bed and shall do likewise tomorrow. I'm most annoyed as they have cut off the water at the mains and I cannot have my usual gallons of tea – they call it *chai* here too. There are lots of chai swindles, of course.

Ian and Wim came and we had two hours in the pool – including one rain shower – which shower was heavy enough to make a kite turn back from the Khartoum run. Did my 100 lengths. We had tea at Ian's flat and then went to Wim's for dinner and to hear some good music. Then we had a discussion on the history of the East in Scriptural times.

At the Bwana's Bible Study we were on the same period. Mrs Jarvis is an expert on archaeology. She has a library of books on the Holy Land sites – including by H V Morton (which she quoted). I gave the Mem Sahib a copy of *Gods, Graves and Scholars.* It is hard to pay back the wonderful hospitality they show. Would it be feasible before I leave to post out some pots of honey? It would be something nice, and something distinctive, to give to the people who have made me so much at home. Last night I was using honey from up on the hills here and it had a delicious *strong* flavour: something between lime and heather. I'll try and bring a jar home. At Jeff's Kiambu farm I took a couple of snaps of the native bee hives: long log tunnels stuck up in the trees. I'll enclose a photo.

14.5.55

Dear Paw,

Over the next week I am going to send home three letters addressed *to myself*. I will number them 1, 2, 3 on the back, and could you please let me know if they arrive OK? Please put them away in a safe place, as they contain stuff that I should hate to be read by anyone. They are the papers to do with the vile Mau Mau oath-takings, and I don't think anyone should read them; but, if you would feel easier having a shufti, do so – only don't let any of the kids see them. Will man ever be 'good, great, joyous, beautiful and free'?

---

* These were 'leaked' documents, and I've no idea, now, how I came to have them. I doubt if the white civilian population knew about what they describe. My father never mentioned them, whether he read them or not – and I never asked. So what exactly was 'oathing'?

'Oathing' began as early as 1947, to engender unity, political commitment and obedience to leaders, using force if necessary. A fee on joining would contribute to Mau Mau's funding. This sounds little different from scores of subversive organisations, but it took on elements that shocked traditional Kikuyu and Christian values and beliefs. People were sometimes terrified into taking an oath in hope of being left in peace, but all too soon moderates were sidelined as extremists took control. This power became corrupt and used as an excuse for personal vendettas, extortion rackets and much else. Violence became endemic, and various native locations of Eastlands in Nairobi became almost no-go areas for the police. Mass oathings took place there, and on the farms (white and black) in rural areas. Murder victims were inevitably mutilated, and thousands of Kikuyu (mainly) would simply disappear. Anderson, in his careful study, called the oathings 'a wicked perversion'; Blundell, one of the saner settler leaders, called it 'a mind-destroying disease'; while in the papers from which I quote it is described as 'a primitive madness'. Of the descriptions of oaths listed in the foolscap pages of notes I'll give just one small sample; there were many variations and grades depending on the oath-taker's rank or standing.

Two new versions have been devised to meet the needs of the terrorists' campaign. The first – *Githaka* (forest oath) – is administered by forest leaders to their followers. Second – *Batuni* (platoon oath) – is gradually being administered to all Mau Mau warriors and 'soldier recruits' by the Batuni; a man thus becomes a full-blooded terrorist. Batuni is mainly as follows:

a. To burn European crops and kill such-owned cattle.
b. To steal firearms.
c. If ordered, to kill regardless as to the victim – even if father or brother.
d. When killing, to cut off the heads, extract the eyeballs, and drink the blood from them.
e. Particularly to kill Europeans.

With the increase in the oaths there followed a like brutalness in the actual ceremony … The oath takers have honoured their vows as the following incidents remind:

a. The Lari Massacre. (Binding the huts with their sleeping families and then setting them on fire).
b. Decapitation and general mutilation of bodies.
c. Bodies (alive) tied up in sacks and dropped in wells.
d. Tortures before death.
e. Exhumation of bodies and eating of the putrefied flesh.
f. Drinking of human blood. (Chief Luka's child was cut in half, its blood drunk and the two halves thrown at the mother, who was then killed.)
g. Death by hanging. (Animals and humans.)
h. Pregnant women slit along their stomachs.
i. Victims held down while their heads are slowly sawn off with pangas.
j. Hamstringing of cattle.
k. Cutting of the ears of certain people who have not taken the oath so as to have them to deal with later, being easily recognisable.

The following describes an oathing ceremony: statement made by Thenu Magu to Messrs Harvey and Hendry:

I was put in a circle and made to take off all my clothes. The whole breast of a ram had been cut off, including the penis; I was made to squat and the meat was placed on my penis and chest. I held it in place and ate one end of the meat. A *ndito* (young girl) stood on one side. The meat and the penis of the ram was forced in the vagina of the ndito, who was having her monthlies. It was given back and I was made to eat parts of it, including the penis and testicles. The girl's name is Wathirra Ngume. She had taken five oaths. She was not a prostitute but is one now. There are ten girls in the camp and all are used when they have their monthlies. (Three of them took the oath in this case; the same girl was used each time.)

Taking oath in the forest:

The group taking the oath have to kill a man and a boy. The head of the man is used, the blood being mixed with the oath-taker's. Both brains and some mugere tree are eaten together seven times. They swear never to reveal whereabouts of arms and ammo. The child's heart is ripped out and, with a nail, pierced seven times.

Women: the oath for women is taken with the tail of a dog which has been cut off and placed up the vagina.

Details from third district:

Only two Meru in gathering uninitiated. 1st ceremony was carried out in the first clearing while the second was being prepared. Called to the 2nd clearing they took off all clothes while the seniors stood with simis[103] and pangas. The oather clasped a live sheep and with it held intercourse and said the words of the oath. In the third clearing were two arches. The first was festooned with intestines, a second had some sacred meru bush leaves added. Hanging from the centre were the sexual organs of a dead female sheep, with other parts as well. Below lay a bowl of blood with seeds and milk in it. The initiate crawled through the first arch and then knelt before the second and had to masturbate through the sheep's vagina so that the semen fell into the bowl. It was then drunk. A young woman was present for exciting the initiate and her blood was also used.

❋ ❋ ❋

RAF Eastleigh
21.5.55

On Tuesday we had a kit inspection and one boy had an amazing lay out on which he had spent hours – yet it had a secret fault: his socks were so old that he had just cut out the feet in readiness to knit new ones. A 'friend', in the preparation asked him to lend something and he had to refuse as he needed the article himself. 'I'll get you for that,' came from the 'injured' one. He did. The SWO[104] inspecting, proclaimed what a good kit layout the lad had, only to be interrupted by the other, who clyped[105] about the socks.

On the Ngong Hills: HB and David Bott with butterfly net (standing), Robin MMinney, Ian, Tony

Their owner is now on jankers. Incidentally, in the Inspection, the three of us had the best layouts of the 120 in the hangar. Common sense of having clothes always washed and tidy – and knowing their whereabouts! It was amazing the wild turmoil that went on the night before. I lay and thrilled myself with RLS[106] stories: 'Thrawn Janet', 'Olalla' and 'Markeim'. We then had a walk through the camp's luxurious new grass. Oh, to smell fresh trampled grass after all this time! Knee deep and scented – wonderful! Butterflies too – and bees.

103 Thin-bladed cutting tools.
104 Station warrant officer.
105 Told tales.
106 Robert Louis Stevenson.

Ian collected John and me for dinner in the New Stanley before which we had a coke in his place (none of us touches alcohol), and a long wandering chat. Then we saw *Pickwick Papers*, which was followed by chai in the PBX at midnight. Rather, we sat on the wall outside as it was cool and bright in the moonlight – and talked. How we talk!

At the Rift the other day a wee Chigogo boy ran up to me and clasped my hand and just would not let go. It was not aid he sought, just some love. His father is dead, his mother in detention and he is so lost. There are so many like that. Another boy, filthy, just sat in the dirt endlessly playing knuckle bones.

I've been amusing everyone with a story from Ken in Germany. At a busy railway station, with many military present, one soldier looking for a bit of fun went up to the Salvation Army lassie on duty and asked sarcastically, 'Will you pray for me?' She reached up and placed a hand on his head and, in a good carrying voice, said, 'Oh Lord, make this man's heart as soft as his head.'

We had a bit of an escapade yesterday. The boy who sleeps next to me refused to get up, so four of us lifted his bed and went charging away to deposit him outside. We only went a few yards when there was a terrific crash and my huge locker fell, sending the trunk on top over the floor and scattering all its contents. There lay a pile of about 50 books, papers, clothes, bottles, booklets and all my junk, all mixed up with stinking medicines. Just as well the ink bottle never broke. We stood in amazement, and then we saw how it had come about. The pole on the bed to hold the mosquito net had caught on a wire running from locker to wall and so pulled everything over. It was a mess. Now it is all fixed again, we have to move! Into a proper billet, a bit like a school dormitory. I'll miss the roomy hangar, though it will be nice away from this noisy, boring shower. We have ferocious arguments with all those who just drink and gamble their time away. We tell them to try living! Life will be a bit quieter without the Lincolns' din just outside. [For reasons now forgotten, the move for John and me at this time was cancelled, so the reproductions of paintings on the locker were undamaged.]

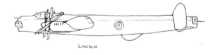

LINCOLN

The eaves of our Signals building are dripping and the ditches are gurgling over the road under the hibiscus and plumbago bushes. The full moon is being tossed about in the rolling clouds beyond the Ngong Hills; yet there is a steadiness about the monsoon – it just comes and comes and then drains away, leaving a world sparkling in the dawn light.

I began typing a letter an hour or two ago but the machine was wanted for work next door, so it's back to the old fountain pen. I hear Hughes is taking 70 folk to the Kelvin Hall to hear Dr Graham. Are you going? I hope so, then I can hear of it first hand. Can you please send cuttings? I hope you enjoyed your Crail visit, Maw. I miss the sea here. Aunt Nell writes saying she wants you to visit Cyprus. Why not? Swimming gala; I just watched, as I was on duty at the time of the heats. That happened in Egypt too! Pity, as it is something

I'm good at. It was hot, so a grand laze. I want to meet more Masai – they are still very wild and uncontrolled but quite friendly. The Archbishop of Canterbury [Fisher] was in Nairobi on Wednesday. Ian said he had seen the new film *The Dam Busters* in London and had tickets for Wimbledon finals. [The winners were Tony Trabert and Louise Brough.]

The Lyons' Den,
Mombasa, 24.5.55

Just after lunch – a very American lunch in a very American home; one full of lively devotion. It is a pity the children are not here, but they are all up at Kijabe. We hope to go there again in June for the Africa Inland Mission's 60th Birthday. The Lyons are fun: Scottish way back, now Americanised.

Strange to be at sea level, and very hot and sticky (80% humidity; even the sea is 80°), a type of heat I have not had for a long time. The house is cool and I look out on to the flowering bougainvilleas and rustling coconut palms with the nuts hanging in green clusters. Weaver birds here are different too. There seems to be a continual flow of guests – one girl, Nancy Graham, from the *Durban Castle* (the liner, you may recall, which wrecked us on the Bitter Lakes!) was at a Billy Graham meeting in the Kelvin Hall,[107] so we shall hear all about that over tea no doubt. We went on board the *Durban Castle* to see her off. We should have asked to see her captain!

The seventeen-hour journey down was very comfortable (*mzuri sana*) in First Class for Tony and me. (John and a Rae Murnane had visited the Lyons earlier.) Meals nothing wonderful, but the railway something to have done. A glorious sunset among the herds of beasts, and then the southern cross and a sickle moon. Ramadan ended yesterday,

and today Mombasa is on holiday. How old it looks. We paid 80/- for first class returns – second class all booked, even with such a big train. You don't go faster for the money. Polé polé for sure — Nairobi dept. 17.00, Mombasa arr. 09.00. Now for a wander, and to wonder! This is Kenya's second-largest town, after Nairobi. There's publicity on Vasco de Gama being here in 1498 – but the traveller Ibn Battuta called in 1327, as a side trip when heading from Mecca to India. He ended up in China! Have you read about him?

Tony in Fort Jesus, Mombassa

---

107 In Glasgow.

The Old Harbour, Mombasa

* On the one Sunday in Mombasa we attended a service at the Lyons' mission – in Wakamba at 09.30 and in English at 11.30. The weather was dry for a change, and everyone hung around afterwards in sociable fashion. We were very hospitably looked after in the Lyons' Den, as their house was called. The sea was a big attraction, and we took the Likoni ferry to visit Shelly Beach and the Shelly Beach Hotel – which still exists, though walking to it today may not be so safe. The modern harbour was very busy, and several liners lay in the Ruiz Reach. The Old Harbour had graceful dhows and other sailing ships, a scene that can't have changed much in centuries. Older buildings like the Law Courts, the English cathedral and the dominating Fort Jesus gave a touch of history, the fort, built by the Portuguese in 1593, made of coral rock.

We saw graffiti of 17th-century sailing ships. The place was certainly ancient. Coins of early Chinese and Persian dynasties have been found, and early Egyptian idols. Trade-wind trade with Arabia had of course existed long before the Portuguese arrived in 1498. For 250 years after that, its history was a bloody tale of sieges and massacres as the Portuguese were evicted and returned, till finally in 1729 they abandoned the island. The British became steadily more active, and in 1895 the British East Africa Protectorate was set up, its capital Mombasa – until the railway penetrated inland, and Nairobi, so central, became the capital.

RAF Eastleigh, 1.6.55

Well, I am back and very happy, for our stay on the coast was most enjoyable. Came back on time after a good First Class, spoilt boys, journey. No man-eaters! Made a point of noting the Tsavo viaduct. On man-eaters, thanks for the Corbett. Everyone has been reading it. We left bags in the hotel and went to see Wim (who was previously in Mombasa for two years) and swopped news, then to the YMCA for tiffin with friends. From there back to town, met Ian (and watched him have lunch) while we talked and then he ran us up to Bwana's. There we met John, and the three of us spent till supper merrily baking. I got a cream horn diploma and an overseer's certificate! A pleasant round-about run home, chatting all the way with the Mem Sahib and Betsy [the memsahib's daughter].

This morning I am bang onto my old watch which is all that is desired as it keeps our trio's days off together. I had five letters waiting, including yours, one from S Africa from Ken Terhoven to thank me for photos, one from a St Andrews lady who sent £100 via me for the Campaign and one from Ken in Germany.

It has been a lovely sunny day and I did a station Cross Country walk (supposed to be a run) with a Sgt who was full of Sergeants Mess grumbles, then I did half my laundry of sticky coast clothes. Coming up in the train we began with a sheet only and ended with two blankets. Cold here in mornings – but dry. Rained solidly in Mombasa, and were we glad of our macs we bought just on the day of going down. Spent more time in the house than perhaps I hoped but did a lot of reading – there were some splendid biographies of people like Moffat, Carey, Studd, Brainerd, etc. Also spent quite a time talking to Mr Lyon, who went out of his way to help us, and I know I learnt much from him. He has been in Africa for over 20 years. We met a fine, old pioneer couple – Rhodes – who used to walk our seventeen-hour train journey to Nairobi 52 years ago. He translated the Bible into Wakamba back then. We sat at his feet like schoolboys. The day we arrived broiled us, and the rest of the time soaked us, and it was hot all the time. Nairobi is just like summer at home. Camp is short of water so there's no swimming.

There's been another prang. Lads kept me a cutting from the *Standard*. Not one of ours but a civvy Dakota flew into the volcanic shambles of Mawenzi, a peak of Kilimanjaro. Crew and 16 passengers killed. The pictures showed bits scattered all over hideous lava cliffs, an inaccessible nightmare of a spot.

---

* In 2004, staying with a friend in the north of England, I chanced to pull from a bedroom bookcase a small stencilled booklet, *The Ice-Cap*, the June 1965 edition of the journal of the Kilimanjaro Mountain Club. In it there was mention of two RAF climbers making an impressive route on Mawenzi in October 1964, from which they observed the Dakota wreckage and scattered bones. As a result a club team set out in March 1965 to retrieve what they could, a difficult expedition with one freezing bivouac, and with several skeletal remains having to be left, being inaccessible with their limited means. The rest were buried under a cairn lower down the mountain.

Mawenzi is a 'Top' of Kilimanjaro, to use Munro[108] terminology, and is a nightmare of jagged pinnacles and huge cliffs of rotten volcanic rock. I came on another story about a pair of climbers coming to grief, one falling to the foot of the cliffs, the other left dangling on the rope in a spot impossible to reach. He was (eventually) retrieved by a marksman firing a shot to cut the rope to let him fall.

---

108 A Munro is one of the distinctive 277 Scottish mountains over 3,000 feet (~ 914 metres), subsidiary summits of which are termed Tops.

The comment about man-eaters goes back to our family enthusiasm for Jim Corbett's *Man-Eaters of Kumaon*. Father bought the first edition of this in India when it appeared (1940) and then sent it home to us. I would subsequently collect and read everything Corbett wrote. He retired to Kenya after the 1947 partition of India and was still there when we came to Eastleigh. As a schoolboy I'd also found, read, and treasured *The Man-Eaters of Tsavo* by J H Patterson, the one to do with the railway.

First published in 1907 it tells the story of two lions which brought the construction of the Coast to Uganda Railway to a halt in 1898 and had thousands of workers (mostly Punjabis) justifiably terrified. The lions killed about 28 people. Shortly after Patterson had arrived, as engineer for bridging the Tsavo River and laying track on either side of it, a Sikh overseer was dragged out of a tent and carried off. They found his head next day. Patterson was faced with killing the killers, and had several hair-raising close encounters before succeeding, the story told in a matter-of-fact style that nevertheless has one gasping. Much of the rest of the book, while interesting about the railway, local customs and wildlife, tells of shooting everything else he could – the first illustration showing his haul of *six* simba, for instance! The Tsavo man-eater 'problem' was mentioned in the British Parliament by the prime minister, Lord Salisbury, because, with Britain pushing hard to gain control of inland Africa, the hold-up had political as well as commercial implications. A film was made about these man-eaters, too, but it was a gung-ho Hollywood version which was readily forgotten. Less well known is the episode of the Kimaa killer, also on the railway.

Near the end of his work on the railway Patterson dined with a Mr Ryall, a police superintendent, in Ryall's inspection carriage – the very carriage that would see the man-eater's horror at Kimaa, a small station about 250 miles from Mombasa. The lion had even tried to claw its way through the corrugated station roof and the trapped *babu*[109] telegraphed 'Lion fighting with station. Send urgent succour.' Several victims had been carried off when an engine driver arranged to sit up one night in a big iron water tank in hope of a shot through a hole cut in the side of the tank. The lion simply knocked the tank over and tried – but failed – to reach the man through the narrow hatch.

Ryall, with two friends, Huebner and Parenti, were travelling up to Nairobi, but decided to try for the lion, and had their carriage parked in a siding. An afternoon scout was fruitless, and after dinner they sat till late without the lion showing. (It was watching them!) Ryall took first watch while the others lay down, Huebner on a high bunk on one side and Parenti, refusing a low bunk opposite, putting his bedding on the floor. Presumably feeling the lion would not turn up, Ryall later took himself to this lower bunk. No sooner had he done so than the lion climbed up onto the platform and pawed open the sliding door to enter the carriage. The tilt of the train made the door slide to a close again, so the lion was trapped inside with the three men.

He sprang at Ryall and to do so actually *stood* on Parenti. Huebner, awakened by the din, saw the lion standing on one companion and attacking the other. He made for the opposing

109 Station clerk.

door which led to the servants' quarters, and this involved vaulting over the raging beast to reach it. He found the door held by terrified servants, but somehow got through. They then tied up the door with their turbans. There was a final loud crash from the shaking carriage as the lion broke through a window, dragging the hapless Ryall with him. His remains were found, a short distance away, the next morning.

After his Tsavo stint, Patterson moved on to the railhead at Machakos Road on the Athi Plains, and pushed the line on to Nairobi, which was then chosen to be the railway HQ. Setting that up was a Herculean task, interrupted by some cases of plague in the sprawling Indian camp. (His remedy was to burn the place down!) He also employed many Kikuyu, and when he left at the end of 1899, 400 of his workers begged to be taken to England with him. He came back in 1906 on a hunting safari, by which time the tiny settlement he had initiated had become the capital, with a population of 6,000; in my RAF days it was 80,000, and now it is 2 million.

6.6.55

Odd to write the date: the sixth is only five minutes old. It is a wonderful night, with a moon in full round brightness. I have just had a flap on the board, as a chap on camp (in labour lines – not ours) has been attacked with a panga. Strange, that as I sit in this peaceful moon light, people half a mile away were quarrelling and in the end fighting. Camp is still except for the distant bark of a dog. Dawn is six hours away and it will be another day of sun, bright and warm.

The other night one of the police lads shot himself. He died in hospital. His wife had run away. Then the other day half the Camp had food poisoning, not badly, but it gave the lazy medics a spell of work for a change. We three escaped, as we did not eat on camp that day! 'A pitiable apology for a dog's breakfast' the Orderly Officer called the meal the last time I was there.

Ian took John, Wim and I to the Kirk's Scottish Country Dancing on Monday. I enjoyed it immensely but felt odd dancing in trousers![110] John was comic, to say the least. I hope to manage a kitchy[111] bit of leave before I come home, and reach the

Scottish Country Dancing at the Nairobi Highland Games, June 1955

---

110 Normally, of course, in a kilt.
111 Wee, small.

northern province which is very wild and beautiful, or maybe use the railway to Uganda! *Chu Chin Chow* is fully booked, so we miss that. More usually it's loud pop keeping the Camp happy. I want to yell *Chuprow!*[112] at times. The enclosed stamps I found blowing down a street so rescued for D. Everyone has flu so I hope we don't catch it, as life is far too interesting to be off. The hangar is perhaps too windswept for germs. We enjoy big bed spaces, and we're largely left alone, with few inspections and reasonable bull.

On Sunday I spoke to the Crusaders for half an hour, about the ascent of Everest. On Saturday the three of us and Wim drove up to Jeff Howarth's farm at Kiambu, a beautiful day with the long view over the Nairobi plains and away to the Mua Hills and the Wakamba land that falls away down to the sea three hundred miles away. Mombasa Island is not very big, but now each square foot of earth fetches £1,000. We spent the first two days just walking on the Island, and second day must have covered a dozen miles. Some dreadful slums and most inhospitable some of them. Still we can now say we know Mombasa a wee bit. It is Islamic of course, of the Indian Ocean rather than of black Africa.

On Friday last Koen Valkoff, the friend of the chap who shot himself, and I were at Wim's and had a very pleasant evening. I gave Koen my *Anna Karenina* in French as I doubt I will ever have time to finish it. I am finding *The Pilgrim's Progress* interesting; not read it for years. We all read it round, as much of it is dialogue. My fancy Bible and Concordance come on night binds. A cup of cocoa now as it is a bit cold.

---

 * The *concordance* mentioned was the newly-purchased volume of Alexander Cruden, a word book of the Bible from which one can track down any verse from one remembered word. Cruden (b. 1701) undertook this mammoth and painstaking task (no computer aid) despite severe mental illness (though one unkind comment suggested that mental illness was a perquisite). The book ranges from Abase to Zuzims. Zuzims? 'Genesis 14:5' Cruden says. They were apparently a people dwelling in Ham whom Chedorlaomer and his gang of ethnic cleansers 'smote'.

9.6.55

Today is the Queen's birthday and a holiday for the Forces – except for telephonists who plod on at our shifts. I had a very busy morning, but this evening is quiet as everyone is away on a binder or at a Camp Concert. I was relieved late, so had to go to town to

112 Shut up!

find lunch (not that I minded), did some needy shopping, and went to the Housewife Exhibition and had a glass or two of squash (gratis) to quench the thirst. I know the girl in the stand. She is doing that for the two weeks and receives £25 for it!! That's about five times what I get for the same time, serving Her Majesty.

What are D's summer plans? Bwana Jarvis is just back from Mombasa and he said the weather was perfect! On Tuesday I missed the baking as I was on duty, but last night John, Tony and I went up early. Had fun with an old steam engine (like a lot of kids!). Tea in the garden as usual – what a lovely bright garden: plumbago hedges, bougainvillea, pepper trees, jacaranda, everything smothered in flowers all the time. Like I recall Hill Crest.[113] There is a pet baby buck there that someone picked up. It happily grazes with the hens! This Sunday there is chance of going to Athi River (the horror) Detention Camp. Permission to visit has come from the Commissioner of Prisons by devious string-pulling. Several old hands have gone home recently from Bwana's, and soon few from pre-Christmas will be left. We love it, of course, as Mrs Jarvis (who can be a holy terror) spoils us frightfully. Bit like Aunt Nellie, only three times the circumference.

13.6.55

I went to the Kirk at 10.30. Ian and Wim were there, and Ian's friend Robin Minney whom we know quite well. We (Tony, John, David Bott of Tony's section, Robin, Ian and Wim's friend Leon) all went to Wim's for *kahawa* [coffee]. At 2pm we set off in high spirits in the cars of Ian and Robin. Each chose a different route out of town to see who would arrive first, and when we rolled over the red roads up to the wooded township of Ngong, Robin, David and John were sitting there as though they'd been there all day. We drove on into the hills: a sort of unpaved Applecross road[114] with stones. The cars stuck twice, but a swarm of kids, at the order of a stern and majestic warrior, helped to push. At 7,000 feet we parked and walked up to the first bump looking over rolling grasslands spotted with trees. There are five hills, and we went up and down three of them before time made us turn: 8,000 feet up and what a view: behind, the plain, then the great drop into the Rift Valley, a great gash 50 miles wide! In the south and north old volcanoes poke up from its floor and away in the south, Kibo [Kilimanjaro's main peak] reared in the haze. Giraffe 4,000 feet below were little dots. It was cool and sunny and very still. The whole Nairobi plain rolled to encircling hills, Mt Kenya, the Aberdares and Mua all dim on the horizons. Oh, how big and so empty – only a few shambas with thin pillars of smoke rising into the air. We walked for three hours. I collected gladioli for the Mem Sahib and David collected butterflies. John collected ticks. (No

---

113 In South Africa, as a boy.
114 It's in the West Highlands. It has gradients of 1 in 5 and hairpin bends, and rises from sea level to a height of over 2,000 feet (626 metres). In Gaelic it's called the Bealach na Bà, the Pass of the Cattle.

one else found any.) We had tea in a place called Happies and then I drove the Ford Consul Fabius home to Ian's where one after the other we delighted in boiling hot showers. Tonight Bwana is talking to our Camp Fellowship, but I'll be at work in the PBX so will miss it.

The weather is wonderful and being back in k.d. even more pleasant. Out of my two years in the RAF I will only have been in 'blue' for about three or four months.

P.S. Just a note, *eck dum*, to let you know my shirt has arrived. Southampton postmark, so it came by sea; *mzuri sana* (many thanks), as they say here. The strike did not hold it up.

25.6.55

John's birthday, so I took him out to lunch and tea and then we went to Wim's. Ian there and one David Bott – ex-Egypt, Jerusalem and Cyprus! [Unsurprisingly, he became one of our gang.] Tony is in hospital, John just out. Nothing much. The whole evening was spent listening to Bach's *Matthew Passion* (again), a glorious piece of music. The day before I was made quite nostalgic by seeing some colour films of the Highlands – all those places I knew. That was after a Youth Service in the Cathedral taken by Dicky, and a hand-round meal in the Old Deanery after. Also films on the Orchestra (technical and scientific; makes the things we heard last night more amazing still).

On Wednesday at Bwana's we had six African medical students from Makerere University.[115] Some first time in Kenya, and all very nice chaps. Bwana gave a lecture on the solar system and it just floored the lot of us. I had some nice chats with three of the lads – two of them Christians and one a self-styled free thinker. On Monday the British and Foreign Bible Society man – Rev Frank Bedford – I know him well – talked for 90 minutes and we all wished it was 900. He had his old Geneva Bible with him and others in Tibetan, Korean etc. He has told me quite a bit about his work at various times. He was at Kijabe, as were the Lyons from Mombasa, for the big conference to celebrate the 60th anniversary of the AIM (Africa Inland Mission). Ian took Keith, David, Tony and me, Wim took Gillie and Elva. Lots of singing and friends of all nations.

PS. I'm really scunnered. That precious blue Aertex shirt, plus white and grey socks, stockings, 2 new vests, 2 new underpants have been stolen from my locker. The Police were quite hopeless. But it sours the atmosphere: might even be a neighbour. Not good.

---

115 In Kampala, Uganda.

7.7.55

Dear Ian

Nice to hear that life in the big city keeps you busy and interested. When I'm demobbed (at Innsworth, just outside Gloucester) it might be an idea for me to get my travel warrant addressed from London to Dollar and manage a couple of days in London with you. I am not 'demob happy' to use the loco, and I don't own a calendar with a big red circle round 'demob day'. I'll be as sad as glad to be out. Today I had a nice bill of 100/- for artist's materials. I want to do two good

Hamish painting in the Ngong Hills

oils – and if they are worthwhile have them framed on arrival for a family present. It's jolly hard to think of something suitable, personal and original – and African. [This was duly accomplished: one painting of the Ngong Hills, one of a rural village.]

We visit the Athi River Detention Camp on Sunday. Officially we are there to 'study rehabilitation methods – with an eye to permanent residence to take up such work, teaching or missionary activities'. Sounds good, and got the Minister's signature. Politics! We are the guests too of a DO[116] whose father was murdered by the Mau Mau. People back home just do not know how horrible it is. Even here it is not talked of. But it is really over. Our Lincolns have made their last raids.

11.7.55

On Friday we had a party at Wim's – to hear Bach's B Minor Mass: Ian has just bought the records. We had a supper of mealies, pancakes, strawberries and cream – as well as drinking and eating hand-rounds all the time. There were the usual four (not three as before) from here – Tony, John, me – and David Bott. Elva Silver was there, and a couple we did not know. We arrived home at five to 12 – as usual.

The Mau Mau amnesty ended yesterday. Not a success.

For the Athi visit I changed into civvy clothes, washed, shaved etc in the exchange, and so got off at once. On the way into a garage we skidded and hit a pump – and soundly rated

116 District officer.

the proprietors for having the concrete both flooded and oily. Wim and Samuel Waruingi (a Kikuyu friend) joined us. I drove Ian's Fabius – on one wide straight of 10 miles I was doing over 60. A wonderful road – and so out of keeping with the rough murram. The main Mombasa–Nairobi road is like a farm track, and you just have to go at it at about 45. Skids on the shale too, but the final thing was a blowout – 100 yards from our destination. Humiliating!

It is hard to say much about the Athi River Detention Camp. It is hard enough to think of it – standing in a compound in the midst of 60 hardcore Mau Mau, some responsible for the Lari Massacre. What sheer hatred on their faces! The ones who had changed were interesting to talk to, and they are usually more educated: teachers, clerks, probation officers and so on. It has given us all a deal to think about. The Commandant was a good chap – full of hope in a position almost hopeless, a religious man, doing the job because he wants to. Most of the workers are volunteers. As you wrote, Maw, 'There is always that heartbreaking why about the wicked things.'

We left after a coke at two, and I drove right into the Akamba hills, so beautiful and so African. And no skiddy roads once off the plains! We had lunch at Puri's Restaurant on a roof-top at four when we reached Machakos, then took the Mua hill road back. Ian drove as I had been going all morning – and that off night duty. Home in the glory of a plain's sunset. Up 8,000 feet with the wind in our faces made us all rosy-cheeked and yawning. Did you read that Kangchenjunga has been climbed? A British team – great!

---

* A picture of Kangchenjunga from Darjeeling hung on a wall at home, bought by my parents when there on their honeymoon. The Kangchenjunga expedition was led by Charles Evans, and the first ascent was made by Joe Brown and George Band. Then Tony Streather and Norman Hardie summitted. A perfect performance.

Ian mentioned this Athi River Camp visit when writing home, so our versions can be compared:

Yesterday Hamish, John, Wim and I went to see the Athi River Detention Camp by special permission of the Minister of Defence. There was a contretemps at a filling station which was an inch deep of water, causing a skid. No damage luckily. All went well till we were within 100 yards of the camp entrance when a tyre burst and had to be changed! However once inside we were greeted by the youngish, ex-officer Commandant who briefed us on the workings and then took us round. All the inmates are detained – not convicts – and comprised about 1,400 of the worst MM offenders; and every 'non co-operator' stoutly denies knowing anything about MM, as we found out when we asked. The camp is spotless and well kept, divided into ten compounds, of which four are for 'co-operators' who have been brought to a state when able to confess to their deeds. The MM committee in each non co-operating compound elects the 'compound leader' – usually a glib English speaker, to impress visitors! Just now there are about 550 'co-operators', the best of whom are used as missionaries to try and convert their ex-comrades – even in other camps. There is a remarkable difference in atmosphere between the two groups – we were in both types of compound – and although I'm not satisfied that all who co-operate do so because of conviction or because they have found a new faith, there are certainly some remarkable results, bearing in mind that most people would say these people had *all* gone too far for *any* to be brought back into the fold. It was all most interesting, and we had a lot of questions to ask. The visit ended about lunch time when after a 'coke' H, J and I went off to Machakos. Wim stayed for lunch, as he was taking back Samuel, a Kikuyu friend of ours who couldn't go to Machakos as he had no pass [his own country, but his freedom so curtailed]. We had lunch about 3.15pm and got back climbing up the Mua Hills and winding along a *lovely* road to the main Mombasa route again – and so back to Nairobi, not without certain further trouble with Fabius, who has been docked for overhaul today.

The detention camps were established to try and wean inmates off, and break the spirit of, the Mau Mau then, depending on confessions and repenting, to have people released. On arrival everyone was screened and categorised, from the hardcore, kept isolated, to those more amenable to re-education. If this sounds a bit like a Soviet *gulag*, it was – and dreadful things were to be done, such guardian powers leading to endemic abuses. The comparison was to be made to Nazi concentration camps.

With hindsight now I rather suspect Athi River was a showpiece screening camp, what with its committed Christian commandant who was genuinely trying to produce reconciliation, a canny choice for when and where (the rare) visitors would be allowed inside the wire. That things were otherwise was suspected at home in the UK, and questions were periodically asked in Parliament; but it was only in late 1955 (after I was home) that Barbara Castle made serious accusations, and it was into 1956 before the press published accusations of torture in the camps. Britain did have quite a lot on its plate in 1956, with the 'troubles' in Cyprus and Malaya, finally quitting the Zone and then, in the autumn, with the collusion of the French and Israelis, staging the ill-fated invasion of Suez. The hangings in Kenya – over 1,000 – exceeded those during the 1945–48 terrorist war in Palestine, the 1950s Malayan insurgency and the EOKA fighting just beginning in Cyprus – or of the

Dutch and French in the East and Algeria.) In 1956 in Kenya the forces quit operations against Mau Mau in the forests. Through all the years of the Emergency it may be noted that 70 per cent of combatants were National Servicemen. At one period there were 11 battalions in Kenya. 1957 would see riots in the Athid River camp. At the end of 1958 there were still 4,688 hardcore people in detention, while as late as 1959 occurred the Hola camp horror, when 11 detainees were brutally beaten to death. The Emergency ended in 1960. Kenya's independence came in 1963.

In 2005, in America, Caroline Elkins' bombshell of a book appeared (*Imperial Reckoning: the Untold Story of Britain's Gulag in Kenya*) which spelt out in detail the endemic, systematic violence and torture in the detention camps. I have not seen this, but received my own personal shock with reading the more accessible *Histories of the Hanged* (2005) by David Anderson: required reading for a proper understanding of a tragic history. (Anderson lists many titles, some by ex-detainees.)

13.7.55

Tomorrow Ian is entertaining a Sqd Ldr from Nicosia, and as I've been there he asked me along. We are going for a long safari in the game park. If he is a nice man I'll give him Aunt Nell's address!

The Mau Mau has meant there are countless children orphaned. One wee chap has been 'surrendering' himself at every police station so as to be taken in, and maybe find a home. Then there are all those whose parents are in prison or detention camps, and all those who are sent into the city every day to beg; all very sad.

Yesterday, off night bind, I slept all morning and then played badminton with John all afternoon, so that I feel crippled now.

On Thursday I went to Ian's office at Government House and then he, Sqd Ldr Spooner from Cyprus, and I went for a delightful run in the Game Park. We saw most things – two big crocs very close! And an aristocratic male lion looking down his nose at us. Their world!

I've just had the bother of dealing with a drunken officer on the phone. Oh, this place! The PBX was a shambles when I took over the watch, and since I cleaned all the gunge from cupboards etc four days ago no one else has done so – and the place stank. So glaikit! They just make more work. Still it is all cleaned now, I've had a wash along the passage, a cup of *kahawa* and a natter with the duty Traffic lad, now a letter or two to write, and then into a few hours of study. Never many calls at night. One thing to look forward to once out, is having more than three nights in bed in a row. John is on duty at Air Movements, but it is a sleeping watch. He'll come down for a natter later; and tomorrow the four of us are going into town, lunch in the New Stanley and in the evening the film *Don Camillo*. I hope it is as good as the books.

John and I took ourselves to the road yesterday and got a nice long hitch to Thika, where we explored and visited the two famous falls. We had our lunch at the Blue Post above the Chania Falls, and explored the garden, which had a pen of swanky crowned cranes. Due to the constant spray from the great Chania Falls, the place is almost tropical. All very beautiful, quiet and deserted. [Elspeth Huxley's *Flame Trees of Thika* would make the spot well known.] Spoke to a man who had been injured in the 'Wavell battle', a real Kenya cowboy, hard as nails and as soft as a kitten underneath. After a few hours we walked up to the main road again, in two hops were back in Nairobi and went up to Bwana's where we played cricket till dusk and then by floodlights. An ample break for tea, to eat our own home baking. The film *Hidden Treasures* was shown: things beyond our ken through the telescope, and through the microscope. The first half, on the stars, is exhausting in its bigness, and then the other side, such things as the 'secret of the snow', the invisible desert flowers, and all the tiny things in water etc. I've seen the film several times. It still amazes. After tea in the lounge there was the usual epilogue.

Two Sundays ago a lad, John, was picked up and saw *Mr Texas*. The next day he came up to the house (as all are invited to) – and he stayed. He is on leave, which finishes today when he prepares for the UK. He was a hapless alcoholic, from a home made miserable by the same curse. Not long ago he was found half-dead in a Mombasa gutter, out of bounds. Half his time in the forces has been 'over the wall'. The film and the message set him thinking and he came back, begging for help, so they collected his gear and he stayed. We befriended him and chatted, and as the days went past he found a new resolve. He ventured down town and came back tipsy. He tried again and came back sober. And then he just, as he said, 'put himself into the hands of God' so 'old things are passed away: behold! All things become new.' As this John finished his faltering testimony that night I think we all had lumps in our throats. Tomorrow he flies home.

Now three in the morning. I have just found mail for me in the cupboard. I hope Ian does not go off to Hong Kong before October, for if we do not see each other then we might not meet for years and years. Next Easter I have an invitation to Holland, where Wim will be. He goes home in December for eight months' leave. He hopes to have a car, and while I am there we can go up the Rhine, perhaps, and then via Belgium to Calais, to cycle to Scotland with me over a couple of weeks. A good idea? I don't really know Europe. I am a very lucky lad – still quite a lad to look at, for on our jaunt to Thika John and I were again asked what school we went to!! Can you do me a favour, Maw, when next you write, and give a brief outline of my history up to the age of returning to UK from South Africa? More or less a list of countries and ships. I'm rather hazy, and so many people ask.

I have just had a police call: some bright spark shoved his fist through a window and was picked up a drunken, bloody mess. In hospital now, so that is dealt with. Eddie, who was with me on the PBX at Deversoir, remarked that we have fewer fire calls here: only five this year, less than one a month, while Egypt had several each month. Well, this afternoon I've had two, and I feel it is time someone else had a turn! The board buzzes then.

Reading *Pilgrim's Progress*, I found this sentence: 'Mr Mnason, a Cyprusian by nation, an old disciple, at whose house we may lodge'. Have to tell Aunt Nell she is an old undisciplined Cyprusian! Just to climax an all-ranks contributing evening – a boozed-up senior NCO is on the rampage because the bar is shut. (It is 03.20!) Sometimes I feel N.S. 'a bad thing' – so many lads go down before its flail. 'Break you, or make you.' I'll say it does. I wish I could do more, though I can look back on some good. One chap confessed that he had tried to kill himself just before I started talking to him … (not long ago one boy did kill himself here).

THE MOTH

I caught a moth at the lamp last night,
I felt it flap in my hand,
I took it out to the dark of stars
But it could not understand.
Straight back to the burning lamp it flew,
Beating its wings on the glass,
I took it out to the dark of stars
But it flopped about on the grass...
I saw the moth by the lamp this dawn
Tattered and dead on the sill,
I took it out to the dark of day –
Where the ants are at it still.

25.7.55

Just taken my chai out to enjoy that subtle, sizzling roar that is the African night. Having written that of course a change: a Lincoln revs up on the concrete – the first of the Squadron to go. On Thursday the Governor, the C-in-C etc will be here for the pukka farewell ceremony. Only the fighters remain, and then one day they will go, we will go, and things will be 'normal'. Will they? They can never be, not while the thousands of weary orphans stand begging on the streets downtown, not while old men remember and torn hearts recall. Kenya is unhappy, there have been such wrongs on all sides. Yet my abiding memory will be of marvellous people, Kikuyu or British, of rich experiences and the glory of the landscape. Where else could one see 'the greatest bird spectacle in the world' [a million flamingos on Lake Nakuru] set against such mountains and plains?

Another big event since last writing is that John and I (after a two-month reprieve) have been moved into a proper billet (Block 9, room 16) – after seven months and two days in a hangar. Almost civilisation again – and the first time since coming overseas that bog and bed are in the same building and less than 150 yards away from each other. And a bedside mat on a parquet floor! Even the cleaning is done by locals, not us. Those still left behind are a bit cheesed off. We went to Ian's for a housewarming of his, and Ian's African servant produced one of his 'very specials' (awfuls!): ham and fish chopped up with macaroni and liberally covered in tomato ketchup. All tastefully surrounded by potatoes and carrots. His best effort was prunes on a platter with a border of roast potatoes. We revived in time to be in by midnight. I've written to Aunt Nellie to say a Sqd Ldr Spooner may get in touch, and asking her to be kind to the man – a good bloke.

---

* In March 1954 a couple of Meteors had been sent from Fayid for a time to undertake aerial reconnaissance work, but this was ultimately done by the heavy Avro Lincoln bombers, which could both pinpoint Mau Mau bases and then bomb them with devastating effectiveness, however jungly the terrain. This as much as anything had led to the real destruction of the Mau Mau. The Lincolns were the unsung heavies of the post-war years, taking over from the fabled Lancasters (with their legends like the Dam Busters raids), only to be rendered obsolete by the early jet bombers. Over our hangar months we came to have a marked love–hate relationship with these six noisy neighbours, but they reminded us we were all in the RAF!

2.8.55

There are certain scenes which will never be forgotten – the first glimpse of Jerusalem lying golden in the sun, the view from above Kyrenia – these are two, but yesterday I found another, even more amazing: the sun setting on the snows of Kilimanjaro. I could never paint it – I can just remember. The clouds were glorious in sunset colours, and as

Kilimanjaro from Amboseli – the highest summit in Africa, 19,341 ft.

we looked they fell apart and there, towering above the plains rose the snowy summit – dazzling in colour – a breathtaking mountain. All around are the great plains and the dried-up lakes, the stunted bushes and thorn trees, the flying game; then, like some great drop curtain the dark mass of Kili heaves up into the clouds – up, up, go the eyes, till 19,000 feet up the clouds fall away to give that glimpse of golden snow, the mountain's size and height overpowering, unspoiled, untouched, old and rich and beautiful. Did you know Kili used to be ours, but Queen Victoria gave it to the Kaiser (her grandson) because he complained Germany had no decent mountains in their bit of East Africa? That is true!

As it was August Bank Holiday Ian was free, so we four had decided on a full-day safari. We did 330 miles, and only the odd 30 miles was on surfaced roads. We were off at 05.45. We saw the dawn rising like a picture: hills and trees black against the yellow sky. As we left the Nairobi Plain the sun burst like a golden shower over the grass, and waking gazelle and zebra raced along the road. A sly jackal slunk off, and the vultures rose grudgingly from a dead something to circle above, then for many miles the murram[117] ran up and down great sweeps of hill: hills barren and rocky, hills covered in bush or golden with long slopes of grass. The clouds formed at 9,000 feet, and several times we nearly entered it. At times it cleared to reveal views – views that cried: 'This is Africa!' – huge views of plains that rolled for ever. After three and a half hours we had reached Tanganyika – 104 miles from Nairobi.

We stopped at the only hotel in Namanga (on the border) and had a huge breakfast: cereals, fruit, eggs, coffee and toast. We piled provisions into the boot and set off into the Amboseli Game Reserve – 1,000 square miles of wild land. Now and then as we drove we would meet a tall Masai warrior who would solemnly raise his hand in greeting (we would return the salute), and now and then we would see their cattle and huts off in the trees. They have a wonderful religion which declares that all the cattle in the world belong to the Masai. Sometimes they go to war to prove it, and the Wakamba[118] find that God apparently agrees. It is not so long since the tribes were face to face – just waiting for someone to make the first stab …

On desperate roads we bashed through 50 miles of roughest Africa – at one place right across 10 miles of smooth lakebed where we touched 70 mph. *Allegro molto.* Our usual rate was 20–30 mph. On the bigger roads you go at 50 mph and hope no big holes come. If you go much slower the car gets beaten to bits on the corrugations. Driving is quite

---

117 Dry red earth road.
118 A tribe neighbouring the Maasai.

thrilling. We stopped at the lodge to lunch (the Baby was full of food!) and to find what was wrong with the car. Could find nothing so dared to go on. Spent 2½ hours with the ranger till only the position of the towering mountain told us where we were. Dikdik, Thomson's gazelle, zebra, lion, lots of elephant (one with an egret on board), giraffe, eland, Grant's gazelle, jackal, vultures, flamingos, ibis, owls, great lizards, tortoise,

wildebeest, hartebeest – these are some of the creatures we saw. One group of three young lionesses would not look up from lying lazily on their sides. David wanted a colour photo so I gave a 'roar'. The result was startling: they all leapt up, one more or less flew over us, another darted off, while the third stood very alert – in a wonderful pose. Click! Later we found a lone cub. Two groups of elephants – one playing in a swamp and the other browsing in the trees. A bird started up before a big male, which reared up with a shout and went thundering past and away.

We had our full share of thrills – from the animals – and from the car. The places it went! We returned to the lodge where we had lunched, and met some friends from Kijabe; five girls and boys with a master on a safari before they go to university in the States. They all hope to return to East Africa. There were weaver bird nests hanging on an acacia tree – just like South Africa. Remember the widow birds, Maw, with long tails? We see them often.

Ian drove coming, so going back I relieved him. John drove on the easy salt flats – he is learning now, seeing I am going soon. It was then we saw the summit of Kili in its glory and stopped to wonder. Dark fell quickly before we refuelled at Namanga and began the hundred miles back – what a fantastic run, almost terrifying. At the end after five hours almost non-stop from the lodge we felt dead weary. And poor old Fabius was feeling sickly but still gave power – steady 40–50 mph all the way while the headlights sent great shadows off every ridge and bump and the corners came rushing at us. Now and then mysterious glinting eyes looked out from the bush; occasionally a frightened gazelle flashed away in great leaps.

The noise was great – and so was our singing. Tony was not too well, and we wrapped him up and he slept. We talked and sang choruses, and the miles slipped past. The countryside was flooded with light and all the stars were bright. Over the hills and far away – hour after hour – mile after mile – we felt just like Toad in *The Wind in the Willows* – only it was real. We stopped at the Kijabe wagon on the roadside where they were supping round a roaring log fire: a happy few minutes.

We reached Nairobi at 10 – our estimate to a minute. One after the other we showered off the red dust, and hot and tired and wind-blown we sat over our Horlicks. We were the first out of camp. We were the last in again. Africa: hot, dusty, hard and big, is putting her spell on us.

On Saturday the three of us lunched with Ian and then went to the Highland Games. We watched the dancing for much of the time – even a sword dance. How my feet itched! It was very pleasant with a bright sun and a great row of eucalyptus behind. We wanted to see the caber being tossed, but every time they failed they sawed off another bit. They were still sawing when we left. Someone will have some nice firewood! Just been told RAF stands for Really All Fun. Must see if we can climb Kili. It is so powerfully *present*. The name sings: Kili man 'jaro. [I did start planning the ascent but, being sent home early, the climb was denied me.]

---

* Ian:

Ian tossing the caber; John encouraging

Last Monday was Bank Holiday and I went to Amboseli Game Park with Hamish, John, Tony and David from the RAF (the 'Terrible Three' now the 'Fabulous Four'). We didn't leave Nairobi till after six but saw the dawn some miles beyond Athi River. We continued to Namanga, stopping en route to chase some giraffe. For about half the way you have flat plains and then more trees and ups and downs. From Namanga we drove across [the border] a few hundred yards, just to say we had been in Tanganyika, then to the only hotel for a very good breakfast at a reasonable price ...

At the Park entrance we caught sight of a quantity of drying poles so promptly set to trying to toss the caber. Managed to a few times. No doubt the Masai have now taken up the sport.

Inside the Park the first animal we saw was a small tortoise which we kidnapped but, except for guinea fowl, and distant zebras and wildebeest [*sic*], drew blank for the next 50 miles to the Safari Lodge. On the way we got a very good glimpse of the snow-capped summit of Kilimanjaro and crossed the dried-up Amboseli soda lake. There was an amazing mirage so it looked as if we were driving to the water's edge though the lake is really quite dry. After lunch we arranged to take a guide – cost 10/- a day.

First I investigated a curious noise when the clutch was in ... the left part of the rear axle was very hot. Assumed lack of oil but after efforts to pour in some through improvised funnel decided it was full enough and the brake was at fault. But the noise sounded something dangerous and a breakdown van would have been rather expensive. We got a party of Americans (whom Hamish knew) to help in the examination. No positive results emerging we proceeded to lunch. [The noise was due to the gear mounting being crammed with dust – as were the passengers.] I think the only animal we missed seeing was rhino … I still haven't seen one, though I met the spoor on the Ngongs … We reached the gate at 7pm after a terrific view of the sun setting on Kilimanjaro and drove through the starlit evening.

12.8.55

Just came from a pleasant singsong in the camp church with our Fellowship. We had sung hymns for half an hour after an opening prayer, and then Jack Shellard (in our billet) gave a talk, followed by general chat and two more hymns to finish. Just now the Duke of York schoolboys (CCF)[119] are on camp, so we had half their contingent present. Several of them we know well from Crusaders. On Thursday there was a parade and the Air Commodore spoke to the camp – just in time to prevent another stushie over food. I never went, but lay and read.

John Cates, Wim Schot, Tony Judd

LATER. A wedding was something different, and I quote Ian's account. The wedding was of Samuel Kimani (lots of Samuels). Ian wrote:

We were all invited to an African wedding at a village on the way to Limuru. The church wedding was in the morning (and the traditional one some time before) and we could only make the reception. Samuel is a Christian friend of Wim's who sells vegetables in the

Samuel Kimani and his bride, William his best man

119 Combined Cadet Force.

market and whose father used to be a chief. At 3pm we found the whole village assembled in age groups outside Samuel's hut, waiting for the pair to emerge. We were given seats of honour, and a friend of Samuel's, a Christian called Livingstone, was stationed to interpret for us. The couple emerged with a couple of child bridesmaids and sat ceremoniously at a table in front while their parents took tea together close by (the wife isn't allowed to accept the tea if her parents aren't present and agree). We were all served and duly partook, and after there were five speeches, one by Wim, which Livingstone translated.

The speeches were all made by convinced Christians, and the organiser of the party (a cousin of Samuel) is a church leader – and all appealed to the rest of the village to learn by Samuel's example. Rather different from speeches at British weddings – but better! The village is right in the centre of the Mau Mau leader's estates: the Koinange family (all of whom are locked up or in exile) being local squires. One of the women doing the tea was wife of Peter Koinange; they say he is the most dangerous Kikuyu still at large, but she became a Christian. Another Koinange was killed at Lari.

The ceremony ended with a large basket being put on the table, and everyone went up to shake hands and deposit a wedding present. I gave a scarf, after advice from Mr Calderwood, who probably knows more about these things than anyone. By the finish there were pots and pans piled high, and everyone was ready for the photographs.

14.8.55

This is V J Day[120] – only ten years ago – when I was staying in Dunfermline with Aunt Iza. The town went mad with relief that war was over at last. Where were the rest of you? Why was I having my birthday in Dumf and not in Dollar? Asante sana for the birthday gifts – so very useful; provided some needed civilian clothes and things. I only bought two books!! I have told people not to send on any more sea mail. This week I will send off a big kit box. We should all arrive together. I hope so, as there are certain presents therein. Saturday (13th) was a very happy day: Ian, Wim and the gang gave me Bach's *Matthew Passion*: four long-playing records. [Willem Mengelberg and the Concertgebouw.] Thrilled to bits.

All our gang went to the Norfolk Hotel (Nairobi's best) and had a happy luncheon party, then – a real treat – we went riding. While the other four were given a lesson, Ian and I went way off into the bush. As we turned to go home the horses showed the usual signs of more zeal and we really let them go. No polé polé, thank you. We had a long, mad gallop, side by side, along a lane enclosed by trees, then through a boma with the totos[121] and hens scattering wildly before us. The ways parted, and we parted: Ian to the left and I to

---

120 Victory over Japan; the end of World War Two.
121 Small children.

the right; a rush into the grass and away over the fields. When we stopped we were quite breathless. Ian got thrown once. [In his words: 'a graceful fall on return to the school, for the horse pecked badly at a bush, swerved and lowered its neck! However, I pride myself on having retained the reins nevertheless.']

I still have the menu from this occasion. The table d'hôte luncheon cost 7/-. Present were Wim, Ian, John and David Bott. 1. Lentil Soup with croutons 2. Fricassee of Tripe 3. Kabob Curry and Rice 4. Grilled Rump Steak 5. Parsley Potatoes, Marrows au Gratin 6. Cold Buffet 7. Assorted Salads 8. Banana Fritters 9. Mixed Ice Cream. Cheese and Biscuits. Coffee served on the veranda. Quite a contrast to tinned meat and powdered potato on RAF Eastleigh.

I lay all Sunday morning, worked my shift in the afternoon and then Ian and Tony came to collect John and me for the Kirk, after which we picked up David at the Cathedral. The Moderator, David Steel, was speaking: one of a series on the Armour of God from Ephesians Ch. 6. He was good, as usual, and has an amazing intellect. I had a chat with him at the close and have fixed a date for a visit to the Fellowship here. Last night we went out to Wim's. It was the night of camp cleaning, and this time the additional bind of a kit inspection. ('Stand by your beds!') John and I had done ours early – what little was not ready – so we were glad to escape the turmoil. We still won praise for our layouts.

I've been informed that I leave Kenya on the 16th October – on a civilian Hermes via Khartoum etc. We'll see.

21.8.55

On Saturday we had a safari up to the Rift Valley Academy as it was too cloudy for Ian to run me up to the Ngongs to paint – and tonight Mr Hollanbeck from there came with another of his tape recordings. On Friday I had lunch in the New Stanley Hotel with a friend with whom, three years ago to this day, we were camping together: David Shannon, in town for two hours – and we meet! And then last night at the Kirk, Laurie Campbell was in for the evening. On Wednesday I was talking at Bahati location and felt, as I did in the Reserve, that those I talked to had a more vital life than any of us. They died for their faith and those left are strong and true, and humble. On Thursday I had the Camp service (Ian came) and then there was Sunday, a day to remember.

I was only in bed at one o'clock, as coming off the board I was caught by a young pilot officer, and we talked on and on, then we were up at 05.15 and off by six, away in Fabius to Athi River. There we left two army lads we'd given a lift to, they making it onto a gharry going to Mombasa. It was to get them well on the road we went so early – and, secretly, hoping to see the dawn from the wild, rolling plains, but it was cloudy and no burst of rich colours; just one minute dark and the next the bright day with animals wandering about and wondering at our presence.

We went up to Kiambu to a Kikuyu service – which 'began promptly an hour and a half late'. Over 80 children – and grown-ups – baptised. I shall never forget the scene: everything outside because the church is too small, with the sea of black faces, row on row. This is where Mau Mau began, yet here is the start of something else. They are far better Christians than we; theirs is the vital faith of the apostolic years. We sat in the Chief's house having tea after – such a contrast to the hell and terror that has been their lot for so many years. Samuel, whom we knew so well, was there, and so was Livingstone with the perfect English and a heart of gold. There were many, many handshakes, the strong 'right hands of fellowship'. It was one of the greatest honours for me to be there.

Ian had taken Tony and me to the service because a friend, whose daughter was to be baptised, had asked him. Chief Koinange was present. The Koinange family are the local squires, and more or less all but Charles are locked up because they were deeply involved in Mau Mau. (Peter Mbiyu, the most dangerous, was in exile in London.) Charles struck me as a bit shady and rather a fence-sitter, but so far he has kept on the right side of Government. He had to leave before the service began, to attend the DO's baruza[122] and then on to David Maruhui's place at Kiambu. (David's father was murdered by Charles' brother – though he got off because of pressure on the witnesses.)

Each of us had an English-speaking acquaintance, mine a Makerere graduate Peter Gacathi, who interpreted where necessary. The usual Anglican lines weren't difficult to follow, even in Kikuyu. The hymns we knew but were slightly varied: Nearer My God to Thee, Come Holy Ghost, Lord Thy Word Abideth. There's only one baptismal service a year. No babies, and all the boys in best khaki shorts, etc. It was delightful, and encouraging. Wim wasn't present so I have been asked to organise a Bible reading study by the people. The DO was agreeable, but we now wait for permission from the DC. [Wim obtained permission. When he left, Ian took over.]

We drove on to the Brackenhurst for a good tiffin (lemon meringue pie – yum! yum!) and set off round the golf course practising archery with Kikuyu weapons we'd bought from

---

122 Official meeting.

the Kamba carvers' stalls. We only lost one arrow. And got covered in ants! We went back to Kiambu to take Samuel into Nairobi.

---

* Samuel W. would write to me in Scotland, saying that Wim was much appreciated. He used the image that in certain times people would wash up on the shore in a strong wave which then receded again but left some good pebbles on the shore. I liked that, especially from someone who had never seen the sea and was obliged to obtain permission from the authorities even to visit his wife and family.

26.8.55

I always think of the new date as the sun rises, usually now glorious in colour and wrapped about with the eastern clouds. It is worth working the night hours to see dawn's glory – and to feel well again. (Did I tell you I have just got over a bad two months: just wabbit[123] physically and other ways.) I came on duty to find my work mate drunk, and three others likewise. They were all arguing about religion and, knowing me, pounced. I felt a bit scared – but then didn't, and gave it to them! When I had finished they just sat silent.

Tonight we lit the candles and had some belated birthday cake [baked by Mother]. It was scrumptious! One boy found a wee 3d piece – which went reverently from hand to hand like some link of civilisation washed up on a desert island. There were just a random four of us in the billet. We found some oranges and bananas and there was the chocolate.

Ian has had to leave his flat in Muthaiga and for 12 days, while he fixes up a wee *banda* (cottage) at Longatta, he has the use of a friend's house, the friend, Courtenay-Bishop, being on leave. Tony, John and I hitched over to the flat where everything was packed and in two journeys helped him move. We washed and dressed for dinner – in a place called The Lobster Pot (frightfully select – and ridiculously expensive). Still, as Tony is posted to Aden this week, it was his farewell. The bill was 42/-. We had the best curry yet in Kenya … We then went back to camp, booked in, then I came out again with Ian – without booking out – and we returned to the house – a lovely place overlooking a wooded valley. I sit on the pillared verandah writing this. Just finished breakfast out here – 2 poached eggs on toast, bread and honey, fruit and coffee. Now 11. Ian went to work at 08.30 and I phoned

---

123 Weak.

up to 'book myself out of camp', as it might be awkward getting in again unobserved in the evening! Shopping after lunch and then up to Bwana's for the rest of the day. Robin Minney has gone off on holiday to Sicily and should be at a new job in Kampala when we get there on our planned Fabius safari.

We have had a move round at work and I now go (1) morning and evening, (2) afternoon and all night, (3) day off, (4) day off. So it is perfect: work two days and more or less live out for the other two. Quite illegal of course, but the SPs[124] are a good lot and it does not much matter, not for erks! One of the boys is cutting grass and it smells lovely. There is a huge grass slope in front of quivery gum trees.

On Monday morning I had a long swim under a sunny sky, and in the evening Wim, Tony, David, John and I went on to the Town Hall where a pre-war world chess champion, Max Euwe, was playing 20 others – simultaneously – a fantastic sight, especially as it was towards the finish and King after King was being turned over. I don't know if Euwe lost a game. We then went and had ice-creams and espressos at a Greek restaurant before coming back – to night work. Last Saturday we had another go at our new sport of archery. Great fun! We all bought Kikuyu bows and arrows while up at the Brackenhurst for tea. They fire very well. I'll bring two lots home (one for David). Good that we will all be home at Christmas – may not come again very often. Thank you for my 'History'. [See Appendix III.] Ian (Lofty) is on loan to the Ministry of Commerce and Industry, and works in the Secretariat. He is often away on safari, visiting airfields. Also has hotels to keep an eye on, so more safaris likely.

---

* Max Euwe was chess world champion 1935–1937, beating Alekhine for the title but then losing the return match. Euwe was a genuine amateur – really the last such world champion. (For non-chess players, in a simultaneous match like this, the expert (Euwe in this case) was enclosed in a ring of tables and would pass from one to the other and make his move before going on to the next board, which gave the challengers the whole time of the circuit round to think up their next move. They would make it as Euwe came to their board and he would then make his move *at once*, and pass on. A game would be conceded by turning the king over.)

---

124 Station police.

5.9.55

We spent Saturday night at Ian's – the last fling of the 'Fabulous Four' (Tony, John, David and self). We were up early in the morning to say kwaheri to Tony. He is posted to Aden, where he may well be for 18 months. I depart next month and Wim about Christmas. John, a three-year man, might even outstay Ian; so our gang of three/four is disintegrating. A Britannia was in. They call on test flights.

We all drove back into camp, collected our stuff and drove out: John and David under the seats and self in the boot (bureaucracy avoiding). Rather ironically, one of the Police chaps tried to thumb a lift as we went through the gate. On Sunday morning we came in the Civil side (Ian has a pass) and we packed Tony's boxes and transported them to Movements. We then 'booked out'. David was singing in the Cathedral choir so he couldn't, and at night, after all was over, he just came in, in the boot. Sunday we had 'early' tea in bed at nine and then went off to dispatch Tony's belongings to him in Aden. We had lunch at the Njangu Inn on the way to the Church of the Torch at Kikuyu. The church was opened about 1930 (the first church was 1899). Various Scottish churches paid for some attractive stained-glass windows. After that, and a puncture, we had a run Ngong way, a look at Ian's cottage at Longatta, and an archery contest (which John won). We're going to go with Mrs Jarvis to the sales to find things for Ian's cottage. It looks just like an old croft house, neat and at home in its surroundings.

---

* On 16 September David flew off to the UK via the Canal Zone. A Britannia flew over, very low, at the time. Wim hoped to be home for Christmas too. The band of brothers was breaking up. On the 17th John and I with Ian and Wim attended the lively Kikuyu wedding of a friend, Peter Mwae. On the 18th there was the Battle of Britain parade on camp, attended by the governor. I even went to the NAAFI – about the only time it is mentioned through Kenya days, an indication of the very different conditions since the Canal Zone. I don't think boils have been mentioned, either. In the two years I never had a night in sickbay. Ian came to a Fellowship night when Wim talked about desperate life in Holland during the war and his career in Indonesia as a conscript afterwards.

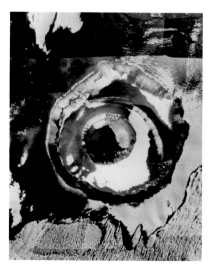

Not an elephant's eye but a composite air view looking down on Kibu, the summit crater on Kilimanjaro

28.9.55

Well, this note is to say that I am back in Nairobi – after quite an adventurous holiday. I drove about 500 miles in that time, and had one accident – incident really. You'll hear of that *baado*.[125] I feel fitter than I have been for ages, quite sun- and wind-blown. Our rough itinerary was as follows:

Monday 19, John and I shop etc and help Ian pack. Then we all come to Camp for Fellowship. Ian our guest this time and he led a good discussion. We picked up five army lads from Rainer's Camp, who go to Bwana's.

On **Tuesday 20**, we set off and had an eventful run to Embu on the slopes of Mount Kenya. We lunched with Jeff Howarth (who has joined the police) at the Izaak Walton, a fishing inn, but missed David Shannon. Then to Nyeri, where we had tea with Alison and her mother. We sat and watched the mountain [Kenya] rising from the mist, visited Baden-Powell's grave, and went on. I drove in the dark round the mountain to Nanyuki. Ian took over and we got stuck in the mud 200 yds from the Mawingo Hotel. In the end we got

Thomson's Falls

Ian and John at the Tea Hotel, Kericho

out, and our helpers then stuck. This is Kenya's most luxurious hotel, and looks like a clubhouse for a home counties golf club, and there's an amazing view of Mount Kenya. I did three sketches and will do an oil of it when I get home. [I did this, in oils, but the result was so poor the painting was thrown out.]

I drove next morning, **Wednesday 21**, to Rumuruti, where we went into the bush to a Game Farm where there is a terrific zoo. Then to the 246-foot[126] plunge of the Thomson's Falls and over Blood Pressure Ridge (9,000 feet)[127] into the Rift Valley, and Nakuru which is Kenya's third city. Up the other escarpment (Mau Escarpment), a tasty high tea in an Inn – Londiani – and then we just drove till dusk fell. We then piled out, and later back in to sleep: Ian in the front, John in the back and self in the boot. I was the only one who slept well – so well I missed the 02.00 Police visit (which made a comic ending to the day).

Thursday 22, breakfast and clean-up in Kericho's Tea Hotel and then down to Lake Victoria. Lunch at

125 Shortly.
126 ~75 metres
127 ~2,750 metres.

the Uganda border and then I drove to Jinja where we wandered over the Owen Falls Dam before driving the 50 miles to Kampala. We stayed with Robin Minney in the Imperial Hotel (his flat not yet ready) and had quite a party.

Friday 23 was my marathon drive to Fort Portal: 200 miles in eight hours, of roads that twisted and turned, only stopping for two accidents and lunch. John kept blowing a bugle out of the window or singing 'So this is the Kingdom of Toro' ('Toro' for 'Heaven' in the pop song). Skids in the black mud. I took the car into the side and stove a mudguard. Ian took Fabius to six inches of a cliff, and that needed a lorry and a dozen men to get us out. We arrived worn and muddy with the Mountains of the Moon, Africa's heart, gleaming silver above us. Over them, the rivers run to the Atlantic by the Congo. Our side they run to the Nile. We spent two days there. We visited and then had dinner with the Omukama of Toro; His Highness and his Palace were the strangest of strange experiences.

Saturday 24: Ian and John set off for Kabale (I hope they made it, for the roads were muddy from the rain) and I set off in a huge lorry back to Kampala. Spent the night in Robin's flat and caught the Nairobi train in the morning: all day, all night, all day. Found friends on board, so a pleasant and scenically wonderful run. I was back by midnight on the 27th.

---

* This safari was really the climax of my time abroad. We were lucky to set off as planned. Fabius was giving serious troubles – or various garages were – and we departed with 'a kind of rattle in the gearbox'. Ian had also spent several days flying about the NFP (Northern Frontier Province) on official business, where the air transport behaved quite as badly. There was one touch of light relief: Victor Mature and Janet Leigh were filming *Safari* on location. Some of the brief letter comments can be filled out from memory, having talked with both John and Ian, and I'll add a couple of incidents from a letter of Ian's.

Alison and Ruth at Nyeri were the daughters of Dr Mackay, a family we'd met at the Jarvis's. I was 'soft' on Alison, to use John's word. We lost touch in the UK later.

Baden-Powell's grave was on everyone's itinerary. I had read his books avidly as a boy in South Africa. His exhortations, with *Jock of the Bushveld*, the writing of Selous[128] and the other game hunters, and the superbly illustrated historical works of T V Bulpin were devoured, and we imaginatively played their games. I recall that as Cubs in Natal we had a maze of boy-sized huts built of grass, reached by secretive passages in the long grass. We were at home in a big landscape, and interested in birds and flowers and creepy-crawlies. In comparison, scouting at home, mostly in village halls, never appealed. I'd lived a dream in Africa; after that, Scotland was too cold a reality.

---

128 Frederick Selous, 1851–1917, explorer and big game hunter.

Robert Baden-Powell, Chief Scout of the World, died in 1941. What we entirely missed was the nearby grave of Jim Corbett, who had only died a few months earlier. That would have interested me far more. Corbett and his sister had finally lived in the banda at the Outspan Hotel, the same banda that had been the last home of Baden-Powell. If Corbett had escaped the horrors of partition in India he ended living on the edge of the Aberdares, a centre of Mau Mau activity, which the RAF bombed regularly. His last books were written at Nyeri: *My India, Jungle Lore, The Temple Tiger* and *Treetops.*

The owners of the Outspan had built Treetops as a game observation post in the top of a huge *ficus*. It offered rough and ready accommodation, and became famous in 1952 when Princess Elizabeth and Prince Philip stayed a night there. Corbett identified wildlife for them and spent the night sitting at the top of the ladder, rifle to hand. In the night, King George VI died and, as Corbett ended his report: 'a young girl climbed into a tree one day a Princess, [and] climbed down from the tree the next day a Queen'.

The Mawingo Hotel had a great reputation, and was enjoyed in every way. Lawns ran down to reflecting water, there was a rose garden, a babble of birds (a paradise flycatcher) and the view, looking out from my bedroom window at dawn, was to Mount Kenya clear against a lush lemon sky. The building itself had clean lines, was comfortable and provided good food. We used hotels in Kenya (most officially *not* for rankers) in a way we could probably not afford today if we returned. Treetops now has the appearance of a city block. (Mau Mau burnt down the original.) The Mawingo is now the upmarket Mount Kenya Safari Club.

Khar Harley's game farm at Rumuruti was appealing because many of the animals, taken in as orphans, were tame. Not many people have had a cheetah rub against their legs and purr. There were hippos in a pool, elephants, huge tortoises, and giraffes to hug. Ian didn't look so 'lofty' alongside a giraffe.

Lofty and Totos at the Rumuruti game farm

* Ian:

So to Nanyuki (Hamish driving), which we reached after dark, having had a splendid view of Mt Kenya on the way. From there to the Mawingo Hotel is only five miles, but 500 yards from the hotel I slithered and skidded to a complete halt, someone having carefully graded the road that morning and then there being heavy rain; so, thick mud. Four Land Rovers passed without towing ropes. Hamish went to summon help. Then a large taxi came, the passenger reluctant to help, but they had to as they couldn't pass us. We got a shaky start and were soon at the hotel, *covered* in mud. The taxi then stuck as well! The people in it simply paid it off and walked to the hotel leaving the owner … At Nakuru we bought a towing rope. [Before leaving the muddy Kingdom of Toro Ian bought tyre chains for Fabius.]

To save money we decided to sleep in the car. What a night! Hamish slept in the boot with the lid nearly closed, John in the back, me in the front. We were in bed by 7.30pm and had to endure till 6.30am. I woke every time I turned. I had the door open and lay flat, sometimes on my back, sometimes curled up or knees in the air. At 2am a police lorry drove up, the officer having spotted my legs wrapped in a blanket protruding through the open door and no doubt expecting a murder at least! However, the corpse came to life. Heavy dew made my feet wet and, in short, we decided not to do it again. Hamish, to aggravate things, claims *he* slept the whole time. In the morning an African bus passed just as he was raising the lid. It must have given them something to talk about.

---

* Thomson's Falls are named after the great Scottish explorer (as are Thomson's gazelle – *Eudorcas thomsonii*). He was still only 25 in 1883 when he pushed inland from the coast to reach the Ngong Hills, went up the Rift Valley to Lake Naivasha, climbed into the Aberdares, saw Mount Kenya's snows (which people had refused to believe existed), and by Lake Baringo finally reached Lake Victoria and explored Mount Elgon before, cannily, turning back.

He was the first person to come out of Masai country alive, in fact had been cared for by them after being badly injured when tossed by a buffalo. When James Hannington (appointed Bishop of Buganda!) pushed on to the Nile in 1885 he was murdered. Thomson's book *Through Masai Land* (1884) is still in print. (A first edition costs four figures.) But somehow Thomson isn't as well known as he should be.

How pushy the grabbing of Africa would be is seen in the railway from Mombasa reaching Kisumu on Lake Victoria in 1901. The whole story of opening the way to Uganda is told in *The Lunatic Line* by C Millar (Macdonald 1972), as good as any history of Kenya.

Thomson was born in a stonemason's cottage in Penpont, Dumfriesshire. In 1879 he went with Keith Johnston to East Africa, and when his leader died he carried on, reached Lake Nyasa and explored Lake Tanganyika. He liked Africans and they liked him. Unlike Stanley he lost nobody on this expedition and never fired a shot in anger. He was 21 at the time. Our age! If that wasn't enough to make him my hero, he also made a daring exploration of the Atlas Mountains of Morocco, a landscape to which I would return over 50 times. He sadly died at the age of just 37 in 1895.

Kericho's Tea Hotel had only recently been built by Brooke Bond when we were there, but had that indefinable air of an old colonial hotel, with spacious grounds and comfort –

and set in a world of tea growing. The tea plantings carpeted the rolling hills with a woolly pile of bright green. Kenya is now the world's third-largest producer of tea.

In 1971–1972 I returned to climb Kilimanjaro as part of a sabbatical year which, after climbing and trekking from Arctic to Atlas to Andes, saw two of us on an intended Cape to Cairo journey. After a good time on Mulanje we sailed for three days up Lake Malawi over Christmas on the *Ilala* (which still operates) and on to Meru for the long walk up Kili. Two other friends joined us for the ascent. Marangu Hut, Mandara Hut, Horombo Hut, Kibo Hut, took us up steadily but at the Kibo Hut I went down with a bug that had been niggling since the lake voyage. The others climbed to the summit and down to the Horombo Hut faster than I managed from hut down to hut. A week later I flew home – and it took me six months to recover. The story is told in my book *Chasing the Dreams*, 2019.

The rest of the Kilimanjaro gang continued into Uganda mere weeks after General Idi Amin had ousted Milton Obote – accusing *him* of corruption, tribalism, and economic policies hurting the poor. (Amin promised an early return to civilian rule, free elections and the release of all political prisoners!) As a member of our party had been one of the lawyers who drew up Uganda's first constitution at Independence, he stayed with the attorney general in Kampala, who was an Indian, and when Amin later cast eyes on his daughter (he was marrying someone of every race and tribe for one of his aberrant political ideas) the girl was promptly shipped off to India. The attorney general was never heard of again. Amin's destruction of a green and fruitful country is one of Africa's saddest stories.

The palace and the Omukama of Toro

The Omukama of Toro, whom we visited in 1955, was one of the many minor rulers still holding sway. He had been in London for the coronation of Queen Elizabeth, and had been one of civil servant Ian's responsibilities at the time. He had said something on the lines of 'If you're ever in my part of the world, old chap, do look me up.' So Ian did. A dirt road led up a gentle hill past fields of bananas to a white arched entrance, past an office to reach the palace, which was rather on the lines of a colonial house with overhanging corrugated iron roof and a balcony running along the upstairs rooms. There was a view down to Fort Portal – and the Ruwenzori, Ptolemy's Mountains of the Moon. His Highness sat on a throne, and anyone addressing him had to prostrate and crawl. Not us, mercifully. The mix of cultures was remarkable. There was a piano, which had been shipped from London. We dined at a table set with all the trimmings of western affluence. The meal was memorable. Something like a meatball which we ate had the most revolting taste of anything I have ever had to swallow, etiquette not allowing me to spit it out. (Years later John recalled this too.)

The Kabaka of Buganda, the most notorious of these rulers, was allowed to return from London exile about this time, but only on condition he transferred power to a council.

Uganda became independent in 1962. A retrospective irony: a corporal serving in the King's African Rifles (Uganda Regiment) and fighting Mau Mau at the time was one Idi Amin.

Robin Minney was teaching at the African University of Makerere, which sat imposingly on one of Kampala's many hills so we visited it briefly: 'a quick dekko' in forces' slang. We also saw Kampala Cathedral beside which a simple stone just bore the name 'Mackay', marking the grave of Mackay of the Lakes, Uganda's pioneering missionary who had started the strong Scottish connection here. When we stopped for petrol a local asked us in a rich Glasgow accent, 'Aye, hoo mony gallons shall ah pit in?'

My *seeing* the Mountains of the Moon was in some ways the climax of the Fabius journey, for the range is only clear of cloud on a handful of days each year. The very name tingles with romance, and the reality was a dream: a snowy crest of peaks rising from the evening mist and washed with the tints of sunset.

After our two nights in the Mountains of the Moon Hotel, Ian and John continued for another week, to Kabale on the Rwanda border. My leave was more limited, so I headed back to Nairobi as described. We had visited the Owen Falls dam at the outflow of Lake Victoria in Fabius. My train journey took me down the Nile as far as Mbulamuti station, where a signpost indicated: Kampala, Tororo, Nairobi, Murchison Falls, Lower Nile, Congo.

Jinja, Uganda: the Owen Falls Dam

I'd listed the place names of our journey on letter paper at the Mountains of the Moon Hotel, which was headed with a rondel showing an elephant in front of improbable mountains. Telephone No: 6, Telegraphs: Romance. What reflected the times even more was how the directors of Imperial Hotels Ltd were listed: 'M Moses (Iraqian), F C Elliott (British), G A Kassim and Hon Ibrahim Nathoo (British subjects)'. Ah well, the litany of the singing African names remains: the Journey to the Mountains of the Moon: 20.9.55: Nairobi, Kahawa, Ruiru, Thika, Saba Saba, Fort Hall, Sagana, Embu, Karatina, Naro Moru, Nanyuki. 21.9.55: Rumuruti, Thomson's Falls, Ol Joro Orok, Blood Pressure Ridge, Nakuru, Molo, Mau, Londiani, Lumbwa. 22.9.55: Kericho, Kisumu, Lela, Yala, Mumias, Bugiri, Iganga, Jinja, Mukono, Kampala. 23.9.55: Mityana, Mubende, Butoke, Kyanjojo, Fort Portal, Toro.

RAF Eastleigh.

3.10.55

John finished leave Saturday and had Sunday off. I had Friday and Saturday off, so we both broke bounds to spend a weekend out at Ian's cottage. I went to a sale in the morning.

The cottage is looking quite well furnished now. The three of us went to see *Tosca* done by puppets: ambitious, and good entertainment. This evening for the Fellowship we had David Steel along to speak. He preaches stunning sermons – in a rich Aberdeen voice.

It feels awful to be back on camp in some ways. On our tour we could be away out in the wilds with the nearest white man a hundred miles away through plains and swamps – little removed from the early pioneers. And yet the toil in the mud, the wheels stuck and the sun broiling and mosquitoes biting … it ends, and we limp into a posh hotel. In a few minutes we lie like lobsters in a bath and gaze at tiled walls and polished taps, we sit by a fire, we dress for nine-course dinners, we sip coffee and talk, we have a singsong from the *Songs of the Savoy* and go to bed on Dunlopillo mattresses with chins resting on green sheets and downy bedclothes. Later, as tonight in the exchange, I spend an hour sweeping the muck out (ashes and paper and all the litter), I sweat and I polish, I answer irate, drunken officers and sergeants, I doze and I go to bed when all the world wakes. Contrasts!

On Wednesday I have to spend the morning visiting people to fix up the Fellowship programme to the end of the year. I have made 13 calls for that today already – one perk of being a telephonist. At lunch time it's kwaheri for Alison this time. We have a kiddy's 'Doctor set' to give her! She is going to St Andrews to do medicine so I'll see plenty of her again, I hope. She is *very* nice. Then I am helping with the building of another extension at Jarvis's. Thursday I work. Friday there is the camp Bible Study to lead, and Saturday I am off up to the Rift. On Sunday we go to Kikuyu for a Service and back for Crusaders. Food preparing for two hours, 'fishing' for an hour, supper, the film and so on. Then as I lie in bed I shall think: 'This time next week I shall be – where?' Elva, another friend, on Sunday last, gave me a lovely photo of Kilimanjaro from the Amboseli. God! This big land is in my heart now. [Elva Silver was a nurse and kept in touch, a good friend of Alison's; and the Nurses' Christian Fellowship met in the Mackay family home.]

I should think all the book parcels have arrived by now. There were going to be another five lots, but they are coming in my two kit boxes. New regulations mean all kit boxes go by sea and are allowed up to 112 lbs. Costs nothing.

I don't think I can go to London: warrants are all made out for the quickest way: Gloucester – Birmingham – north. London would be at my own expense, and I can't afford it. My big trip here, when films are done and so on, will have cost about £20. It was a fantastic tour – full of fun and wonder, thrills and spills, both so worrying and so carefree in its wanderings. Dismal with the car in the mud and tropical rain, glorious in the wonder of seeing the Mountains of the Moon.

LATER. Been listening to the radio. Depressing to hear more trouble being stirred up in Cyprus by EOKA, with strikes and riots and the Turks retaliating – and both now anti-British. Seems incredible; everywhere we travelled in Cyprus last May seemed so peaceful. Among the majority of people it probably was. Peace, family security and work are what most just want, but it takes just a small number to turn life upside down. Like Hitler. Like, often enough, in our own turbulent history. There's a kink in the human make-up. But you will hear far more about what happens there than we do.

---

* Gillie was John Gilliebrand, ex-Palestine Police, who was one of ten people I had to enrol to talk to the Camp Fellowship up to the end of 1955. Diplomatically, I had Eastleigh's Padre Must, also R G M Calderwood of the Scots Kirk, Colonel Dare of the Salvation Army, Revd Frank Bedford of the Bible Society and Mr Hollanbeck from Kijabe with a tape about the conversion of the one-time crook Jim Voss, Laurie Campbell from Kikuyu, Dr John Winteler with colour slides of the Holy Land, and Ken Matthews of a trip from Land's End to John o'Groats. Organising all that was my last frantic self-imposed task in Kenya. The name David Steel is not unfamiliar, as Scotland's first presiding officer; this Nairobi David Steel was his father, minister of St Andrews from 1949 to 1959, and later moderator of the Church of Scotland. John Winteler is Mrs Jarvis's brother. They go back to reformers who were 'out' with John Huss.

I was lucky to see something of Kenya again in 1972 on a Cape to Kenya stravaig.[129] Nairobi had become a city with motorways and modern buildings, but the Nairobi Game Park still had plenty of wildlife. I'd been ill on Kilimanjaro and lost nearly two stones in weight and had little strength, but we were well looked after by John and Anne King and entertained by the Mountain Club of Kenya – Alasdair, of our gang, showed them Andes slides at a meeting at Wilson Airport. We dined in the Norfolk and the New Stanley for old times' sake, visited the Alliance High School at Kikuyu (Laurie Campbell well remembered), Nanyuki, Thomson's Falls, Nakuru, the Italian POW chapel, the World View and Lake Nakuru to see the million flamingos, then departed by Jumbo from Embakasi Airport with both Mount Kenya and Kilimanjaro in view. Just why I'd had this big African safari calls for a story indicating how one thing can lead to another, even as years roll on. Wheels within wheels.

In the late 1960s or early 1970s I was coming off a remote Munro when I met an older man who explained he was after completing a second round of the Munros now he was retired. (As a youngster he had romped round the Munros and Tops in 1939; Munroist No 8.) We chatted away as hillgoers do, and he offered me a lift in his car, parked not far below on a track (*sans* permission no doubt) while my camper was away down on the main road. He lifted the boot's lid to light an old primus and bring a dixie of water to the boil – the first time I had ever seen a brew-up carried out in the boot of a Rolls-Royce. We kept in touch thereafter; I visited his home in Edinburgh occasionally.

He must have been a Rolls-Royce man (or was it the same car?), for he and his wife had once driven a Silver Shadow overland from Kenya to India and then on to the UK. We

---

129 Jaunt, wandering, walkabout.

found we had some East African experiences in common, but he had explored extensively; entertaining notes in Scottish Mountaineering Club journals described the unlikely Mount Mulanje or the Chimanimani Mountains – which, thanks to him, a friend and I would climb on our 1971–1972 Cape to Kenya wanderings which ended, for me, ingloriously on Kilimanjaro. (He did complete that Munros second round in 1978, and died in 1994, a fine old man indeed.)

In 2018 a book was published about his unique World War Two experiences; D M Guss: *The 21 Escapes of Lt Alastair Cram*. Cram! Heavens! While I was a humble airman-telephonist in Nairobi, Cram had been a prosecutor/judge involved with the Mau Mau. He compared the Kenya camps to those of the Nazis – as only he could know, having been a POW of the Nazis, and ironically, one of the judges thereafter at the Nuremberg War Trials.

10.10.55

I was given my medal today – the Africa General Service Medal with KENYA bar. The ribbon is black or dark green stripes on yellow, so is affectionately or otherwise called the 'bumblebee'. Last use of my Housewife to sew on the ribbon. In my RAF's Assessment of Conduct, Proficiency and Personal Qualities I was marked 'Exemplary' which in the *Devil's Dictionary* I'm sure will be defined as 'never got caught'.

Had a lovely yet sad last weekend. Yesterday up at Kikuyu saying goodbye to Laurie, a great person. Lunch and tea there and an African BB[130] service in the afternoon. Then to Bwana's. On Saturday we had a film too instead of Bible Study: the story of the Cross with regards to Barabbas: 'Which Will You Have?' (sniffles from big boys!). I was chuffed to have completed the Camp Fellowship programme. Quite a job! And I won't hear any of them. Now time to close the evening watch – I've been instructing a u/t all evening, so nothing much else done, and thinking he wasn't needed, if they'd let me stay on as I offered. I wanted the Kilimanjaro trip. Being home will make up for that of course.

15.10.55

This is Jambo and Kwaheri. My last letter as an airman abroad! Two years! Why, I can picture the very stones on the path I shall wander up to Devon Lodge. This is being written up at the Jarvis's before tea out under a pristine sky, and the showers of blue jacaranda

---

130 Boys' Brigade.

blossom that keep falling into the cups and onto the cakes. I can remember as yesterday, when on Boxing Day John, Tony and I lay with Dicky Smart under the summer sky and gazed into the same blue trees. The jacaranda year has gone round and they bloom again. There are pink oleanders, and white daturas scenting the dusk. A noisy bulbul. I'll be miserably sad leaving the red soil of Africa with its limitless horizons and exotic features. I feel I was marked as a boy and now the brand is deeper. Africa! [As mentioned earlier, I would come to spend something over 13 years in Africa – but most of the years were spent in the far north-west of the continent: Morocco and the Atlas Mountains.]

We have just been to Government House – where Ian is working – and also to the Legislative Council where the Sergeant at Arms showed us round. A very modern building. Ian and I had lunch in the New Stanley, and they played a selection of Highland airs for me. Nine leisurely courses. Buzzing waiters. And nice to relax with the eyewash and flannel past – there *were* times when we all detested the RAF, but overall it has been a wonderful two years, full of fun and excitement – and rich experiences.

I saw my plane as we passed Camp today – a Hermes. The record-breaking Canberra [in December 1954 a Canberra had set a new record for a flight from London to Cape Town] and a Britannia were there as well. I've too much weight, so Ian has a grip full of stuff to send on somehow. I'll get the Baby on as hand luggage. I also sent off a parcel of books and papers, all which will arrive long after I do. Travel will take about as long from RAF Innsworth to Dollar as it does from Nairobi to the UK. I'm fit the Doc says, but he advises all returning to UK to take a week of complete rest. Not difficult! Crail may be the answer. Then what a lot to do and sort out! *Wapi kwenda*[131] now, eh? I have got thinner but tougher. I have not wasted these years. Expectations were surpassed. At sunrise tomorrow the last and saddest farewells to this land, and then north. North to so much else that I love.

---

* Ian, Wim and John saw me off from Eastleigh at dawn on 16 October. I've kept a flight bulletin, issued at 09.55 as we flew over the White Nile and in ten minutes would be over Khartoum and the junction with the Blue Nile. Next port of call, Wadi Halfa (Sudan), where a meal would be served. We stopped over at Luqa in Malta, and from Hendon I was back in Innsworth, near Gloucester, where the overseas journey had started. (Personnel and Training Command HQ is still based at RAF Innsworth.) From there it was on to Crewe to catch the Midday Scot for home.

I had tried everything to stay on in Nairobi, even offering to do another six months, for our gang were, very much at my instigation, set on climbing Kilimanjaro, at 19,341 feet the highest mountain in Africa. With Tony in Aden and myself in the UK, John alone was left of

131 Where are we going to?

John (5th from left) – the survivor of Fabius – on top of Kilimanjaro

the Terrible Three. Months later I would receive a telegram with the succinct text: 'SURVIVORS FABIUS CONQUER KILI', and later still a photo of John on top of Africa, sitting with Hollanbeck girls from Kijabe High School (Africa Inland Mission) who had organised the climb.

Tony planned to return to Eastleigh on leave but some Op saw the flight cancelled. He was moved to RAF Habbaniya (Iraq) and on it closing was sent to RAF Akrotiri in Cyprus. He did visit Babylon ('Something, if not Jerusalem' – Jerusalem by then forbidden territory). He informed me of Ian being rerouted home by the Cape (on the *Braemar Castle*) as the 1956 Suez debacle had closed the canal. A gang saw Wim off just before Christmas; he's going on to work in India. Wim did come and tour Scotland, and later visited with his wife Bertha and three lovely daughters. He finally worked in Geneva, during the years when I was regularly visiting the Alps, so I saw them most summers. Once he had retired I visited them in the Netherlands, and they came to Scotland again.

About a dozen enjoyed Christmas 1955 at Bwana's. Their children, Elizabeth, Jenny and Michael, were home. Alison's sister Ruth was there. There was a big picnic at Lake Naivasha. Much was made of the Scottish honey. Later, the Jarvis parents were to depart on a six-month holiday in Europe. They sailed on the *Kenya Castle*.

John was the last of our trio to leave Kenya and, as soon as he was home, met up with Ian and Tony (all London-based), and then came for a few days in Scotland. He was missing Kenya, partly I'm sure because of a young lass out there (but that soon ended with a 'Dear John' letter). We met as our erratic lives allowed, the last time seeing him at his home in the New Forest dangling a grandson on his knee. Ian I met now and then in Scotland (though my spare bed was six inches too short) and met or stayed with him over the decades in the London flat he shared with his partner. I'd had no idea he was gay till, not long after leaving the RAF, he had written me a long, agonising letter from Kenya. John is probably correct in suggesting that Ian's 'coming out' at that time 'cost him his K'.[132] When I left Kenya, Ian was heavily involved with the demanding Royal Commission, 'a high-powered office boy', at one time secretary to 23 committees. The Commonwealth Office turned down his request to have his time in Kenya extended. Oddly, against normal practice, when home again as a principal he was given Kenya affairs to deal with.

Bill Blakey ended his RAF days as corporal i/c wireless (fitting aircraft) at RAF Aldergrove in County Antrim. He had already married and found a home, and two days after demob took up a teaching post in Maryhill in Glasgow.

---

132 Knighthood.

Ken, a busy Methodist minister, and I eventually lost touch, but in 2019 he rang me out of the blue and we had a very long and pleasurable catching-up.

I originally transcribed some of these letters for these friends, but twice since, over the years, I've come on additional letters and have been persuaded, on various counts, that some selection should be made public. Sadly, 60-plus years on, I'm the only survivor of our happy band of brothers, so there's almost a duty to publish, to tell how it was to be young in the RAF in the 1950s when the British Empire was facing up to its demise.

I have added a few more notes, for history is so often rewritten according to current political manipulations, and viewpoints change – but this is how it was for me *then*, living it. Some things I said back then I perhaps regret, on some matters I have radically changed my views; but this book tells of what I encountered, experienced and recorded, and so it has to stand, a young man's testimony to life. Fewer and fewer Suez veterans turn out to march on 11 November, and soon they, we, will all have walked into the sunset, our memories evaporating into the little clouds of history.

Squad, halt! Left turn. Stand at ease. Stand easy. ... Dismiss!

Appendix I: Glossary

Abbreviations, acronyms, foreign words, jargon, slang used in the Canal Zone (Z), Kenya (K) or within the family, often with Far Eastern or Scottish origins (F).

a.c.2	Aircraftman second class (lowest rank), thereafter a.c.1; LAC, leading aircraftman; SAC, senior aircraftman
akka, akker	a piastre (money in general) (Z)
asante (sana)	thank you (very much) (K)
assis	soft drink, orange-based (Z)
ATC	Air Traffic Control
AWOL	absent without leave
baado	shortly, soon (K)
billet	accommodation
bind	committing work, often inescapably boring (e.g. night bind for night shift)
bint	girl, young woman, prostitute (Z)
bob	one shilling
boma	stockade (K)
bull	polish to a high degree of shine; a general term for unavoidable, demanding work
Bwana	Mr, boss, title of respect (K)
CCF	Combined Cadet Force
chai	tea (Z)(K)
chakula	food (K)
charge	noted misconduct, leading to some form of punishment.
chati	large jar for cooling water (Z)
Chuprow!	Shut up! (F)
clype	tell tales (F)
CO	commanding officer
C of E	Church of England
C of S	Church of Scotland
Cpl	corporal
crabbit	grouchy (F)
cushy	easy, soft, comfortable (e.g. 'a cushy billet' = 'a good posting')

DC	district commissioner
DI	drill instructor
diarrhoea	went by many names: gippy or gypo tummy, the runs, the trots, squitters …
dhobi	laundry (F)
DO	district officer
dudu	a creepy-crawly (K)
dwam	trance, daydream (F)
ek/eck dum	at once (F)
EOKA	Ethniki Organosis Kyprion Agoniston, Cyprus's National Organisation of Warriors
erk	new recruit (RAF), lowest ranker.
eta	estimated time of arrival
felucca	a traditional Nile sailing boat; very picturesque from a distance
fizzer	a charge, usually leading to punishment
foostie	fusty, mouldy (F)
gash	rubbishy, unnecessary
GCT	General Classification Test
gen	topical knowledge, information (once you've acquired it, you are 'genned up')
gey drouthy	very dry (F)
gharry	lorry usually, but could be any vehicle (in Z)
girn	grumble (F)
glaikit	stupid (F)
haunless	handless, or 'all thumbs' (F)
housewife	sewing kit
HQME	Headquarters Middle East
i/c	in charge
Imshi!	Buzz off! (or ruder) (Z)
Jambo	Hello (K)
jankers	punishment following a charge, often meaningless
JAPIC	Joint Aeronautical Photographic Intelligence Centre
kahawa	coffee (K)
KAR	King's African Rifles; a 'native' regiment
k.d.	khaki drill
khediveruler	of Egypt
kitchy	small (F)
kite	aeroplane
klefty wallah	thief (Z)
k.t.	tropical kit
kwaheri	goodbye (K)
LAC	see a.c.2
maalish /maleesh	never mind, forget it (Z)
MEAF	Middle East Air Force
mealies	maize, sweetcorn (F)

memsahib	a woman of status (K)
mkubwi	big (K)
MMG	Mission to Mediterranean Garrisons
MO	medical officer
MP	military police
MT	motor transport
mucker/mukker	pal, friend, crony (Z)
murram	dry red earth (road surface)
mzuri sana	very good (K)
NAAFI	(pron. Naffy): Naval, Army & Air Force Institute
NCO	non-commissioned officer
NS	National Service
ODs	other denominations (other, that is, than C of E)
OO	orderly officer
oo	out of order
OR	other ranks
P&O	Peninsular & Oriental Steam Navigation Company (shipping line)
panga	hacking blade used in fields (machete) (K)
PBX	private branch exchange
pdq`	pretty damn quick
peely wally	pale and wan (F)
piece	sandwich (F)
PMUB	Presbyterian, Methodist, United Board (of Baptists and Congregationalists)
PO	pilot officer
polé polé	slowly (K)
POM	potential officer material
POM	a brand of powdered potato (Z, K)
poochie	any creepy-crawly (F)
pukka	correct, genuine, praiseworthy (F)
RC	Roman Catholic
REME	Royal Electrical and Mechanical Engineers
SAAF	South African Air Force
SAC	see a.c.2
SAO	station admin officer
scarting	scratching (F)
scunnered	disgusted, fed up (F)
shamba	small farm (K)
shufty/shufti	look at something (Z)
simba	lion (K)
simi	a thin-bladed cutting tool
skite	skid, slide (F)
snafu	adopted Americanism: Situation Normal, All Fouled/Fucked Up
SPs	Station police
Sqd Ldr	squadron leader

square bashing	initial service training
Stella	Egyptian-brewed beer (Z)
stravaig	jaunt, wandering, walkabout (F)
SU	Scripture Union
swindle	communal group setup/sharing (e.g.: tea swindle)
SWO	station warrant officer
SYHA	Scottish Youth Hostels Association, now Hostelling Scotland
tedapah	not to worry (F)
tholl	endure (F)
thrawn	stubborn (F)
tiffin	midday meal (F)
toto	infant (K)
unfundie	Honourable Sir, similar to the Arabic *Effendi* (Z)
u/s	unserviceable (out of order)
u/t	under training
wallah	person (e.g. *dhobi wallah*, laundryman) (Z)
Wapi kwenda?	Where are you/we going? (K)
WO	warrant officer

Appendix II: Bibliography

General

The following are studies of National Service in general, perforce with the greater part concerning the military. Between them they recount first-hand experiences from a wide range of servicemen and officers and their worldwide postings, much of which will be familiar to those who served in the RAF.

Royle, Trevor: *The Best Years of their Lives: The National Service Experience 1945–63.* 1986.

Hickman, Tom: *The Call-up: A History of National Service.* 2004

The titles above are thematic and chronological, and based on the words of those who served. The first title, below, is a more literary work, and experiences recounted are from a more cultured source (officers mainly) who would become well known (e.g. Alan Sillitoe, David Hockney).

Johnson, B S: *All Bull: the National Service.* 1973.

Baxter, D: *Two Years to Do.* A rather grim two years in the ranks (UK) with the Royal Army Service Corps.

Chambers, P and Landreth, A (eds): *Called Up: the Personal Experiences of 16 National Servicemen.* 1955. Not many RAF contributors, but giving an interesting variety of experiences.

Clerk, David Findlay: *Stand By Your Beds.* 2001. The only full autobiographical study in the RAF (AC2 to flying officer).

Findley, Douglas J: *White Knees, Brown Knees.* 2003. The most valuable work for RAF interests (he served as an airman at RAF Deversoir) but also a deeply researched record of the harsh realities for all who served, and died, in the Zone, and their shameful non-recognition by government.

Forty, George: *Called Up. A National Service Scrapbook.* 1980. (Pictorial; but the RAF and the Canal Zone don't seem to exist.)

Ions, Edmund: *A Call to Arms; Interlude with the Military.* A five-year break (army officer's) from academia. (Korea and the Zone briefly mentioned)

Thornhill, Michael T: *Road to Suez: the Battle of the Canal Zone.* 2006. An indispensable study of the years leading up to the 1956 debacle, when British forces were most involved in the Zone.

NB There are too many books for me to mention about the so-called Suez Crisis of 1956 with its worldwide implications. I had left the RAF before then.

Shindler, Colin: *National Service.* 2012. A readable history told through 30 wide-ranging contributors who served all over the world between 1946 and 1962.

Fiction

All these authors make use of personal experience in their National Service days:

Lodge, David: Ginger, *You're Barmy*. 1962 *et seq*. The first and best NS story: an army setting in Germany.
Thomas, Leslie: *The Virgin Soldiers*. 1966. Popular when published; army setting in Singapore/Malaya.
Wesker, Arnold: *Chips with Everything*. 1962. This is a play with its setting an RAF training camp.
Williams, Gordon: *The Camp*. 1960. Set in an RAF base in Germany.

A surprising number of autobiographies by 'celebrities' in various fields have comments or chapters on National Service experiences; these reflect the gamut from utter antipathy to congenial praise. A few I can think of are Brian Blessed (his experiences hardly matched his name!), Michael Caine, Peter O'Toole, Hugh Grant, Peter Hall, Bob Monkhouse, Keith Waterhouse, Auberon Waugh, Robert Robinson, Jackie Charlton, Michael Heseltine, and Tony Hamilton and his brother Geoff.

Canal History

Burchell, S C: *Building the Suez Canal*. Cassell 1967. A well-illustrated account, of what was an extraordinary effort by the visionary, determined Ferdinand de Lesseps.

Mau Mau

Anderson, David: *Histories of the Hanged: Testimonies on the Mau Mau Rebellion in Kenya*. 2005. The most balanced and thoroughly researched of the studies into Britain's response to the Mau Mau atrocities; not pleasant reading, showing irregularities, brutality, irresponsibility, and deceptions persisting up to the highest levels.
Elkins, Caroline: *Imperial Reckoning: the Untold Story of Britain's Gulag in Kenya*. 2005. (The book won a Pulitzer Prize in the USA where published.)
Kariuki, J M: *Mau Mau Detainee: the Account by a Kenyan of his Experiences in Detention Camps*. A calm account; the author, a loyal supporter of Jomo Kenyatta, who was assassinated in 1975 (Oxford 1963).

A few other personal accounts would appear in the following decades (noted in Anderson).

Cyprus

Durrell, L: *Bitter Lemons*. 1957 (et seq). Lived near Kyrenia 1953–1956, and writes about his experiences.
Gunnis, Rupert. *Historic Cyprus*. 1947, 1973. A historian's dry description of all the Cyprus known sites of antiquity. I still own the copy I bought then. Many of the sites have since been destroyed or left derelict with the island divided on religious and cultural lines.
Thubron, C: *Journey into Cyprus*. 1975. A 600-mile trek through the island, the north still undeveloped.

Jerusalem

Montefiore, Simon Sebag: *Jerusalem. The Biography*. 2011. A balanced, readable 700 pp of complex and often bloody history.
Morton, H V: *In the Steps of the Master*. 1934. Still readable travel descriptions of Biblical sites.

Kenya

Miller, Charles: *The Lunatic Express*. History Book Club 1971. A fascinating account of building the Uganda Railway and also a good historical introduction to the history of the British in East Africa. Well-illustrated and an extensive bibliography. A good read.

APPENDIX III: THE BUILDING OF THE SUEZ CANAL

The celebrations for the opening of the Suez Canal must have been amongst the most spectacular and extravagant ever. The debt-ridden Egyptian ruler, Khedive Ismail, cheerfully lashed out £E1.5 million (or £100 million in today's money). He had been by far the largest financial contributor to 'de Lesseps's mad dream'. Ismailia had been named after him, and to that place he invited 4,000 people from all over the world to join the festive occasion. A thousand would sit down to the 24-course banquet in a specially built palace. Ismailia had been turned into a garden city, and on the desert edge 3,000 Arabs had been settled with tents and flocks and families to add the exotic to the spectacle. There were camel rides and military parades. 'Conspicuous spending' is the term best summarising those November days in 1869.

The chief guest was the wife of Napoleon III, Empress Eugénie (de Lesseps's cousin) but there were royal yachts and rulers from Prussia, the Netherlands and Russia. Emperor Franz Joseph of Austria-Hungary had sailed in in his imperial yacht *Greif*. Over 80 ships had steamed into the newly built Port Saïd, named after the previous ruler, Mohammed Saïd (to whom, more than anyone, a canal owes its existence at all). Fifty yachts followed Empress Eugénie's *Aigle* through to Lake Timsah and Ismailia, roughly the canal's midpoint. Among all the glitter and glamour, Ferdinand de Lesseps sat quietly, in plain evening dress, no doubt recalling the seemingly insurmountable battles, financial and technical, since the idea of a canal had caught his interest on landing as vice-consul in Alexandria in 1832 – except he hadn't landed at first, as he had been quarantined on board the *Diogenes* because of a (false) cholera alarm.

To pass the time he had been reading the tomes of the *Description de l'Égypte*, the scientific report from the explorations during the time of Bonaparte in Egypt (1798–1801) – but they, wrongly, considered a passage impossible, thinking there was a difference of 30 feet in the level between the Red and Med Seas. Many thousands of years earlier people had known better: in the time of the Pharaohs a canal had run from Zagazig on a branch of the Nile through to where Ismailia would be, and on via the Bitter Lakes to Suez. Some system like this came and went right through to Roman times, and was only lost to the desert by the Ottomans. Red to Med had always been an important trade route, but when Vasco de

Gama found the way round the Cape it opened up a less complex route, which, even though considerably longer, lay beyond Ottoman reach or danger from Red Sea pirates.

De Lesseps was in Cairo for five years from 1833, and was fascinated by the idea of a canal. He met everyone with the slightest connection, like the Frenchman who was the sultan's irrigation and engineering adviser; he befriended Thomas Waghorn, the Englishman who ran an overland service from Suez to Cairo, a coaching route that sounds rather like something out of Hollywood's films of the Wild West. This route a decade later was bringing Bombay mails to London in a month, rather than three via the Cape (4,600 miles against 10,400). In 1857, the British, until then the fiercest opponents of a canal there, would beg Egypt to allow them to move their forces that way following the 'Indian Mutiny' (history is full of ironies).

De Lesseps studied maps and old references to canals, and very clearly had a dream of what might be, but in 1837 he was transferred and for the next 20 years followed a distinguished consular service, married and had a family. He resigned in 1849 and, with his wife dying a few years later, he was left with the administration of the family's estate. Life must have seemed far from Egypt and the canal dream. Yet he had throughout the years corresponded with engineers and surveyors in Egypt and elsewhere. In 1852 he wrote a detailed memo on the canal project, but the Egyptians were not interested and, as mentioned earlier, the British (with Palmerston as their prime minister) were strongly against the idea – and Britain had the ear of the sultan at Constantinople (Istanbul), Egypt's overlord. Their opposition continued, even after canal work had started. At one stage the sultan stopped all work on the canal – and Egypt had to pay out £3 million in reparations. The bold de Lesseps had started the work with only a third of the finance on board, and it would be the Viceroy Mohammed Saïd and the Khedive Isma'il who in the end largely paid for the canal.

The initial work was all pick and shovel, verging on slavery, but the time had come, Europe was industrialising, trade was becoming an essential for economic growth, sail was being replaced by steam, and wood by steel, so de Lesseps created the technology necessary as they progressed – and succeeded, a magnificent feat.

The infrastructure required was huge: extreme logistics because of desert sand and rock. Before work could proceed fresh water had to be sourced, which would see the ancient canals renewed and extended. Nile water flowed to Ismailia and was piped to Port Saïd and, as the ill-reputed Sweet Water Canal of my RAF days, south to Suez. Three rocky ridges of higher ground had to be blasted through (a final reef on the Shallufa cutting was only cleared the night before the grand opening). Ali Pasha, grand vizier of Turkey, was chief guest when the dam holding back the Red Sea water was breached to flow into what would be the Bitter Lakes.

And it all happened because de Lesseps in his Cairo days of the 1830s had befriended a fat little prince escaping the strictures of the palace. This was Saïd, overweight, miserable, whom de Lesseps, generally acting as the benevolent uncle, would let loose in the consulate kitchens (to stuff on spaghetti) and teach to ride. In 1854 de Lesseps read that Saïd had succeeded an uncle as viceroy in Egypt – and immediately saw his chance, seized it, and during the course of a royal tour in Egypt with Saïd sold him the idea of the canal across the isthmus, and won the concessions needed to proceed. The rest, they say, is history.

Britain tried hard to derail the project, but with Palmerston dead and a growing empire in the East, even the politicians saw sense and would then swing rapidly to the other extreme: control Egypt, control all. Saïd died in 1863 and was succeeded by Ismail: both men – physically huge, indulgent, extravagant and erratic – regarded the canal as their project (off stage, de Lesseps, smiling). They would beggar Egypt for it.

In 1875, hearing how desperate the khedive's finances were, the British PM Disraeli seized an opportunity to purchase what would be a controlling 40 per cent of the canal shares from Ismail. The story has become legend: Parliament was not in session, the Treasury inaccessible, but over a dinner with the Cabinet, Disraeli went ahead. His private secretary was sent to the banker Lionel Rothschild to ask for £4 million. Just like that!

'What is your security?' he was asked.

Came the reply: 'The British Government.'

Rothschild nodded, 'You shall have it,' and continued with his dinner.

But how to protect their interest?

In 1882 a revolt gave the British the excuse (foreshadowing 1956!), and they bombarded Alexandria, invaded, and took control of Port Saïd, Ismailia and Suez. Through various treaties, constitutions and puppet rulers the British controlled Egypt for the next 75 years. In May 1956 the last British forces left the Canal Zone; then in July, while Nasser was broadcasting to the nation, his forces took Port Saïd, Ismailia and Suez. The canal that ran through Egypt now belonged to Egypt and Egypt alone. (A large indemnity was paid to the Suez Canal Company.)

De Lesseps saw the canal as a gift to the world, open to the ships of all nations – which it was, and, with a few blips, has remained. Work on the canal never stops both for maintenance and improvement; when opened it was 127.2 feet wide; in 1939 its width was 367.2 feet and by 1959 it was 495.4. In 1955 the number of ships using the canal was 14,666. Joseph Conrad called the Suez Canal 'a dismal but profitable ditch'.

Its importance as a trade route in the 21st century, however, was underlined by the 250,000-tonne container ship *Ever Given* getting jammed across the canal for six frantic days in March 2021.

According to a BBC report on 29 March, when the ship had just been freed:

> Lloyd's List showed the stranded ship was holding up an estimated $9.6bn of trade along the waterway each day. That equates to $400m and 3.3 million tonnes of cargo an hour, or $6.7m a minute.

> Looking at the bigger picture, German insurer Allianz said on Friday its analysis showed the blockage could cost global trade between $6bn to $10bn a week and reduce annual trade growth by 0.2 to 0.4 percentage points.

Approximately 10 per cent of the world's total trade and 10 per cent of the world's oil trade flows through the Suez Canal each year.[133] As a result of the block, over 400 ships had been forced to kick their heels in the canal, and it took until 4 April to clear that immediate backlog. The knock-on effects on supply chains worldwide lasted for several months.

Meanwhile, Egypt is doing quite nicely out of the canal; in June 2021 the head of the Suez Canal Authority, Osama Rabie, said it had netted Egypt 'the highest revenues in the history of the canal … a record $5.84 bn in the last tax year, despite the coronavirus pandemic's effect on world trade as well as the six-day blockage'.[134]

I closely watched the *Ever Given* saga as it was played out on the world's screens. The technology brought into play would have fascinated and delighted the practical dreamer de Lesseps. I hope he was looking down, and smiling.

---

133 Faucon, McFarlane and Hodari, '*Energy Industry is hit by Fallout'*, *Wall Street Journal*, 26 March, 2021.
134 *Al Jazeera*, 11 July 2021: Egypt's Suez Canal reports record revenue despite blockage crisis.

APPENDIX IV: THE *EMPIRE WINDRUSH*

The loss of the *Empire Windrush* interested all of us who had seen her pass along the Suez Canal, particularly on this last voyage (letter of 29.3.54). She had left Japan in February (with forces personnel, including wounded, from the Korean War) and had called at Hong Kong, Singapore, Colombo and Aden before reaching Suez. (There had been a minor fire on leaving Hong Kong.) On board were 1,276 passengers, including women and children, and 222 crew. At Deversoir she left the Great Bitter Lake for the canal run to Port Saïd and then on into the Mediterranean. In the early morning of 28 March there was an explosion and a fierce fire in the engine-room.

Four crew were killed, but two did manage to escape the inferno. All electrical power failed so the firefighting squad's hoses were useless, the watertight doors – power-operated – could not be closed, likewise the public address system; and steam whistles couldn't operate to rouse sleepers. There was also great difficulty launching some of the lifeboats from the same lack of power. There were 22 lifeboats, all made use of. Several ships were soon on the scene: Dutch, Italian, Norwegian and the P & O *Socotra*. These conveyed the rescued to Algiers where the French Army or Red Cross cared for them till the aircraft carrier HMS *Triumph* took everyone to Gibraltar to be flown home. HMS *Saintes* managed to attach a tow on *Empire Windrush* but had made little distance before the still-burning ship sank, two days after the original, still unexplained, explosion.

In 2018, when I'd found what had been my missing letters from this period, there was much on the media about the 'Windrush Generation', and curiosity led me to find out if that operation 70 years before had been by the ship we'd seen in the canal. I found the details above of what finally happened to the ship, but then wanted more of her history.

Several vessels acquired by Britain for carrying troops were called *Empire* plus the name of a river. The Windrush is just a minor tributary of the Thames, so an odd choice. But this ship had been launched with another name, in another country.

She had been the *Monte Rosa*, launched in 1930 as one of five Hamburg Süd Company ships with *monte* (mountain) names to become emigrant ships to South America. *Monte Rosa* was the only one to survive World War Two: one *monte* sank near Tierra del Fuego in the year *Monte Rosa* was launched, one was sunk in an air raid, another was badly damaged and scrapped after the war, and the last was scuttled by the British in 1946.

Monte Rosa hadn't had much of a charmed life either. When the Nazis came to power in 1933 she was made part of a 'Strength through Joy' programme to provide cheap sea holidays. (She ran aground in the Faroe Islands but was refloated next day.) With World War Two she became a barracks ship, acted as troop-carrier for the invasion of Norway, then became a recreational ship for the crew of the *Tirpitz*, parked, inactive, in a fjord for the duration. *Monte Rosa* was one of several ships deporting Norway Jews – of whom all but two would not survive Auschwitz. *Monte Rosa* was attacked and supposedly hit in March 1944, and in June the Norwegian resistance managed to attach limpet mines to her hull in Oslo. These exploded at sea but only caused minor damage. In 1945, as a hospital ship she was damaged by a mine, repaired at Gdynia (Gdansk) but then set sail with 5,000 German refugees aboard, fleeing the advancing Russians. She was captured at Kiel, becoming a prize of war, and the British converted her into a troopship under the name *Empire Windrush,* operating to the Far East. Just one voyage took in the Caribbean – but from that her name would uniquely live on.

In June 1948 the *Empire Windrush* docked at Tilbury and 1,027 passengers disembarked, 802 of whom came from Caribbean addresses, mostly in Jamaica. Sixty-six passengers came from Mexico; there were Poles (many soldiers) who had made their way there from Siberia, to India and the Pacific; they too had been granted permission to settle in the UK. The disembarking was given much publicity, and as a result the name became a shorthand for West Indian migration; those who settled are today's Windrush Generation. (A square in Brixton was renamed Windrush Square in 1998, and in 2008 a heritage plaque was installed at Tilbury. And in 2019 a memorial was erected in Waterloo station).

In May 1949 the *Empire Windrush* had caught fire on a voyage from Gibraltar to Suez. The ship was towed back to Gibraltar. In February 1953 in the middle of the Indian Ocean, 200 miles south of the Nicobar Islands, *Windrush* came on a small cargo ship, *Holchu*, adrift and with no sign of her five-man crew. Another ship nearby, the British freighter *Ranee*, was taking the first-ever shipment of rice, 7,540 tons of it, from Communist China to Ceylon. When men from *Ranee* boarded the *Windrush* they found food prepared in the galley; there was no shortage of fuel, food or water; the ship was in good condition; her cargo of rice was safe. *Ranee* towed the *Holchu* to Colombo but the fate of her crew remains a mystery. *Holchu* normally just operated between the Andaman and Nicobar Islands.

In 1954 the *Empire Windrush* ended her many lives as described. The Hamburg Süd Company (which built our ship) has not forgotten her; one of its modern container ships sailing the seas at the time of writing bears the name *Monte Rosa*.

APPENDIX V: MOTHER'S HISTORY OF HAMISH'S EARLY YEARS

Born: Colombo 13.08.34. Jessie Simpson godmother.

1936   March: P&O *Rajputana*. Ian missing while bathing Hamish. Suez Canal. Next 2½ years in Galway, Carrick Castle, Dunfermline.

1938   Oct: Colombo. P&O *Ranchi* via Suez Canal.

1939   Yokohama, Japan. P&O *Ranchi*. Mum and Dad up Fuji 03.09.39.[135]

1940   David born 15.12.40. Akija Beach holidays. Nikko.

1941   Late Jan.   *Asama Maru* to Kobe. Icicles on ship's rigging. *President Munroe* (maiden voyage) to Shanghai, Hongkong (you ashore in kilt), Manila, Singapore.

         March: to Klang

         15.12.41   David's first birthday party. Air raid. You: 'Shame David's disturbed on his birthday.' [A pocket diary makes it clear that the family life of mahjong, cinema, haircuts, club, sport had gone on uninterrupted till this point.]

         16.12.41   Sent off to safety of a tea estate.

         23.12.41   Back to Klang. Air attacked on road. Sailed on wee *Ipoh* from Port Swettenham, towing barges.

         24.12.41   Raids. Returned to Port Swettenham.

         25.12.41   Raids. Hamish missing in garden. [Whence my piece of shrapnel in knee – still there.] Sail again. Jap prisoners in hold. Malay guards. Captain amuses you with card tricks. Sea View Hotel. During dinner, you at door, half-naked, shout across, 'Mummy, David's yelling'. Bad raids. Shelter – singing.

1942   1.1.42   Dutch *Marnix van St Aldergende*. Batavia. Durban. Uncle John and Aunt Nellie [Father's sister]. Uncle Jim [Father's brother] and Aunt Edith and Cousin Dickie. To Highbury School, Hillcrest. Various homes, upcountry, Natal.

         Feb. 42   Father escapes Singapore. Bombed and sunk. Escape across Sumatra. Colombo. Durban.

1943   Feb. 43   Father to Madras [Father would be in Calicut in 44, Karachi in 45–47].

1944   Durban flat, awaiting ship. Train to Cape Town.

---

135 The day World War Two was declared; a coincidence.

July   *Andes* to Liverpool via Freetown. David lost before leaving port.

Glasgow with Simpsons. Dollar. Carrick Castle. Dollar settled. Big brother shock of brothers! [Father didn't see Ian for nigh on nine years because of the war. He and widowed grandmother almost went out to Japan in 1940 'for safety' – !]

Aunt Nellie's husband was an army doctor and she a nurse, and they were meeting the refugee ship officially. When we came down the gangway they had a surprise. Nothing like having a scattered family.

Living in South Africa too were Father's brother Jim, with his wife and young teenage son Dickie. An older brother, Bunny, had vanished over Germany, serving in the South African Air Force. I rather hero-worshipped Dick, an outdoor type who spent his life in locust control work. Some of the time we lived beside the Valley of the Thousand Hills where I roamed with Zulu friends, unaware of apartheid. South Africa is a country for boyhood, and I relished the two years there. Africa can be infectious.